All scriptures are from the King James Bible

© All rights Reserved 2012
Publisher
Good Shepherd Writing and Publishing LLC
A subsidiary of Shepherd Ministries
Dr. Willie B. White

Topical Discussions
- ◊ Blessed Hope in God and our Savior Jesus Christ
- ◊ Jesus The Promised Messiah
- ◊ God and His People
- ◊ Christ Saves
- ◊ A Christ Centered Community
- ◊ A Redeemed Community
- ◊ God's Covenant Community
- ◊ God's Plan For His People
- ◊ God And His People
- ◊ Knowing God's Instructions
- ◊ Hope In Jesus Christ
- ◊ Salvation Through Jesus Christ

Audience

This devotional is designed to inspire Christians the world over and point the way to Christ for non-believers.

The aim of this devotional is to provide daily inspirational thoughts with Biblical background for practical applications as well as promoting Bible study and meditating on God's Word. Also, daily readings from this devotional will establish a deeper love for God and a more intimate relationship with the Lord.

At the conclusion of this devotional it is the author's desire that the reader will proclaim the good news of the gospel beginning in his or her Jerusalem, Samaria, Judea and the world over in obeying the great commission that was issued by Christ Himself (Matthews 28:19-20). In doing so others will come to Christ and God's kingdom will grow; thereby further winning this spiritual warfare against Satan and his army.

Therefore, read, meditate, pray and be filled with the Holy Spirit.

Blessed Hope In God And Our Savior Jesus Christ

Who is Jesus? John 1:1-3; 14

In the beginning was the Word, and the Word was with God, and the Word was God. The same was in the beginning with God. All things were made by Him; and without Him was not any thing that was made. And the Word was made flesh, and dwelt among us. (and we beheld His glory, the glory as of the only begotten of the Father) full of grace and truth.

John answer's our discussion question by presenting Jesus as "the Word" of God and in doing so John states that God in these last days spoke to humanity through His Son. God in times past spoke to humanity through His prophets. John presentation of Jesus as "the Word" of God is presenting Jesus as the manifold wisdom of God and the perfect revelation of the nature and person of God (1 Corinthians 1:30; Ephesians 3:10-11). Jesus being presented as "the Word" of God reveals the heart and mind of God (John 14:9).

John presents three main characteristics of Jesus as they relate to Him being "the Word" and they are (a) Jesus as "the Word" in relation to His Father; Jesus was pre-existing from eternity. He is divine having the same nature and character as His Father. (b) Jesus as "the Word" in relation to the world as it was through Jesus Christ that God created all that exists and now sustains the world. (c) Jesus as "the Word" in relation to humanity as He became flesh through the gateway of the virgin birth. Jesus' coming to earth as man and God was for the purpose of being the sacrificial Lamb of God.

Verse 4 presents Jesus as the light of the world as His light embodies God's truths and these truths light the way for all who believe on the name of Jesus.

Jesus is the Savior of the world who was in the beginning with God when the world was formed.

The Church: Matthew 16:18

And I say also unto thee, That thou Peter, and upon this rock I will build my church; and the gates of hell shall not prevail against it.

The Greek form of the word "church" is referred to as an assembly of people coming together in a congregation to worship God. With that being said let's look at the representations of the church. (a) The church is looked upon as God's people or the redeemed believers made possible by Christ's death (1 Corinthians 1:2; 10:32). (b) The church is the people who have been called out of the world by God Himself unto salvation in His kingdom. (2 Corinthians 6:16-18). (c) The church is the temple of God and the Holy Spirit who is God in the third person (1 Corinthians 3:16; 2 Corinthians 6:14-7:1). (d) The church is the body of Christ which is comprised of the body of baptized believers (1 Corinthians 6:15-16). (e) The church is the bride of Christ (2 Corinthians 11:2; Ephesians 5:22-27; Revelation 19:7-9). (f) The church is seen as spiritual fellowship among believers and God as this includes the Holy Spirit, unity in the Spirit (Ephesians 4:4), and baptism in the Spirit (Acts 1:5; 2:4). (g) The church is the spiritual ministry of all believers who have been gifted with different gifts by the Holy Spirit. (h) The church involves an army of believers locked in a spiritual warfare with Satan. (i) The church is seen as the pillar grounded in the truths of God (1 Timothy 3:15). (j) The church is seen as a people of future hope centered on Christ's return for His bride—the church (John 14:3; 1 Timothy 6:14). (k) The church is both the visible and invisible body with the visible being the building and invisible being the believers who are joined together in Christ by faith (Revelation 2:11; 7:26). ***The church!***

Call on Jesus: Romans 10:9-10

That is thou confess with thy mouth the name Lord Jesus, and shalt believe in thine heart that God hath raised Him from the dead, thou shalt be saved. For with the heart man believeth unto righteousness and with the mouth confession is made unto salvation.

If the question were raised, Why call on the name of Jesus? There is power in the name of Jesus as He is our Lord and Savior. The one who died for the sins of the world and was raised for our justification. How is there power in the name of Jesus? Jesus is God's Son who was there in the beginning with God during the creation process. Jesus is God in the flesh and He is the Word of God. It is our belief in Jesus that we have eternal life; however, there are some things that all believers must do, and they are (a) admit that they are sinners, (b) confess their sins and then (c) turn from their sins. The three step process to repentance.

Our scripture verses provide the essentials for salvation for all believers, which are; (b) all must confess with their mouths and, (b) believe in thine heart that God hath raised him (Jesus) from the dead, thou shall be saved. In verse 10 which states that in the heart is where salvation begins. A man believeth unto righteousness and his confession is to salvation. Salvation means that all who believe have been freed from the bondage of sin and the separation that sin brings. Jesus' death on Calvary bridged the gap that once existed between humanity and God as Jesus' death and resurrection is the center of our salvation.

More importantly, all who believe will spend eternity with God as the believer has accepted Jesus as Lord of his/her life.

We have discussed the saving power of Jesus; let's look at His powers to heal all manner of diseases, His comforting powers when we are burdened with the troubles of this world. Jesus has the power to give sight to the blind, make the lame walk and dumb to talk as well as the power to raise the dead. More importantly, Jesus has all powers in heaven and earth in His hands as this leads both believers and non-believers to completely trust Jesus with his/her life. During Jesus' earthly ministry He demonstrated His awesome powers by the many miracles He performed mainly authenticating His deity to all who witness and believed Him. Reflect with the writer if you will on the incident when Jesus turned water into wine for the wedding party. There is the woman with the issue of blood when she touched the hem of His garment she was made whole. There is the lame man, who Jesus told to take up his bed and walk; who can forget the blind man that Jesus made an ointment from spittle and dirt placed it on the man's eyes and told him to go and wash. This man gained his sight and went his way praising God. Jesus exhibited His power over death when He called Lazarus from the grave after being dead four days. This incident was to show His powers over death and all who believe on the name of Jesus shall live forever with Him.

In can be concluded then that the powers of Jesus are because He is God in the second person and all members of the Godhead work together for the good of mankind.

Believe on Jesus as there is power in His name.

Sin And Death: Romans 6:1

What shall we say then? Shall we continue in sin, that grace may abound?

Today's topic begins a three day discussion on sin and its consequences, believers being dead to sin and being alive in Christ, but for today our focus discussion is sin and its definition.

Sin can be defined as a transgression, a wrongdoing, or a sin against God or wickedness or injustice (Romans1:18 1 John 5:17). Sin can also be defined as a lack of love. Matthew 22:37-40 speaks of loving God with all thy being and thy neighbor as thyself. Being that God is love and anyone who lacks the love of God is subject to wrong doings and lawlessness and is seen in defiance to God's law of love (v. 19; 1 John 3:4). Sin can be defined as a moral corruption in humans that supersedes human good intentions. Sin causes humans to commit unrighteousness and all manner of evil against one another and is rooted in human desires of disobedience to God's moral laws. In a word sin is selfishness at its center is self pleasures while these pleasures are in direct opposition to God.

Sin entered the human race through the disobedient act of one man, Adam (5:12) and since that dreadful day sin has had negative affects on the human race both physically and spiritually. Sin caused a spiritual divide between man and God which made it necessary for Christ to pay man's sin debt. Sin caused God's anger and He pronounced the whole world guilty.

Sin separates man from God.

Believers Dead To Sin: Romans 6:2-10 *God forbid. How shall we, that are dead to sin live any longer therein?*

What does it mean to be dead to sin with Christ? All who believe in Jesus Christ and have accepted Him as their personal Savior has died with Him because believers are in union with Him. Therefore, believers are alive with Christ and will live forever with Him.

The believer's water baptism expresses his/her burial and resurrection with Christ as it portrays the believer's rejection of sin and all the consequences it brings. Also, being dead to sin represents the believer's continual faith and commitment to Christ and His righteousness as this results in the believer's continued flow of God's grace and mercy. Additionally, believers being dead to sin means that the believer will live in union with Christ in His resurrected life. Verse 6 makes a profound statement on being dead to sin in that the "old man" has been crucified (put to death) with Christ on the cross so that all believers were raised with Him to a new life; meaning the old man's nature and unregenerated self is no longer controlled by sin, but once regenerated the believer is Christ-centered and controlled with godly desires.

One final note on being dead to sin in that all believers died to sin in the eye sight of God and was born again by the Spirit and has been given the power of Christ to resist sin and its evil deeds. **Believers died to sin and are free to live for Christ daily.**

Alive in Christ: Romans 6:11-23

For the wages of sin is death; but the gift of God is eternal life through Jesus Christ our Lord.

What does it mean to be made alive in Christ? Being alive in Christ means that each believer has accepted Christ as his/her personal Savior and Lord and committed him/herself to a life of righteousness and obedience to Him and His ways. Believers that are alive in Christ are those who have become regenerated souls and are no longer under the control of unrighteousness but are under God's grace and mercy when justice was demanded.

Believers being made alive in Christ cost God His only begotten Son done in love for the human race to repair a broken fellowship with humanity. **What love!**

Being alive in Christ gives the believer the opportunity to live with Him forever and live in perfect harmony with the Godhead. Being alive in Christ, believers manifest the righteousness of Christ in our daily lives for a sin riddled world to see. Also, being alive in Christ believers has the indwelling Holy Spirit who gives the believer power to boldly witness Christ the world over. Being alive in Christ believers become part of a royal priesthood, a holy nation and a set aside people doing the Will of God. Lastly, believers being alive in Christ are in the body of Christ-the church. Being alive in Christ believers will live for an eternity as stated in verse 23, which provide the alternative to living in sin.

Dead to sin alive in Christ-Christ is alive so are believers.

Election and Predestination: Ephesians 1:4-5

Having predestined us unto the adoption of children by Jesus Christ to Himself, according to the good pleasure of His will.

Election and predestination are the focus of today's discussion as they relate to God, Jesus Christ and the believer and the blessings of each. A biblical definition of election is being chosen by God for all believers who believe in Jesus Christ. Election is Christocentric, which means "He hath chosen us in Him (Ephesians 1:4). Christ as the elect is the foundation of our election and our union with Christ is the basis of our election whereby we become members of the elect (Ephesians 1:4-7, 9-10, 12-13). Our election comes through faith in Jesus Christ. The "in him" is through the redemptive death of Christ that God forms His elect people and this election is to salvation as salvation is offered to all who believe.

Predestinate means to decide beforehand as it relates to God who decided beforehand in Christ the ones that will be His elect, meaning true believers who makeup the church, the body of Christ. God predestinated His elect to be the following: (a) called (Romans 8:30), (b) justified (Romans 3:24; 8:30), (c) glorified (Romans 8:30), (d) confirmed to the likeness of His Son Jesus Christ (Romans 8:29), (e) Holy and blameless (Ephesians 1:4), (f) adopted as God's children (Ephesians 1:5),(g) redeemed (Ephesians 1:7), (h) for the praise of His glory (Ephesians 1;12; 1 Peter 2:9); (i) recipients of the Holy Spirit (Ephesians 1:13; Galatians 3:14), (j) recipients of an inheritance (Ephesians 1:14), and (k) to do good works (Ephesians 2:10).

True believers are chosen by God.

Believers Sealed With The Holy Spirit
Ephesians 1:12-13

In whom ye also trusted, after that ye heard the word of truth, the gospel of your salvation in whom also after that ye believed, ye were sealed with that Holy Spirit of promise.

A Seal is looked upon as a form of identification and all believers have the identifying mark of the Holy Spirit. The seal of the Holy Spirit is God identifier of believers that shows His ownership. The seal of the Holy Spirit is visible to God but is invisible to the believer's naked eye. What is visible to the believer's naked eye is the demeanor of the believer when the Holy Spirit is present in his/her life (v5). Also, believers know that they belong to God through the regenerating work of the Holy Spirit as He renews and delivers the believer from the power of sin (Romans 8:1-17; Galatians 5:16-25). Additionally, the Holy Spirit provides each believer with the knowledge that God is our Father.

Believers being sealed with the Holy Spirit he or she is better able to witness Christ, while being drawn closer to God as the Holy Spirit builds the body of each believer into a holy temple of God. Being sealed with the Holy Spirit believer's inner being is strengthened thus he/she is given power to maintain the Christian faith in unity while reaching full Christ likeness. Lastly, being sealed with the Holy Spirit, each believer has the assurance that our redemption is real and we are adopted sons of God; as the Holy Spirit is our protector and guide.

The seal of the Holy Spirit is our heavenly driver's license-- what an identifier!

His Workmanship: Ephesians 2:10

For we are His workmanship, created in Christ Jesus unto good works, which God hath before ordained that we should walk in them.

Who are His workmanship? Believers in this scenario are the workmanship as we the believers are workers for Christ. Being workers for Christ, believers are to live holy lives before men so that our good works can be seen by Christ who is in heaven. Being the workmanship for Christ mean that we are to continue carrying the gospel message to the world as commissioned by Christ Himself (Matthew 28:19-20) as it is our mission to make other disciples for Christ.

The question now becomes how do we make disciples? We make other disciples through our lifestyles, our witness as this is to begin in our homes, communities and then carry the gospel message abroad. Also, being workers for Christ we are to minister to the sick, feed the hungry, visit the homebound, give comfort where needed because Christ said "what you do to the least of these you do also unto me" (Matthew 25:40). Christ was the perfect example for doing the will of His Father and we as believers are to do likewise in following Christ's example of ministry. It is noteworthy to mention that we are not saved by our good works but because of our salvation we do good works. James 2:17, which states "faith if it hath no works is dead." Does your works exemplify your faith? True faith always manifests itself in obedience to God as it relates to our works.

Our works speak to our faith.

Jan 10

Jesus Tempted: Matthew 4:1-11

...Jesus was led up of the Spirit unto the wilderness to be tempted by the devil.

Today's topical discussion is on Jesus being tempted by Satan after Jesus' baptism in the Jordan. Satan tempting Jesus was an attempt to stop or hinder Jesus from obeying the Will of His Father. Had Satan been successful in getting Jesus to bow to the wishes of him then the plan of Salvation would have been null and void, neither would there be any hope for believers. Jesus being both human and divine relied on the power of the Holy Spirit as well as using scripture to deflect the fiery darts of Satan. Scripture records three failed attempts by Satan to tempt Jesus; the first attempt was Satan wanted Jesus to turn stones into bread, but Jesus quoted scripture (v. 4) on each occasion. Satan was bound and determined not to be defeated as he tried again by telling Jesus that if He is the Son of God for Him to cast Himself down and he would give his angels charge of Jesus. Notice how Satan confused scripture and too many who may not know the truth will be fooled by Satan's lies. On Satan's third try he showed Jesus all the kingdoms of the world and told Jesus if He would bow down and worship him these kingdoms would be His. Finally, Jesus told Satan that he was not to "tempt the Lord thy God." Questions that come to mind are what was Satan thinking? Did Satan recognize Jesus for who He was and what Jesus' mission was? Did Satan think Jesus being God would be fooled by his lies and cunning tactics?

The message from this passage of scripture is that Satan is on his mission to destroy God's kingdom and will use every strategy known to man in his efforts to be successful as it was Jesus' mission to destroy the works of Satan. Christ won the battle on Calvary and this makes Satan a defeated foe and he will never succeed in his mission. However, he will continue trying to mislead and confuse the minds of believers. A well known fact of his deception is when he caused Eve to believe his lies by misquoting scripture. It is wise for all believers to know the truth for themselves. Believers are encouraged to put on the whole armour of God because we as believers are constantly being bombarded by Satan's wickedness. Lastly, Jesus is our perfect example of dealing with Satan.

Who is Satan? Satan which means accuser or adversary was created by God as a perfect and good angel who was in charge of the choir in heaven. Satan rebelled against God because he wanted to become greater than God. Satan's rebellion resulted in him being kicked out of heaven and since then he has made it his mission to destroy God's kingdom. The war between God and Satan has been ongoing since. It was Satan's lies and deception that caused the fall of the human race (Genesis 3:1-6) which resulted in the separation between God and humanity, but Jesus is the bridge that closed the breach.

In closing this discussion, just as Jesus was tempted by Satan, so will all believers and as Jesus withstood Satan's tactics so can believers with the indwelling of the Holy Spirit to aid us as He did Jesus.

Jesus overcame temptation on our behalf.

Patience In Temptations: James 1:2-4

My brethren, count it all joy when ye fall into divers temptations; Knowing this, that the trying of your faith worketh patience.

How do we define temptation? Temptation can be defined as experiencing difficulties or adverse situations in our lives. Often times these difficulties or temptations are from the world in which we live or from taking direct hits from Satan. We are never to say that our situations/temptations are God inflicted, but He does sometimes uses these situations to test our faith in Him and to develop perseverance which leads to a godly character in each believer. Another school of thought is that the trials we face are to test our sincerity and commitment to God as He already knows our faith and commitment, but He wants us to know the extent of our faith and commitment. It is noteworthy to say that when experiencing trials we must ask for patience to endure, while knowing that God the Holy Spirit is there with us to provide the strength and patience to endure.

Job is a perfect example of being tried by the fire who endured unto the end as he never lost faith in God. In his humaneness he became weary and wanted an audience with God, which God granted; in the end Job realized his unworthiness. Verse 4 brings out the purpose of patience, which is to make us perfect that we may want for nothing. Perfect or perfection is seen as having a right relationship with God as evidenced by our love, devotion and total dedication to God.

Patience equals perfection.

Obeying the Voice of God: Luke 5:5

..Simon answering said unto Him, Master, we have toiled all the night, and have taken nothing; nevertheless at thy word I will let down the net.

Our lesson study takes place where Jesus had been teaching on the Lake of Gennesaret when He saw the two fishermen washing their nets when He entered into the boat of Simon Peter. Jesus asked Simon Peter to move a little farther away from shore, which Simon obeyed; there Jesus began to teach more people what thus saith the Lord. After Jesus' session was complete He instructed Simon to "launch out into the deep, and let down your net for a draught" (v. 4). Again Simon Peter obeyed and he caught so many fish until his partner was called over to share in the catch which was enough to fill both boats.

What was Simon Peter's reaction? Peter recognized that he was a sinner in the presence of God and fell on his knees and prayed. Peter like many of us realized that there is more to be gained by obedience than disobedience. When Jesus asked Simon Peter to follow Him so that he would become fishers of men, Peter immediately left occupation, friends and family to follow Jesus. **Have you heard the voice of Jesus and obeyed?**

All believers have been called by God for ministry, but the question becomes do we hear and obey like Simon Peter? Obeying the voice of Jesus yields a bountiful harvest as we are destined for greatness in God's vineyard. Believers are to become fishers of men just as Simon Peter and the other disciples.

Hear and Obey.

Four Kinds Of Soil And Their Fruit
Luke 8:5-8, 11-15

A sower went out to sow his seed; and as he sowed, some fell by the way side; and it was trodden down, and the fowls of the air devoured it.

In today's discussion we will focus on Jesus teaching regarding how the gospel message will be received by all who hear the Word of God. A parable is understood to be an earthly story with a heavenly meaning. Another thought on parables is that it reveals the truth about God's kingdom for all whose hearts are prepared to receive the truth and conceal the heavenly truth for the unprepared hearts. Jesus used parabolic teaching during His teaching ministry because of its effectiveness in getting His message across to His audience. It is noteworthy to say that there will be conversions, but the fruit one bears depends on how one responds to God's Word (Mark 14).

The sower in this parable is God Himself and the seed is the Word of God (v.11), and the soil are the people. The wayside seed are those that heard the word, Satan came to rob and steal God's Word from the heart of those believers (v.12). The rock soil are those believers who hear and believe, but lack a solid foundation (roots) and when temptation arises they fall away (v.13). Next we have the thorny soil which represents all those that believed and went forth but were choked to death with worldly concerns and Satan's lies and this soil bears no fruit. Lastly, the good and fertile soil is those who believed with an honest heart and kept the word in their hearts; this soil produced fruit.

Which soil do you represent? Good soil!

Caring For One Another: Galatians 6:2

Bear ye one another's burdens, and so fulfill the law of Christ.

What does it mean to care for one another/our fellowman? To care for our fellowman is simply to provide whatever supports the person needs whether it is financial assistance, medical or prayer in the time of sorrow. Scripture reminds us that whatever we do for the least of God's children we also do to Him and on the Day of Judgment our service record will be read. Also, caring for our less fortunate expresses the love of Christ as He loved and cared for all. Wherever there was a need Christ met their need without questions or hesitations. We are to do likewise and in doing so we manifest Christ in our lives.

More importantly, in caring for the needy we are showing love as we are commanded to love all. It has been said many times that you get back what you send out; meaning if your give sparingly you reap sparingly and if you give in abundance, then you will reap likewise. All humanity is God's creation and all are created in the image and likeness of God; therefore, we are all alike on the inside regardless of our outer differences.

Lastly, if our fellowman asks for a hand would you turn a deaf ear or would you be lead by the Holy Spirit in meeting the need; just as Christ would often meet physical needs to address the person's spiritual need.

Caring equals love and love is care in action.

Restore Our Brother: Galatians 6:1

Brethren, if a man be overtaken in a fault, ye which are spiritual, restore such a one in the spirit of meekness; considering thyself, least thou also be tempted.

What is the definition of restore? To restore something is to return it to its originality. In the case of humanity our broken fellowship with God was restored by Jesus Christ and His shed blood on Calvary. Individual restoration is based upon true repentance by returning to Christ with a full commitment to Him and His ways.

Often times a believer can aid in the restoration of a fellow believer by reaffirming the benefits of being in fellowship with God and other believers. If our fellow believer is one of a leadership position, then the fallen soldier must be reminded of the moral qualifications of God's leaders. All leaders are under the moral obligations to live godly lives before others; living ungodly lives before his/her followers may be a stumbling block them.

More importantly, believers should pray for our fallen brother/sister as we all are being tested by the adversary and our response to him depends on our spiritual armour. All believers are encouraged to dress for a spiritual warfare by putting on the whole armour of God (Ephesians 6:11-18). Lastly, our fallen brother/sister is not to be ridiculed while in their fallen state, but instead we are to extend a helping hand in leading them back to God. Reading and meditating on God's Word daily is our best offense from becoming victim to Satan's traps to where restoration is necessary.

In humanity's fallen state Christ became our restorer, believers are to lend a hand to our fallen brothers/sisters.

The Model Prayer: Matthew 6:9-15

After this manner therefore pray ye; Our Father which are in heaven, Hallowed be thy name. Thy kingdom come, thy will be done in earth, as it is in heaven.

Our scripture records Jesus' model prayer which includes six petitions and addresses three concerns and they are (a) concerns with the holiness of God, (b) concerns for ones personal needs, and (c) concerns regarding sin and the willingness to forgive.

Let's look at the petitions in this prayer beginning with verse 9 which expresses our worship of God as our heavenly Father while recognizing who He is and what He has done for all humanity. Also, in verse 9 we pay adoration to the heavenly Father as He is worthy of all our reverence and should be exalted and glorified.

Verse 10, our prayers should express our concerns for the kingdom of God here on earth while recognizing that the fulfillment will be in the future. Also, in verse 10 believers must desire the spiritual presence and manifestation of God's kingdom as this includes the assertion of God's power among His people. Then we are to align our wills with the Will of God and His purposes will be fulfilled in our lives.

Verse 11 asks God to supply our daily needs and we have the assurances that He will according to Philippians 4:19. Verses 12 and 15 addresses the issue of forgiveness, if one wants forgiveness, then he/she must be willing to forgive others as God forgave all humanity. God's forgiveness is the basis for our forgiving.

Lastly, verse 13 addresses our concerns for being delivered from all evil as Satan is our adversary who is constantly trying to hinder God's kingdom building.

Pray!

The Lord's Supper: Matthew 26:26-30

And as they were eating, Jesus took the bread, and blessed it, and brake it, and gave it to the disciples, and said, Take, eat, this is my body. And He took the cup, and gave thanks, and gave it to them, saying, Drink ye all of it.

What is the significance of the Lord's Supper? The significance of the Lord's Suppers is related to the past, present and future of the believer's salvation. We see from our scripture text that Christ Himself instituted the Lord's Supper as this was His last Passover meal He would share with His disciples before His sacrificial death at Calvary. This Passover is associated with the spring festival associated with the Israelites departure from Egypt. It is celebrated as the Passover of the Hebrews houses when the death angle passed over where the blood was painted on the door posts. Jesus' crucifixion occurred on "the preparation of the Passover"; (John 19:14) Jesus became our Passover lamb. Jesus' blood would take away the sins of the world. It is noteworthy to say that Jesus was the perfect sacrificial lamb who was worthy to die for the remission of sin.

This brings a question to mind, What is the importance of the remission of sin? First, the remission of sin involves the forgiveness of sin which is what God did through the shed blood of His Son Jesus Christ. Forgiveness was necessary because of humanity's sin and man had become alienated from God and through forgiveness reconciliation was made possible. Second, God's forgiveness of sin involves making no account of man's sin; this is if it never occurred. This is the difference between animal sacrifices and Christ's sacrifice. Third, the term remission means "to pardon", "take away", "cover over", "to cancel", or "to send away." Jesus' sacrificial death on the cross took away our sins, but to receive our pardon one must truly repent of their sins, which involves admitting to their sin, confessing their sins and then turning away from their sins. It is noteworthy to say that divine forgiveness is an ongoing process for believers so that we may maintain our saving relationship with God (Matthew 6:12, 14-15; John 1:9).

Now that we have taken a panoramic view of the Lord's Supper, let's look at the three areas of significance of the Lord's Supper beginning with the **past;** it is the remembrance of Christ's death for the believer's redemption from the bondage of sin and its condemnation. It is a form of thanksgiving for the many blessings and salvation that God made available through Christ's sacrificial death at Calvary. Christ's death is a motivating factor in aiding believers from falling away and reverting back to sin.

The **present** significance of the Lord's Supper is the fellowship that believers have with Christ and one another. All believers share in the benefits of His sacrificial death as we all become one in the body of Christ (1 Corinthians 10:16-17). It is through the Lord's Supper that all believers share in the presence of the risen Lord in a special way (Matthew 18:20; Luke 24:35). Also, it is through the Lord's Supper that we as believers reaffirm the Lord ship of Christ and our commitment to do His will and remain loyal to Him while resisting sin and carrying out His commission as recorded in Matthew 28:19-20.

The **future** significance of the Lord's Supper is the foretaste of the future kingdom of God. It is in the future that all believers will be with the Lord as it is viewed as one big glorious hallelujah celebration. In the future significance, the Lord's Supper looks forward to the time of Christ's imminent return for His people, the church (1Corinthians11:26). More importantly, participation in the Lord's Supper is made meaningful when done in sincere faith and with true devotion to God and His Will.

The Lord's Supper is one of the ordinances of the church as it is done in remembrance of Christ shed blood and broken body for all humanity. The Lord's Supper and baptism are the two ordinances of the church as both symbolize our relationship to and with Christ.

God's Faithfulness And Man's Unfaithfulness
1 Corinthians 10:6-13

There hast no temptation taken you but such as is common to man, but God is faithful, who will not suffer you to be tempted above that your are able, but will with the temptation also make a way to escape, that ye may be able to bear it.

Beginning in verse 1 of our discussion text we see God reminding Israel of His faithfulness to them and their unfaithfulness to Him. Israel's behavior is an expression of their ungratefulness for God's grace and mercy. God reminded Israel how He brought them through the Red Sea on dry land and was a protective covering for them while traveling in the wilderness and even provided meat and water that they didn't have to toil nor draw. What God wanted in return was for Israel to be true to Him and worship Him, but instead they worshipped idols.

God's judgment on Israel is a stern warning for believers under the new covenant as He will not allow sin to go unpunished. In verses 11 and 12, God provides encouragement against sin and the believer's fall from grace (v.12). Verse 13 highlights the faithfulness of God because He has provided the Holy Spirit to aid His people in overcoming temptation. It is noteworthy to say that God in His grace through the Holy Spirit is there when our temptations become too great for us to bear and secondly God always provides His people with an escape route to flee sin and temptation. The grace of God is found in the blood of Jesus, His Word and the indwelling Holy Spirit all working in concert to keep all believers from sin and temptation.

Is our unfaithfulness due to a lack of faith and trust in God?

God's Deliverance In a Time of Need: Psalm 107:13-22

Then they cried unto the Lord in their trouble, and He saved them out of their distresses.

In this psalm, David talks about the goodness of God toward man and that His mercy lasts forever and for this praises of thanksgiving are in order. The preceding verses outline the many ways in which God expresses His deliverance for His people. More importantly, in the time of trouble when all else fails man can call on God and in His faithfulness, and goodness He delivers each time. Verse 13 drives home the point. It is noteworthy to mention that much of our suffering is self-inflected, but nevertheless, when man reaches the point where his/her self-sufficiency fails he/she calls on the Lord and He is faithful to deliver.

What does this say for God and man? Regardless of man's concept of self-sufficiency his existence is embedded in God. It says that God is faithful regardless of our relationship with Him and all our hope rests in God. God is our deliverer and each person can dial 111 and there is never a busy signal. In the OT God Himself delivered His people and in the NT our deliverance was provided through Jesus Christ. **What a great God?**

In every situation of our lives all humanity has the assurances that God is our deliverer because His service record reads faithful, trustworthy, dependable and merciful.

If the question were raised, who else can deliver all humanity from every situation? The answer would be only God.

The King's Prayer: 2 Kings 20:1-7

Then he turned his face to the wall, and prayed unto the Lord, saying, I beseech thee, O Lord, remember now how I have walked with a perfect heart, and have done that which is good in thy sight. And Hezekiah wept sore.

Our scripture text highlights the power of sincere prayer and God's deliverances. This scene opens with King Hezekiah on his death bed of affliction and God sent His prophet Isaiah to see the king with a message, which was for the king to set his house in order because death was certain. Upon receiving this grim news the king immediately went into prayer to God and his prayers was heard and answered. God in His goodness extended the king's life by fifteen years.

What does this say about King Hezekiah's walk with God? Hezekiah walked with God and had great faith and trust in God that He would hear his prayers as he was healed and God delivered both the king and the city from their enemies. **What a prayer answering Go!**

What this says for believers today is that the closer we walk with God the better our relationship is with Him. Our prayer lives are essential to our daily lives as God desires a close fellowship with His people. Another point is that when we as believers go to God in sincere prayer we must possess the confidence that He has the ability to deliver if that is His Will. The Bible records many faithful prayer warriors who God has delivered from their sticky situations; remember the Hebrew boys and Daniel-God can and will do the same for you and I.

Pray in sincere faith-He answers.

Doctor Jesus: Matthew 9:27-34; 11:2-6

And when He had come into the house, the blind man came to Him; and Jesus said unto him, Believe ye that I am able to do this? They said unto Him, Yea Lord.

During Jesus' earthly ministry He healed all manner of diseases without prescription, or any other of today's medical instruments. He simply used His divine powers and when words were necessary He spoke, and when anointing was the order of the day that too was applied. Our scripture verses highlight some of Jesus' healing the many who desired a healing from Him.

The lessons to be learned from Jesus healing ministry is that (a) He is the master healer, (b) He has powers over sickness and death, (c) He is God in the flesh, and (d) to be made whole one must have faith in His ability to heal. These questions come to mind, do you believe in the healing power of Jesus? Do you believe that Jesus is the master healer? Do you see Him as the spiritual healer of man's sins? Upon accepting Jesus as your personal Savior, He becomes your spiritual healer from the sins of this world; then all believers are made whole to eternal life to live a sick-free life. This reminds me of the words to a song; "go tell somebody of the goodness of the Lord, tell somebody of the man who set me free, tell somebody of the man who saved my soul from misery." ***Tell somebody about Jesus who died for you and me. Jesus is the healing balm in Gillian.***

The Disciples' Missionary Journey
Matthew 10:1-8

These twelve Jesus sent forth, and commanded them saying, Go not into the way of the Gentiles, and into any city of the Samaritans enter ye not. But go rather to the lost sheep of the house of Israel.

Jesus' twelve disciples had witnessed Jesus perform many miracles which included healing the sick of their diseases, and often times the healing was an opportunity for Jesus to meet the spiritual needs of the person.

In today's text we see Jesus commissioning His disciples to heal the sick, cast out devils and preach the kingdom. In commissioning His disciples and all believers Jesus gives the necessary power to perform these acts. Matthew 9:38 talks about praying "thy will be done" before undertaking a mission of ministry prayer is one of God's own principles as His powers are released through our prayer requests.

The purpose of the disciples and all believers' missionary journey is to wage war against all evil forces that existed in our world then and now. In addition to healing and casting out evil, we as Disciples of Christ are to preach "the kingdom of heaven is at hand."

In our missionary journey some will hear and be saved just as many were saved during Jesus' earthly ministry. We as Disciples of Christ are to continue the work of Jesus by saving the lost. If the question were raised, what is the mission of the church? It is finding and saving the lost. Lastly, the church is looked upon as the spiritual hospital of the world. The church is the bride of Christ who is its head and it is made up of baptized believers.

Join Christ and His mission of saving the lost.

Jan 23

Great Faith: Matthew 8:5-13

And Jesus said unto the centurion, Go thy way; and as thou hast believed, so be it done unto thee. And his servant was healed in the self same hour.

Today's discuss will focus on the faith of one person's concerns for another's well being as this illustrates the love and concern that all should have for our fellowman. The Centurion in our text sought Jesus for His healing powers for his servant who was on his death bed, but felt unworthy for Jesus to enter his household. The Centurion still expressed great concern for his servant as well as great faith in Jesus' ability to heal.

Some lessons that are highlighted in this text are (a) humility, (b) faith, (c) concern for others, and (d) recognizing Jesus and His power. The Centurion acknowledged his unworthiness to be in the presence of the Lord, while stating his powerful position but lacked the power of healing. Therefore, he humbled himself before the Lord and asked for the needed help on behalf of another. While expressing his concern for his servant he was manifesting the love of Christ which is commanded by Christ Himself. It is noteworthy to say that the Centurion had a right view of self and Christ as this is a requirement of humility. Lastly, the Centurion's faith was the key ingredient in his request as this is true for all who pray or make requests of God.

How do we define faith? Faith is our belief in someone or something. Ones faith in Jesus Christ is what saves all who believe and is freed from sin. Faith the size of a mustard seed will work wonders.

How great is your faith?

Jan 24

Baptism: Matthew 28:18-20
Go ye therefore, and teach all nations, baptizing them in the name of the Father, and of the Son, and of the Holy Ghost. Teaching them to observe all things whatsoever I have commanded you and lo I am with you always, even unto the end if the world.

Today we will take a look at the word "baptism" and its meaning as it relates to Christ and the Christian life. Baptism is defined in the Student's Bible Dictionary (P.38) as immersion, submersion (Romans 6:1-4). Baptism in itself does not save, but it is symbolic of a person's salvation and signifies the believer's obedience to Christ. The water baptism process is symbolic of a person being buried in the earth and being raised from the dead as this is what happens when we speak of being buried with Christ to sin and rose with Him to a new life. Also, the believer being raised to a new life in Christ is the eternal and resurrected life each believer will have in the future (Romans 6:1-6). Mark 10:38-39 and Luke 12:50 equates baptism to the suffering and death of Christ and Christian baptism is the sharing in Christ's death and resurrection as well as the other events that brought Christ to these events (Romans 6:1-7; Colossians 2:12).

John the Baptist baptized with water and preached repentance; the Christian baptism has the same elements as John's baptism did, which are repentance, confession of sin, begin a new life with evidence of such, the coming judgment, a focus on Jesus Christ and His spirit.

Now that we have looked at baptism and Christian baptism, let's look at baptism in the Holy Spirit. Baptism in the Holy Spirit has several doctrinal teachings and they are: (a) it is intended for all who have professed Christ as their personal Savior have the indwelling Holy Spirit. (b) One of Christ's key goals while here on earth was to baptize His followers in the Holy Spirit. (c) Baptism in the Holy Spirit is seen as a distinct operation separate from His regenerating works. (d) Baptism in the Holy Spirit is being filled with the Holy Spirit (Acts 1:5; 2:4). (e) Being baptized in the Holy Spirit mean the believer receives personal boldness and the power of the Holy Spirit to do great works (Acts 1:8; 2:14-41;4:31; 6:8; Romans 15:18-19; 1 Corinthians 2:4). (f) Being baptized in the Holy Spirit brings the believer into the fullness of Him and His prophetic ministry and supernatural gifts for a lifetime of witnessing Christ with power. (g) Lastly, being baptized in the Holy Spirit brings each believer into a relationship with Christ that is renewed (Acts 4:31) and it is maintained (Ephesians 5:18).

If the question were raised, what are some evidences of being baptized in the Holy Spirit? Some trade marks of being baptized in the Holy Spirit are each believer will manifest a great love for God and seek to magnify and glorify His name. Each believer will have an increased awareness of God's love and a closer relationship with Him. There will be a greater appreciation for scripture and its truths. An additional evidence of being baptized in the Holy Spirit is the believer's love and concern for his/her fellowman, and there will be the turning away from sin and a greater desire to please God and live holy lives. ***Being baptized in the Holy Spirit is a blessing.***

Calling Sinners To Repentance
Luke 5:27-32; Isaiah 55:1-3

And after these things He went forth, and saw a publican, named Levi, sitting at the receipt of customs; and He said unto him, Follow me. And he left all, rose up ad followed Him.

The call for sinners to repent has been and continues to be an open invitation from God as recorded in Isaiah 55:1-3, where God is extending an invitation for all to attend His heavenly feast. God invites all humanity come without money and without price as money at His house party is no good. God tells all that partake of His bread and water they will never hunger nor thirst again. God also states on His invitation that ones soul shall delight in the fatness of His heavenly feast. **What a feast!**

Jesus extends the same invitation during His earthly ministry, which He makes plain in verses 31-32. He was seen often in the company of unbelievers and when asked why He kept company with sinners, His reply was that He came to save that which was lost.

If the question were raised, why has God's salvation invitation remained open for such a long time? It is God's desire that all be saved, but He knows that some will fail to repent and be lost. Also, God's open invitation is due to His love and longsuffering. His longsuffering is giving all unbelievers an opportunity to repent. Unrepentant sinners are outside of God's protective seal of salvation and stand to loose the blessing of eternal life. Question, who wants to live in hell (this sinful world) then die and go to hell?

Repent-become heaven bound where joy and happiness reign.

God Loves His Children: Hosea 11:1-4

When Israel was a child, then I loved him, and call my son out of Egypt.

God paints a vivid picture of His love for Israel and all humanity while speaking through His prophet Hosea. See, Israel in her idolatry had forgotten God and what He had done for her forefathers. During Hosea's prophecy, Israel was in complete spiritual apathy as all manner of crimes and violence were common place. To gain the attention of Israel for her idolatry God warned Israel that her own ways would result in destruction of the land. Israel had turned from worshipping God to idols as they were being led into spiritual apathy by their leaders, the king, priest and false prophets.

These questions come to mind, are modern day society guilty of the same spiritual apathy as Israel? Aren't sin and all manner of crime just as rampant in today's society?

The lessons from this scripture are that everyone should seek to know God for themselves for He is the only true and living God who first loved all humanity when man was estranged from Him. To know God one must read and meditate on His Word daily and ask for divine interpretation of the scripture. Resist evil temptation by relying on the indwelling Holy Spirit who is there to guide, teach and protect all who yield to His leadership.

In closing, God's love is manifested in His grace, mercy, and faithfulness, longsuffering and open invitation for repentance.

God's love for His children is never ending. Accept His love and be saved.

The Father Hears: John 11:38-44

And I knew that thou hearest Me always; but because of the people which stand by I said it, that they may believe that thou has sent Me.

Today's discussion is taken from a very familiar passage of scripture where Jesus raises Lazarus from the dead. If the question were raised, what is the importance in this scripture passage? There are several messages here, first, many of the followers in the crowd didn't believe in Jesus, second others didn't know Him, and third Jesus calling Lazarus from the dead was a sign pointing to Jesus' resurrection to life. Also, Jesus' raising Lazarus from the dead showed what God will do for all believers for they too will be raised from the dead (14:3; 1 Thessalonians 4:13-18).

A note of observation here is that Jesus prayed to His Father before He called Lazarus from the grave. This highlights the power of prayer and Jesus belief in prayer also His dependence on His heavenly Father as Jesus stated on many occasions that He came to do the will of His Father.

There were two outcomes from Jesus' raising Lazarus from the dead, and they were (1) many Jews believed on Jesus, and (2) the Pharisees, the Jewish religious leaders of Jesus' day sought to kill Him (vv 45-53).

The lessons learned from this scripture passage are (a) Jesus is the life and the resurrection and all the dead in Christ will be raised with Him unto eternal life. (b)There is power in prayer and all believers should seek to do the will of God. (c) Jesus is our perfect example of a prayer filled life.

Pray God Hears!

Sincere Prayers: Matthew 6:5-8

...When ye pray, use not vain repetition, as the heathen do, for they think that they shall be heard for their much speaking.

Our scripture text provides some helpful advice on where and how to pray; it suggests that every one should have a private place to talk to God one-on-one. This passage of scripture also suggest that when in prayer do not do as the hypocrites do as they pray in public for notoriety or the praise of men because this is all they will receive. Jesus is our perfect example for being alone with God in prayer; scripture records the many instances where Jesus would steal away in private to pray. **Look at the results of Jesus' private time in prayer with God!**

If the question were raised what is the importance of secret prayer? Life in the Spirit Study Bible list three important reasons for secret prayer and they are (1) pray in the morning to commit our day to God, (2) pray in the evening to give thanks to God, and (3) pray when prompted by the Holy Spirit as this doesn't have to be a long prayer just simply state what's on your heart. God, our Father promises to openly reward sincere prayer with His answer and His presence. It is noteworthy to say that our most honest prayers are those that are sincere, short, and direct and to the point when talking to God for He knows our desires before we ask, but He wants His children to come to Him with our requests.

These questions come to mind, when, where and how often do you pray?

Your Prayer Closet: Matthew 14:22-33

And when He had sent the multitude away, He went up into a mountain apart to pray; and when the evening was come, he was there alone.

Again we are discussing prayer and the when's, where's and how's prayers are most effective. Today's scripture depicts Jesus sending His disciples ahead while He retreated up into the mountains to be alone with God in prayer. Spending time alone with God is essential to both believers and non-believers prayer lives for several reasons which are (a) our time with God should be free of distractions, (b) our time with God should be in holy adoration for Him, and (c) our time with Him should be in sincere honesty and in true faith. Jesus' actions express the value of His "me time" with God while realizing the importance of prayer. Even though Jesus was both human and divine He realized that prayer was essential to His spiritual well-being. This is true for all believers in both the OT and NT.

Another school of thought of the importance of being alone with God in prayer is to prevent spiritual decline in ones life. If this does occur then one must take corrective actions in the form of making God first in our lives so that the hunger and thirst for His presence is renewed. It is well documented that ones prayer life is critical to a close fellowship with God. Starting your day with the Lord is a vital component to holy living.

In closing, prayers are important, but our prayer closets "me time" with God is most important.

Love Your Enemies: Matthew 5:43-48

...Love your enemies, bless them that curse you, do good to them that hate you, and pray for them which despitefully use you, and persecute you.

In reading our topical discussion text, this question came to mind, what profit is there to love only your friends? There is no profit in the eyes of God when one loves only his/her friends. When this occurs we are in violation of the second commandment which states we are to "love our neighbor as thy self." Your neighbor could very well be someone you consider your enemy. Verse 44 states, "Love your enemies, bless them that curse you, do good to them that hate you, and pray for them that despitefully use you and persecute you."

We are commanded to love one another because God loved us when we didn't love Him and the magnitude of His love was manifested in His Son Jesus who went to Calvary for the sins of the world. **What love---there is no "greater love hath no man that a man would lay down his life for his friends" (John 15:13).** How can we say we love God whom we have never seen and hate our brother? Are we being hypocritical when this occurs or do we have a true vertical relationship with God? If our brother/sister is living an unholy life we are to hate the sin but love the person. Love is the core of our being because God breathed the breath of life in to each of us.

We have the capability to love and we must love all men-friends and foe.

Jan 31

The Holy Spirit: Exodus 3:14; Genesis 1:1
John 1:1-3; John 14:16-17

..The Spirit of truth whom the world cannot receive, because it seeth Him not, neither knoweth Him; but ye know Him; for He dwelleth with you, and shall be in you.

Let's begin this discussion by asking who is the Holy Spirit? The Holy Spirit is the third person in the Godhead. Members of the Godhead are comprised of God the Father, God the Son, Jesus Christ, and God the Holy Spirit. The Holy Spirit is divine and is a member of the Godhead. He is eternal, omnipresent, omnipotent, and omniscient as He operates coequally, coeternally and coexistently with the other members of the Trinity as one unit.

The Holy Spirit was present during the creation process; He is seen as the spirit that was "moving" (Genesis 1:2) over creation. He was preserving and preparing creation for God's further creative activity. Psalm 33:6 authenticates the presence of the Holy Spirit by stating "By the word of the Lord were the heavens made; And all the hosts of them by the breath of his mouth." As He was active during the creation process, He remains active in the lives of all humanity today and will continue until Christ return. Also, it is noteworthy to say that scripture has it that without the Holy Spirit there would be no creation, no universe, no humanity, no Bible to read God's holy Word. Neither would there be power to proclaim the gospel message (Acts 1:8). Without the Holy Spirit there would be no faith to believe, no holiness to live by, no new birth for Christians which is called regeneration, neither would there be any Christians.

Now that we have looked at the involvement of the Holy Spirit is in human life, let's look at the emblems that are associated with the Him and they are (a) wind, (b) fire, (c) water, (d) oil, (e) seal, and (f) a dove. He can be grieved as He possesses a relationship with humanity. His activities are (a) He reveals, (b) He teaches, (c) He witnesses, and (d) He intercedes for mankind. There are some thirteen names/titles that are associated with the Holy Spirit; some are Spirit of God, Spirit of Christ, Eternal Spirit, Spirit of truth, Spirit of Grace, just to name a few.

We have looked at the Holy Spirit's emblems and some of His titles, let's segway to His role in God's plan of redemption. He was active in the redemptive plan during the OT era as He anointed special people for special assignments and duties. In the NT He is the agent of salvation convicting all of their guilt while revealing to the truth about Jesus Christ. He was the empowering agent during Jesus' wilderness temptation by Satan. He is the agent who baptizes all in the fullness of the Spirit, thus giving believers the power to witness Christ and effectively work as God's ambassadors in the entire world. It is through the Holy Spirit that God gives different gifts to edify the body of Christ. Lastly, it the power of the Holy Spirit that empowers believers to combat Satan's daily attacks as these attacks are designed to disrupt God's plan of salvation and His kingdom building.

Let's close with this question, what is the doctrinal teaching on the Holy Spirit? The doctrinal teaching on the Holy Spirit is that He is part of the triune God, which is essential to the teaching of the Christian faith.

The Holy Spirit is God in the third person.

Jesus The Promised Messiah

Feb 1

Jesus Presented And Revealed To The World
Luke 2:25-35

And behold, there was a man in Jerusalem, whose name was Simeon, and the same man was just and devout, waiting for the consolation of Israel; and the Holy Ghost was upon him.

The background setting for today's discussion is in keeping the law and customs during that time period that after about eight days of purification of the mother and circumcision of the male child sacrifices were to be offered. Mary and Joseph were following the customs and law when they took baby Jesus to the temple there they encountered a devout and just man of God named Simeon. Simeon was performing his priestly duties when Jesus' parents presented Him in the temple according to the custom. The Holy Spirit had revealed to Simeon that he would not see death until the consolation of Israel.

When Simeon looked upon the child he knew he had seen the promised Messiah and his wish had been granted by God. Seeing God face to face is the desire and greatest blessing for all Christians. Both Simeon and Anna, a prophetess offered praises to God as this was the dawning of the Messianic era as there would be a new spiritual awakening; many would witness an increased presence of the Holy Spirit as prophesied. Jesus the Messiah came to save the world—both Jews and Gentiles from the bondage of sin (vv32, 35).

Jesus presented in the temple and revealed to the world as Lord and Savior as He is God who died to set men free, but He rose with all power. He is constantly being revealed daily to new believers.

Hallelujah Christ is alive!

God Judges All: Romans 2:1-11

But we are sure that the judgment of God is according to truth against them which commit such things.

Why were God's judgments necessary? All manner of sin had become common place among all humanity and especially the Gentile nation (Romans 1:24) and God gave them over to a reprobate mind. What this means is that God abandoned this society of people. This is because their sinful lifestyle did not glorify and honor God. God is the righteous judge who cannot and will not look on or tolerate sin. God is longsuffering giving sinners time to repent, but if there is no repentance, then judgment is assured.

From our scripture text, we see God judging both Jews and Gentiles alike because the Jews were committing the same sins as the Gentiles (v.1), and in verse 3 Paul admonishes the Roman believers that just because you are God's chosen people don't think that you will escape His punishment from your sins.

Verse 11 answers the question as to why God judges all, which is "there is no respect of persons with God." In verse 6 which also states that God will render to every man according to his deeds (paraphrase); this means if you sin, punishment will follow and if you do good then your reward is eternal life which is the basics for salvation.

The question now becomes, who would fail to honor and glorify their creator and sustainer of all life, or the one who can kill both body and spirit?

Live a righteous life and receive your reward-eternal life.

God's Words Preached To The Gentiles
Acts 13:44-49

And when the Gentiles herd this, they were glad, and glorified the word of the Lord, and as many as were ordained to eternal life believed.

The setting for today's topical discussion is Paul was expounding on the Word of God to the Jewish believers, but after they left the synagogue the gentile believers approached Paul asking him to share the Word of God with them the next Sabbath so that all could hear the Word of God. When the Jewish religious leaders witnessed the whole city coming to hear the Word of God being preached they became angry and tried to hinder the spread of God's Word by speaking against what Paul was preaching. What did Paul do? He became bolder in his message of Christ and told them that the Word came to them first but they rejected it, therefore it was necessary for all to hear and believe on Christ (v.45). There are two declarations in this verse and they are (a) when the Jews rejected the Word they declared themselves unworthy of salvation, and (b) God's Word is for all as God always has a spokesperson who is ready, willing and able to preach Christ in spite of opposition.

The reaction of the Gentiles upon hearing the Word of God as recorded in verse 48 makes a profound statement of gratitude and the power therein for all who hear and then believe. Verse 49 substantiates the power of the Word and the growth of God's kingdom.

Share God's Word for there are those who want to hear and will believe His Word.

The Brightness Of God's Glory
Isaiah 59:20-21; 60:1-5

Arise, shine; for the light is come, and the glory of the Lord is risen, upon thee.

Isaiah paints a glowing picture of Christ as our redeemer coming out of Zion. Isaiah pictures Christ as a glowing light that will come as a bright light manifesting the glory and majesty of God Himself.

Christ is the promised Messiah who will redeem His people from the bondage of sin. Christ will come to those who will genuinely turn from their sins (repent) and commit themselves to serving the Lord. God also promises that all who repent of their sins and accept His Son as their Savior then God's spirit will come upon them (Acts 2:4; John 16:13) and His words will never leave their mouths. This scene will be perpetuated for generations to come and the result is that God's kingdom will continue to grow.

The prophecy of the redeemer has been fulfilled in the NT and the continued preaching Christ and His glory as all nations and leaders/rulers/people come to share in the light of Christ and witness Christ to others. The "all" includes all humanity. Scripture states that every knee shall bow and every tongue shall confess that Jesus is Lord. Verse 4 solidifies that all will come to Christ and will have glory in the brightness of the light. It is note worthy to say that I am witnessing more and more people acknowledging Christ as Lord.

The light of Christ sheds light on the darkness of sin and the need for His redeeming power.

Walk In The Light: Revelation 21:22-27

And the city had no need of the sun, neither of the moon, to shine in it; for the glory of God did lighten it, and the Lamb of the light thereof.

In John's vision while marooned on the Isle of Patmos he saw the New Jerusalem and what it will be like. The City of Jerusalem will be squared with twelve gates and walled which represents security for the believers. The twelve gates represent Israel (v.12) and the twelve foundations represent the church (v.14) as these representations are the continuity between God's people in both the OT and NT as He is the God of all believers for all the ages.

In the new City of Jerusalem the brightness of God and His glory will provide the necessary light as there will be no need for city lights, moon light as there will be no night and no need for "the light of the sun". It is believed that the light of God will be the light for the saved who will "walk in the light" of God as He promised that day and night will never pass away (Psalm 148:3-6; Isaiah 66:22-23; Jeremiah 33:20-21;25).

Residents of the City of Jerusalem will have been cleansed from all abominations as they will have been washed in the blood of Jesus—the Lamb of God. Therefore, believers from all nations will have earned the right to "walk in the Light" of God. There we will be singing, shouting and praising God. **What a glorious time that will be?**

Accept salvation and spend eternity with God, His Son and the Holy Spirit—the Godhead in the New Jerusalem.

Christ Pleased Not Himself: Romans 15: 1-4

For even Christ pleased not Himself; but, as it is written, The reproaches of them that reproached thee fell on me.

If the question were raised why is self-denial so important? The appropriate answer is that all believers are Christ-like who denied Himself for the sake of others. Romans 14:15, 20 talks about how self-denial promotes the work of God and when we disregard the conviction of others we destroy God's work. Another point on self-denial is that when other believers and new babes in Christ see self-denial in more mature Christians this causes the weaker Christians to grow in Christ.

It is most important for all believers to remember Christ and His self-denial during His earthly ministry. Throughout scripture Christ always indicated that He was doing the will of His Father so that His heavenly Father would be glorified. What does this say about Christ's self-denial and we as believers? It says that we as believers like Christ have no reputation to be gained in God's kingdom building. Why? Because it is about the creator and His glory and honor for He is worthy of all honor, praises and glory. It is note worthy to say that we as believers have no eternal life to give; our mission is to witness Christ and His saving powers. Christ denied Himself to fulfill His mission at Calvary as this pleased His Father to become humanity's sacrificial lamb in bridging the divide between God and man. **What a sacrifice?**

If Christ denied Himself why can't you and I in making disciples for Christ?

Peter's Faith: Matthew 16:13-20

And Simon Peter answered and said, Thou are the Christ, the Son of the living God.

During Jesus' earthly ministry and as His popularity grew, many began to wonder just who Jesus was which prompted the question from Jesus to His disciples, which was "Whom do men say that I the Son of man am" (v.13)? Many felt that Jesus was John the Baptist, while others thought that Jesus was Elias, and others thought that He was Jeremiah, or even one of the other prophets (v.14 paraphrase), but when the question was asked directly "Who do you say that I am? Peter answered quickly "thou are the Christ, the Son of the living God." The question now becomes what brought Peter to this conclusion? First, the Holy Spirit was working through Peter to make known to him that Jesus was the Christ. Second, Peter knew Jesus was no ordinary man to perform the many miracles he had seen Jesus perform. Case in point, Jesus displayed His deity when directing Peter and his partners to launch out into the deep to catch more fish. Another miracle that Peter witnessed to authenticate his faith that Jesus was the Christ, the promised Messiah was the leaven bread for the Pharisees and Sadducees (vv 5-12). Then there was the feeding of the five thousand with two fishes and five loaves of bread and the amount of food left over.

Peter exhibited his faith in Jesus when asked to "follow me and I will make you fishers of men" and Peter immediately left family, friends and occupation of fishing to follow Jesus. Another point on Peter's faith in Jesus was when he began to walk on the water as Jesus walked on the water. Peter was successful until he took his eyes off Jesus. What does this say for you and me? Peter's actions make a profound statement concerning his commitment to following Jesus. The question now becomes, are we equally as committed to Christ? Each believer's answer is reflective of the believer's personal relationship with Jesus.

Symbolically believers can walk on water as long as Jesus is our focus, but when believers take our eyes off Jesus, we begin to sink in our Christian walk. The following questions come to mind, how strong is your faith in Jesus? Are we Christ centered? Does the world see Christ manifested in your daily walk?

Now that we have talked about Peter's faith and some specifics that enhanced Peter's faith, let's talk about the everyday life of faith. For Peter to leave his family and occupation which provided life's necessities took great faith that all would be well. Scripture omits details of this aspect of Peter's decision-making. How would we handle the decision? This brings into focus two thoughts which are the young ruler who wanted to follow Jesus but first wanted time to bury the dead and Jesus instructed him to "let the dead bury the dead." The other is taking no thought for today because today will take care of itself. God said in Philippians 4:19 the He would supply all our needs, this includes family as well as individual disciples (Peter and the rest). Peter's faith exemplifies true faith in God as being led by the Holy Spirit.

True faith and commitment equals a closer walk with God.

Know the Voice of Jesus: John 10:22-30

My sheep hear my voice, and I know them, and they follow me.

  The setting for today's topical discussion takes place with Jesus entering the temple in Solomon's porch and was met by the Jewish leaders questioning His identity if He was really the Christ. Jesus gave His questioners an interesting answer by telling them that He had told them but they refused to believe Him or His works (v.25). In verse 26 Jesus gave the reason why His questioners would fail to believe Him and it was because they were not His sheep (people) which supports verse 14 which states, "I am the good shepherd, and know my sheep, and am known of mine." Jesus continues His conversation with His questioners by telling them that His sheep hear His voice and follow Him as He knows each of His sheep (v.27). What this verse means is that true believers of Christ hear and obey the voice of Jesus and they follow Him. Hearing and following Jesus is a continuous activity that believers must do daily. Furthermore, following Jesus gives eternal life.
  Another school of thought on knowing the voice of Jesus is that true believers are in close fellowship with Him as there is safety and security in following Jesus. As stated in Romans 8:35-39 that nothing can separate us from the love of God; no amount of tribulation can accomplish that feat.
  Know the voice of Jesus-your shepherd and follow Him for He is the good shepherd.

Feb 9

Believe the Good News: Mark 1:9-15

..The time is fulfilled, and the kingdom of God is at hand; repent ye, and believe the gospel.

If the question were raised, What is the good news? The good news is commonly viewed as the death, burial and resurrection of our Lord and Savior Jesus Christ. Another thought on believing the good news is that God had fulfilled His promise to send the Messiah who would save the world from sin and Jesus the Savior was living proof of a promise fulfilled. Just as God the Father was faithful in keeping His promise Jesus would fulfill His mission of dying on the cross for humanity's sins. Another school of thought on believing the good news of Jesus Christ is that He willingly disrobed of His glory in heaven to be subjected to human limitations and rejections by man all for the good of man.

In our scripture text we see Jesus being baptized in the Jordan River by His forerunner John the Baptist and when Jesus immerged from the water other members of the Godhead authenticated Jesus' deity and His earthly ministry was to begin. The good news in this scenario is that God the Father is pleased at the Son's work and ministry. Because of the unity in the Godhead they knew what lay ahead for the Son. Lastly, Jesus humbled Himself for baptism as a symbol for what His sacrificial death would represent--the removal of sin---Jesus was sinless.

Good news! Jesus is providing salvation for all who believe.

A Cry For Help: Mark 9:14-27

And straightway the father of the child cried out, and said with tears, Lord, I believe; help thou mine unbelief.

Today's topical discussion is based on Jesus and His healing ministry had and how He attracted a great crowd of followers. In this crowd was the father of a demonic possessed boy who required being set free from his demonic captures. The father had tried everything he knew to do with no success; he even asked Jesus' disciples, but instead they brought the boy and his father to Jesus.

Some important lessons from our scripture text and they are (a) a lack of faith by the disciples to heal the boy (v.19), (b) the father's display of his love for his son and his desire for his healing, (c) the healing power of Jesus, (d) the father's faith in Jesus, (e) Satan knows Jesus and His power as he is no match for Jesus. (f) Jesus is still in the healing business. (g) We are no match for Satan in our own strength, but with the power of God through the Holy Spirit we can and will be victorious over Satan. (h) We as believers need faith the size of a mustard seed to do great things in the name of Jesus. Faith will conquer our unbelief as it did the father in this text.

Questions that come to mind are What does this say for our cry for help? Are we at our lowest ebb before we cry out to Jesus for help? ***Our cry for help is just a prayer away.***

Jesus As Lord Saves: Acts 2:29-36

Therefore let all the house of Israel know assuredly, that God hath made the same Jesus, whom ye have crucified, both Lord and Christ.

The writer, Dr. Luke is making a profound point as to who Jesus is and His saving powers by comparing Jesus to David. The writer points out to the Christians church that David died and remained dead, but Jesus died on Friday and rose on Sunday whereby making Him God's Son the one who can save all who believe on His name. Another startling comparison being made is that they were witness to Christ's resurrection and His ascension back to heaven and is now sitting on the right hand of His Father. David didn't rise from the grave nor did he ascend into heaven. The most startling comparison is that God the Father has made Jesus His Son both Lord and Savior—as He is being God in the second person who died for the sins of the world; David had no saving power.

Jesus as Lord saves because He became the perfect sacrifice for all humanity which required a sinless person and Jesus met all requirements to become the Savior of the world. He had an earthly mother and God as His Father as He was conceived by the Holy Spirit. Only Jesus' shed blood for the remission of sin could pay humanity's sin debt. No other person was found suitable, not David, not Elijah or any of the other prophets—only Jesus the God man.

Jesus is our Savior because He is the anointed One slain from the foundation of the world.

Have Faith In God: Mark 11:20-25

...Have faith in God. For verily I say unto you, That whosoever shall say unto this mountain, Be thou removed, and be thou cast into the sea; and shall not doubt in his heart, but shall believe that those things which he saith shall come to pass; the shall have whatsoever he saith.

Faith can be defined as ones belief and to have faith in God is to put our trust in the one true and living God who is the creator and sustainer of all that exist. Having faith in God is the faith that God imparts to us to trust Him at all times. Throughout the Bible, God is the object of our true faith. Luke 6: 12 talks about God being the object of prayers to Him and Luke 11:42 speaks of God being the objective of our love towards Him. Romans 3:18 also speaks of God being the objective of fear in reverence.

The Bible records notables who had faith in God and were rewarded for their faith; Abraham believed God and began to travel to an unknown land, but because of his faith he was counted as righteous. Noah believed God and by faith began to build the ark when there was no rain for 120 years and because of his faith he and his entire family were saved. Enoch's faith in God caused him to walk so closely with God until he did not see death. The faith of Daniel and the Hebrew boys caused them to refuse to worship idol gods and because of their faith in God they were delivered from the fire and the lion's den. **What great faith?**

Faith in God will result in our deliverance regardless of the situation. Faith in brings salvation. Have faith!

Keys To God's Kingdom: Matthew 16:19

And I will unto thee the keys of the kingdom of heaven; and whatsoever thou shall bind on earth shall be bound in heaven; and whatsoever thou shall loose on earth shall be loosed in heaven.

Keys represent an entry into some places, but keys in this scenario represent the authority to enter into the kingdom of heaven. Also, keys in this scenario represent the loosing and binding of things in heaven and earth and the one with that authority is Jesus Christ. This authority was given to Jesus by His Father God who also gave Jesus the authority to delegate His authority to Peter and the church for the purpose of carrying out the great commission as recorded in Matthew 28:19-20.

Peter and the church were given keys (authority) to save lost souls through proclaiming the gospel message of Christ and in doing so they would make other disciples for Christ. Also, the church has been given the keys (authority) to bind demons and all manner of diseases, set free the captives from their sins, addictions, and sickness and free them to salvation. Binding and loosing victory have been accomplished through Jesus' work on Calvary's cross.

The church has been given the authority (keys) to stand firm on the Word of God and against the adversary because of Jesus' assurance as recorded in Matthew 16:18, which states "Upon this rock I will build my church and the gates of hell shall not prevail against it." Church, you have been given authority (keys) to be a force to be reckoned with for God in His kingdom building as this authority was given by God Himself through His Son Jesus Christ. ***Exercise your authority/keys.***

Jesus And The Samaritan Woman: John 4: 5-26

Jesus saith unto her, I that speak unto thee am He.

Today's discussion setting takes place with Jesus traveling to Samaria and meeting a Samarian woman at Jacob's well. A conversation ensued between Jesus and the woman while His disciples were gone into the city. Jesus being God and all knowing knew that this woman would come to the well to draw water and Jesus met the woman at a point of mutual interest to get her to where He wanted her to be which was on a spiritual plane. In other words Jesus used well water for His topic of discussion to get her to see that He is the living water and all who drink of Him will thirst no more. During the course of their conversation, the woman surmised that Jesus was a prophet because of His statement of giving everlasting water.

Their conversation turned to worship and where and how to worship the true and living God. The woman had heard of the promised Messiah but failed at this point to recognize Jesus as the Messiah. Finally Jesus told her "I am he" (v.26).

It was through this woman's encounter with Jesus and conversion that the entire town was saved. The Samaritan woman witness Christ to every one she met and her testimony was so powerful that others believed on Jesus. Some questions come to mind which are, is your encounter with Jesus life changing? Do you witness Christ? How believable is your testimony? In witnessing Christ does it matter the person's nationality? It didn't with Jesus. If Jesus came today and asked who have you told about me what would your answer be?

Living a life in and for Christ we are to witness Christ everywhere and to everyone, because Jesus in this scenario did not allow racial differences to become a barrier in saving many souls and neither should we. He used one woman to save a city.

The Samarian woman serves as an example for us today in our witness because we never know who is seeking the love of Jesus in all the wrong places.

> Feb 15

Grow In Christ: 2 Peter 1:3-14

According to His divine power hath given unto us all things that pertain unto life and godliness, through the knowledge of Him that hats called us to glory and virtue.

In verse 3 of our scripture text Peter outlines all that is needed for Christians to grow in the knowledge and truth of God. First, Peter tells us that the "divine power of God hath given all things that pertain to life and godliness; through the knowledge of him that hath called us to glory and virtue." The meaning of this verse is that through the love of God our Father and the salvation of Jesus Christ who is making intercession for us in heaven and the indwelling Holy Spirit believers have all the components to live holy and godly lives for God and before men. Also, anyone baptized in the Holy Spirit by Christ's spirit and remain in communion with God and His Word has the ability to live a holy and godly life. It is note worthy to say that no human addition to God's Word is required for believers to grow in Christ and the knowledge of Him.

Peter goes on to outline the characteristics of virtue as they relate to Christian growth and those are (a) faith, (b) knowledge, (c) temperance, (d) patience, (e) godliness, (f) brotherly kindness, and (g) charity which is love. In verse 10, Peter encourages all believers to add these virtues in order to make ones election sure. Believers' election is our salvation spending eternity with God.

How do we grow in Christ? Christians grow in Christ by taking on the virtues outlined in our discussion text.

Feb 16

John Bears Witness To Jesus: John 1:6-8

There was a man sent from God, whose name was John. The same came for a witness of the Light, that all men through Him might believe. He was not that Light, but was sent to bear witness of that Light.

What does it mean to be a witness? To be a witness to something or for someone means to give an account of what you know first hand or have seen. However, in John's case he was anointed by God before birth to be the forerunner of Christ as he, John was filled with the Holy Spirit to preach repentance and to baptize with water. More importantly, John's ministry was set for him before his birth and in obedience to his calling John began preaching repentance because the coming Messiah was to follow him and He was the light of the world.

John was to bear witness to the light, who was Jesus Christ whose mission was to take away the sins of the world through His death and resurrection. John presented such powerful messages regarding repentance for the kingdom that many believed he was the light, but John was only a witness in his efforts to prepare the hearts and minds for the true light---Jesus Christ.

John was an eye witness to Christ because he lived during Jesus' day, but what about you and I in bearing witness to Jesus? Our witness must be a faith witness as we have seen Jesus through our spiritual eye. Also, we have the powerful testimonies of those gospel writers, apostles, disciples and prophets who walked with Jesus.

Our spiritual eye witness is a powerful account of Jesus as Lord.

Accept Jesus: John 1:9-11

He came unto His own, and His own received Him not.

Regardless of John's preaching about repentance and bearing witness to the light of Christ many who heard John rejected Jesus. In rejecting Jesus as the light of the world what were they rejecting? Jesus was being rejected as God's Son who came to save the world from the darkness of sin, but on the other hand all who heard and accepted Jesus and His gospel message and recognized that it is through Him that they may see God's truth and be saved (v. 9). If a light is shinned in a dark room the darkness dissipates; on a spiritual plane the same occurs in our lives when we accept Jesus as the light of the world.

Scripture tells us that the world was made by him, and He came into the world in human form to bring awareness to the truth that He is the co-creator and sustainer of all that exists and offering salvation. He is worthy of all humanity's acceptance as He lights our way out of darkness into a marvelous light---the light of Christ. Accepting Christ is an act of faith and knowing who He is and His power to save man's soul. By accepting Jesus as Lord ones faith is on constant display as this is an attitude change for a lifetime. Accepting Jesus carries rewards of salvation, everlasting bread and water, becoming adopted sons of God and a crown of life waiting for us when we get to heaven.

Blessing! Blessing!

Who Is Jesus?: John 1: 14-18

And the Word was made flesh, and dwelt among us, (and we beheld His glory, the glory as of the only begotten of the Father) full of grace and truth.

Let us explore our subject question and conclude who Jesus is. First, Jesus is the incarnated Christ which is to say God became flesh and took on humanity's form. Jesus being God in the flesh remained perfect in His divinity and free of sin (v.14). In order to ransom humanity from the bondage of sin a sin free person was required and Jesus fulfilled all the requirements. Second, Jesus is the "Word" who became flesh.

Third, Jesus was begotten of the Father born not by the will of flesh but by the Holy Spirit (v.13). Also, being gotten of the Father does not mean that Jesus was created sometime during the creation process, but it shows His relationship to His Father as He is part of the Trinity and was eternal from the beginning. Further proof of Jesus' Sonship was witness at His baptism in the Jordan River when God the Father and the Holy Spirit met Jesus when he came up out of the water and God the Father declared "his is my beloved Son in whom I am well pleased" (Matthew 3:16-17).

Fourth, Jesus is both truth and grace as it is through Jesus that both truth and grace is available to all who believe (Romans 5:17-21).

Lastly, Jesus is the Savior of the world as He came into the world to be the light of the world for all men to see.
Jesus is Lord and Savior.

Jesus Authenticates His Deity: John 2:1-10

Jesus saith unto them, Fill the waterpots with water. And they filled them up to the brim. And He saith unto them. Draw out now, and bear unto the governor of the feast. And they bare it.

Early in Jesus' ministry He attended a wedding ceremony where wine was being served and the wedding party depleted their supply of wine and He was called upon to do something, which He did. Jesus instructed the servants to fill water pots with water and when tested wine came forth.

Attendees at this gathering should have suspected that He was no ordinary man to turn water into wine—but they didn't. From all outer appearances Jesus looked as any other man, but He held all the powers of His Father. However, Jesus' mother knew her Son was special that she had given birth to the Savior of the world. Even though He walked and talked as a natural man, but He spoke with the power of God.

It is note worthy to say that Jesus turning water into wine was one of the many miracles performed authenticating His deity. As a result of these miracles many believed and were saved but many were not.

Question, what miracle in your life must Jesus perform for you to believe He is the Christ God's Son? Believe: (1) In His heavenly conception and that He is God's Son. (2) He died on Friday evening and rose early Sunday morning with all power both in heaven and earth in His hands. (3) His salvation invitation remains open to all who accept Him in faith. (4) He is coming again soon for His bride-the church.

Jesus is God.

Feb 20

Miracles: John 2:11; Numbers 14:22

Because all those men which have seen my glory, and my miracles, which I din in Egypt and in the wilderness, and have tempted Me now these ten times, and have not hearkened to my voice.

How do we define miracles? The Student's Bible Dictionary (P.156) defines miracles as "God's intervention in humanity, nature, and history (Numbers 14:22; John 2:11)." Also, "miracles can be defined as signs, wonders, or mighty acts. Miracles carry out God's purpose or reveal God."

The many signs and wonders recorded in John's gospel endorse Jesus' activities as the work of God and offer proof positive that Jesus is God's Son in the flesh as they further validate His deity and authority to do His works. It is note worthy to say that of the gospel writers John's gospel highlights Christ's deity. Another purpose for the many miracles Jesus performed was to call humanity into faith in Him and not the miracles itself. Case in point, Jesus giving sight to the blind and making the lame to walk as well as casting out demons from those possessed, namely Mary Magdalene who became a devout follower of Jesus. She was the first at His tomb on Resurrection Sunday and saw that He had risen as promised.

It is noteworthy to mention that God used the angel and His glory to make the announcement to the shepherds of Jesus' birth and where to find the baby as well as the clothing Jesus would be wearing.

Scripture warns us of the false signs that will be performed by the antichrist in the end-times to deceive many.

True believers will know the truth by trying the spirit by the spirit-God's Spirit.

Feb 21

Jesus and Nicodemus: John 3:1-13

...Verily, verily, I say unto thee, Except a man be born again, he cannot see the kingdom of God.

During Jesus' earthly ministry, His fame had spread to the point that wherever His travels took Him His profound teachings and miracles preceded Him. On this particular journey there was a man from the Pharisees named Nicodemus who had heard of Jesus' teaching and wanted to meet Him. What was so profound about Nicodemus was that he knew Jesus was from God as confirmed by His powerful teaching. Nicodemus inquired about getting into heaven, but Jesus' reply (v.3) on being born again puzzled Nicodemus which prompted further explanation from Jesus.

The essence of Jesus' explanation to Nicodemus was regeneration/rebirth which is of the spirit-rebirth/born again is the foundation teaching of the Christian faith. Without a rebirth no one will enter into the kingdom of heaven and receive eternal life and salvation which is through Jesus Christ. Rebirth/regeneration is a faith issue which begins in the heart which is what Jesus was explaining to Nicodemus (vv 7-8). In verses 11-13 Jesus made plain His teaching on rebirth by using earthly things to make His point as He did on numerous occasions.

Jesus marveled at the fact the Nicodemus was a leader of the Jewish people and failed in his understanding of the doctrine of being born again. A puzzling question comes to mind, how many would-be Christians lack the understanding on rebirth/being born again as Nicodemus? One must believe that Jesus is God's Son and accept Him as his/her personal Savior and His atoning work on Calvary they will be saved.

It is note worthy to say that regeneration/rebirth is necessary because prior to all believers turning to Christ the non-believer is spiritually dead because of sin and the person is living in their inherited sinful nature. Without a rebirth no one is capable of pleasing God (Romans 8:7-8; 1 Corinthians 2:14; Ephesians 2:3). In other words regeneration/rebirth is a transitioning from the old self to a new life of Christ. Even though the physical body doesn't change the change is manifested through the lifestyle of the new believer. The new man or repentant sinner is ready to conform to the holiness of God and form a right relationship with God.

Scripture is silent as to whether Nicodemus repented, but it is believed so because he sought Jesus and in recorded Biblical history and from personal knowledge that anyone who meets Jesus is a changed person. Case in point, the woman at the well was changed and her repentance saved the entire city. Then there are Jesus' disciples when they first encountered Jesus their lives were changed forever. Then there is you and I who no longer walk in the darkness of sin because of our encounter with Jesus the light of the world, the Savior who saves each and everyone He encounters. It doesn't matter if we lack the understanding like Nicodemus are doubters like Thomas, Jesus the master locksmith can and does change/unlock the locked/unrepentant hearts of man. Seek Jesus as Nicodemus did for Jesus is waiting with an explanation on "being born again" and extending salvation.

Believe and be born of the spirit-a spiritual birth is unto eternal life.

Feb 22

Giving God's Way: Deuteronomy 15:7-11

Thou shalt surely give him, and thine heart shall not be grieved when thou giveth unto him; because that for this thing the Lord thy God shall bless thee in all this works, and in all that thou puttest tine hand unto.

Our focus topic brings this question to mind, how do you give? The answer is found in verses 7-8 which states, "If there be among you a poor man of one of thy brethren within any of thy gates in thy land which the Lord thy God giveth thee, thou shalt not harden thy heart, nor shut thine hand from thy poor brother. But thou shalt open thine hand wide unto him, and shalt surely lend him sufficient for his need, in that which he wanteth." What these verses are really saying is that all who have been blessed with plenty are to give liberally to those in need as God blesses the cheerful giver.

Also, in obedience to God's law those that have are expected to obey God and give to the ones in need Deuteronomy 24:19-21; Leviticus 19:10) God cares about all humanity and it is His desire that the ones in need are cared for by those who have plenty. New Testament scriptures encourage giving to those in need through the many circumstances that can and does befall our fellowman (Matthew 25:31-36; Galatians 6: 2, 10).

However, in today's society we see the haves constantly striving for more with a disregard for the poor, this is not God's way. Scripture has recorded that much of Jesus' ministry was to the poor and disadvantaged, and in Matthew 6:1-4 Jesus expects His people to give generously to the poor and disadvantaged.

Give like the Lord!

Continued In Prayer: Acts 1:12-14

These all continued with one accord in prayer and supplication with the women, and Mary, the mother of Jesus; and with His brethren.

While Jesus was on His way back to heaven some of His followers were standing gazing up in the sky, Jesus questioned them as to why were they doing such (v.11). Jesus had given His disciples their instruction which was to go to the upper room and tarry for the Holy Ghost and when the Holy Ghost/Spirit came He would give them power to witness boldly (v. 8) for Him.

In obedience to Jesus His followers returned to the upper room where Peter, James, John and the rest of the disciples were and there ensued a prayer meeting. They all were on one accord in their prayers and supplication and when this happens we know great and powerful things happen—the Holy Ghost/Spirit came in a mighty way. The prayer group consisted of both men and women as they devoted to Jesus and His ministry. When the Holy Spirit came three thousand souls were saved.

The lesson here is that prayer changes things as there is power in prayer and our faith holds the key to answered prayers. Another lesson from our text is that God kept His promise of sending the Holy Spirit, and the obedience of Christ's followers. Moral—constant prayers in the lives of modern day believers are essential. Both written and unwritten, OT and NT, and the age of grace provides profound testimonies of the results of constant prayers by the saints of God.

Pray because prayers are always in order.

Persecuting The Church: Acts 8:1-4

And Saul was consenting unto his death, And at that time there was a great persecution against the church which was at Jerusalem; and they were all scattered abroad throughout the region of Judea and Samaria, except the apostles.

In an effort to stop the growth of the church, there was a man named Saul who had made it his mission to persecute all Christians-the church and stop its growth. He had received a letter from the governor to find, and persecute/kill all Christians. Saul was so dedicated to his mission that he was ready to die for his mission and it appears from the widespread persecution of the church many persecutors felt the same and this resulted in the church being scattered throughout the region of Judea with the exception of the apostles.

Stephen had been stoned to death for his preaching Christ and Saul/Paul on his way was met by Jesus on the Damascus' Road and was questioned by Jesus "Why persecuted thou me?"

What man meant for harm God turned the situation around to begin an ever greater work for the church. Saul's conversion was instrumental in furthering the work of God's church. Paul established many churches throughout Asia Minor and he and the other apostles suffered many hardships for their church work.

Today we do not have to suffer for our church/Christ work, but the question now becomes how are we promoting God's church? Is it through our witness and aiding the poor and disadvantaged we encounter? Are we promoting the church in our giving as God has given to us?

In spite of persecution the church continues to grow.

Phillip Preaches To Samaria: Acts 8:5-24

Then Phillip went down to the city of Samaria, and preached Christ unto them. And the people with one accord gave heed unto those things which Phillip spake, hearing and seeing the miracles which he did.

Evidence of continued church growth is witnessed by Phillip's preaching Christ to the Samarians and their response. The church was being widely persecuted and Phillip being a devout man of God journeyed to Samaria to preach the gospel of Christ and God authenticated the gospel message with miraculous signs that were performed (vv 5-7).

What are the results of Phillips preaching? Verses 12 and 14 records that many Samarians who heard the Word of God believed and were baptized, this includes the sorcerer Simon who believed and was healed of his evil spirits. Also, these new believers in Jesus experienced salvation and the regenerating work of the Holy Spirit as well as the power of God's kingdom (v.12). After the Samarians' conversion Peter and John came to Samaria and prayed that they receive the Spirit after the pattern that was experienced at Pentecost.

The church growth witnessed by the Samarians is the direct result of what happens when Christ is preached and the Holy Spirit's convicting work of regeneration-souls are saved, lives are changed, other disciples are made. What we have then is a Christian community committed to God and His kingdom building. More importantly, there is power in the name of Jesus and all who believe on the name receives power to tell others as Phillips and the apostles.

Proclaim the gospel message as commissioned by Christ in obedience to Him (Matthew 28:19-20).

Feb 26

Men And Women Believing And Accepting Christ
Acts 17:1-15

..Many of them believed; also of honourable women which were Greeks, and of men, not a few.

Paul's missionary journeys carried him to many places throughout Asia Minor preaching Christ and he was successful in that many who heard the Word of God believed and were saved. Many of those who were saved were people of affluence as this proves that the gospel is for all who hear and believe. Throughout Paul's journey he established many churches while adding to the kingdom of God.

Another school of thought is that Paul's missionary journey solidifies the growth of the church and ones dedication to Christ after an encounter with the Lord. Also, it speaks to the issue of Jews and Gentiles desiring to hear the Word of God. Paul's missionary journey is evidence that he was in total obedience to the great commission given by Christ Himself (Matthew 28:19-80) as well as many of the leading ladies who played an integrate part in church growth.

It is note worthy to say that in many of the cities that Paul visited the people wanted verification that the doctrines he was preaching were actually from God. In verifying these doctrines some searched the scriptures daily for themselves. Daily Bible reading promotes Christian growth, truth and knowledge of Christ for all believers both then and now.

It can be concluded then that preaching Christ leads to men and women coming to Christ and this leads to salvation.

The great invitation; come to Christ.

Lydia A Servant Of God: Acts 16:14-15

And a certain woman named Lydia, a seller of purple, of the city of Thyatira, which worshipped God, heard us; whose heart the Lord opened, that she attended unto the things which were spoken of Paul.

Today's discussion focuses on a woman servant of God who did not allow her position in society to deter her from serving God and His ministry. Lydia was a seller of purple in the city of Thyatira and when she heard Paul expounding on the Word of God her heart was pricked and became a great ally of Paul and his companions. Lydia and her household were baptized, and then she proceeded to open her house to Paul so they could continue preaching Christ and worship continued and her home became the first church in Philippi (v. 40).

History records Lydia as the first European convert to Christianity at Philippi. Being that Lydia was a convert meant that she was a proselyte as was many of the other women who met for prayer by the river. Lydia continued her service to the Lord so much so that Paul called her a servant who labored with him in the ministry.

Lydia's service to the Lord and her church work is an example of the many women who have and continues to be instrumental to church and in the church. Women are looked upon as being dedicated and devoted to the Lord and their service work for God. Case in point, Dorcas/Tabitha is considered the first female disciple who did many good works and after she died her community sent for Peter to come and pray and restore her to life.

Lydia a faithful servant!

Women Serving God
Matthew 26:6-13; Acts 18:2-3; 18; Philippians 4:1-3

And Paul after this tarried there yet a good while, and then took his leave of the brethren, and sailed thence into Syria, and with him Priscilla and Aquila; having shorn his head in Cenchrea; for he had a vow.

Women have been a very important part of the church and community service for the Lord beginning in the OT era and this trend has continued throughout the NT and church age. The character of those women is that they were dedicated and committed to God and their service work reflects such as reflected in our scripture texts. Christian women are devout servants of God while utilizing their many God given talents. It doesn't matter the position, women serve with humility and grace as women are humble, submissive, loving and devoted.

To make the point of women and their long history of service to the Lord; let's highlight a few beginning with Moses' sister Miriam who was a prophetess and worship leader who led the women in song and praises to God after they crossed the Red Sea. Miriam continued her worship service leadership while the children of Israel sojourned in the wilderness. Another woman serving God was Dorcas or Tabitha who used her gift to make tunics for the women in her community and did so with grace, love and humility that her ministry is looked upon as one of giving. Also, Dorcas is looked upon as the prototype for First-Century deacon. Then there is Mary, John Marks mother who was a confidant of the apostles and she opened her home for worship service as many were held in her home. Mary and her love for God were instrumental in her son and his work for the Lord. History records these sisters Tryphena and Tryphosa from Persis as being of the Romans church and good friends of Paul as they labored much for the Lord (Romans 16:12). In Acts 12:13-16 we find the service work of Rhoda a door keeper as she answered the door for Peter upon his release from jail. Rhoda was a young girl who was in the company of other Christians praying for Peter's release. Another notable woman servant is Phoebe who was so committed in her service work for the Lord until Paul gave her high praise as she traveled to Rome for her church Paul considered her a "servant" which is translated as deaconess. Then there is the husband and wife team of Priscilla and Aquila who expounded the Word of God and the wife always esteemed her husband. Lastly, we have the woman with the alabaster box anointing Jesus with precious ointment at Simon's house in Bethany. Scripture states that she was anointing Jesus for His burial. This woman's act was a portrayal of her love, and devotion for the Master Jesus.

The commonality of all the women depicted in our topical discussion is that they all had a deep and committed relationship to God and the church growth. It is also note worthy to say that these servant/women of God used their gifts and talents for the Lord. Positions of service and their position in life were of no importance because the motivating factor is service to God. Christian women in today's church carry the same devotion, love and commitment; whether serving as a doorkeeper/usher, nurse, singer, deaconess or worship leader they are committed to serve.

Christian women serving God is a precious commodity as we are the nucleus of the Christian community.

God And His People

Work In God's Vineyard: Matthew 21:28-32

But what think you? A certain man had two sons; and he came to the first, and said, Son, go work to day in my vineyard.

Today's scripture talks of a man having two sons. The father asked one son to go work in his vineyard, the first son said no, but repented and went to work in his father's vineyard. When the father asked the second son, he told his father that he would go, but failed to keep his word.

The moral of this story is that God is calling workers in His vineyard—the world to win souls for His kingdom. According to the great commission, believers are to work in God's vineyard by witnessing to others telling them "the wages of sin is death, but the gift of God is eternal life" (Romans 6:23).

The harvest is great, but the laborers are few, meaning that the above scenario proves that many who say they will go witness Christ will not. There are far too many who profess Christ will not share the good news of salvation while there are those who say "no because I don't know what to say will go in spite of reservations."

What does this say about a committed heart? Are you willing to say what God has done in your life? He saved all believers' souls from sin and shame now believers can shout the victory. Committed believers are willing workers in God's vineyard as there is much work to do—***winning souls.***

Mar 2

Petitioning God's Mercy: Psalm 74

O God, why hast thou cast us off fro ever? why doth thine anger smoke against the sheep of thy pasture?

This Psalm is a cry/plea for God's mercy as the opening verse asks "Why hast thou cast us off for ever? Why doth thine anger smoke against the sheep of thy pasture? What is occurring in this psalm is that God was punishing His people because of their evil ways as this prayer is warning for us that God will not tolerate sin indefinitely; eventually we suffer sorrow and calamity. In spite of our suffering and pain God's hand of mercy can be seen as He is seeking a repentant heart.

In the psalmist prayer he recounted the numerous misdeeds that had been committed against God, His sanctuaries and His statues/ways as there were little regard for God's covenant. The psalmist also spoke to God of His awesome powers and that there remain in the land those who revered and trusted Him. It was those faithful that the psalmist pleaded for relief.

The lesson to be learned here is that regardless of society's overall wicked condition, there remain God's faithful believers who can and will go to God in sincere prayer. "The prayers of the righteous availeth much."

It is noteworthy to say that in the midst of our suffering God through the Holy Spirit is present giving comfort to all who call out to Him as He gives us the strength to persevere to the end.
God is merciful!

Mar 3

Samuel The Lord's Prophet: 1 Samuel 3:10-21

And the Lord came, and stood, and called as at other times, Samuel, Samuel. Then Samuel answered, Speak for thy servant heareth.

Our lesson setting takes place with the Lord explaining to Samuel what He will do in Israel and what the results were going to be, which were that "the ears of every one that heareth shall tingle." God was preparing to bring judgment on the house of Israel as Eli was the prophet at that time and God was not pleased with what was happening to His people. Eli's sons were not living according to God's moral laws and statues, and God was going to purge Eli's house of their sins.

Samuel was a student of Eli and was at Eli's house when God called him to service. Samuel was a small child when he was called into service for the Lord. Samuel went on to become a great prophet for the Lord as he was the first to hold the office of prophet. He gathered around him other prophets which became known as "the company of prophets." It was through Samuel's leadership that these prophets were mentored and instructed in God's Word.

The question now becomes why did God call young Samuel to speak for Him to His people? The call was necessary because of the spiritual corruption in the priesthood and overall spiritual decline among God's people. Samuel was to be an example of faithfulness to the Will of God, and to call people to repentance as this would lead to a spiritual revival.

The moral is that God always has a spokesperson who will speak a word.

A Family of Believers: Galatians 6:10

As we have therefore opportunity, let us do good unto all men, especially unto them who are of the household of faith.

What does it mean to be a family of believers? It means that we who profess to believers are born into the family of God as we have been baptized in the spirit by Jesus Christ Himself, and with that designation we as believers have certain responsibilities and duties as they relate to fellow believers.

Most important being in the family (God's) of believers means that we are to follow His example of helping all who are in need and most of all share His Word.

If the question were raised what are our duties as fellow believers? We are to bear one another's burdens which entail providing financial aid when necessary as well as other means of supports. Also, it is the duty of those who are taught the Word of God to provide and give support to those in five fold ministry and the faithful teachers and elders as recorded in Ephesians 4:11. Those who refuse to give support when the means are available show selfishness and this is ungodly and will reap destruction. As this destruction will take place "in due season." While on the other hand for those who provide the necessary support to our fellow believers, elders and teachers will reap their rewards and eternal life (Matthew 10:41-42).

Lastly, being a family of believers' means that we are a part of the Christian Community and we as believers are God's ambassadors.

Families of believers show your colors, God the Father, God the Son, and God the Holy Spirit.

Promise Of a Prophet: Deuteronomy 18:12-22

The Lord thy God will raise up unto thee a Prophet from the midst of thee, of thy brethren, like unto me; unto Him ye shall hearken

The situation had become grim to the point that all manner of forbidden practices were occurring in Israel that God said, "For all that do these things are an abomination unto the Lord; and because of these abominations the Lord thy God doth drive them out from before thee." Verse 15 speaks of God promising to raise up a prophet from among the people, meaning that He had someone ready and waiting to speak God's Words to the people.

The conditions had come to the point that the people didn't want to hear the Word of the Lord nor see His fire that were sure to come again. To prevent God's judgments from raining down like fire, it behooves mankind to hearken to the voice of the Lord as spoken through His prophets/spoke persons.

God also informed the prophets that if you speak and the people fail to listen, then they will be held accountable, but if you fail to speak my words then you will be held accountable. The moral here is that God always has a spokes person and when He says go and speak for Him, then go because God is true to His Word in that He never leaves or forsakes His own. As He was with His OT and NT prophets He will be you and I today when we speak what thus said the Lord.

God fulfilled His promise of sending the ultimate prophet in Jesus Christ.

Jonah Prayed: Jonah 2:1-9

Then Jonah prayed unto the Lord his God out of the fish's belly.

In Jonah's attempt to escape God's call to go preach to the people at Nineveh he was caught up in a fierce storm at sea and was thrown over board, but thanks be to God there was a great fish waiting to carry Jonah to where God wanted him to be.

It was in Jonah's lowest ebb that he called on the Lord in prayer from the belly of the fish, and the Lord heard Jonah's prayer. This was Jonah's prayer for deliverance and God being the merciful God that He is delivered Jonah. The lessons Jonah learned was that regardless of where he traveled he could not escape the reaches of God nor could he flee God's mercy. Another lesson learned by Jonah is that obedience is better than sacrifice.

The question now becomes, what lesson is there in these verses? The lessons for us today is that (a) Jonah prayed a prayer of deliverance and thanksgiving, (b) it doesn't matter our condition, God can and will deliver as He hears the repentant hearts, (c) believers are never to give up hope regardless of our current situation and we must cry out to God with sincerity for He hears and answer's, and (d) all humanity's salvation is in the Lord.

What does this say about prayer? Prayer is our communication with God and our faith in our prayers is the key as our faith represents a truly repentant heart.

Pray as Jonah!

Jonah Obeyed God: Jonah 1:1-3; 3:1-9

And the word of the Lord came unto Jonah the second time, saying, Arise, go unto Nineveh, that great city, and preach unto it the preaching that I bid thee.

After Jonah's brush with death and him seeing there is no fleeing God when He has an assignment; Jonah in obedience to God preaches to Nineveh and the people believed the Word of God. It is note worthy to say that before Jonah's fish experience he felt that the people of Nineveh didn't need to hear from God, but this wasn't God's view of the situation as it is God's desire that all humanity be saved through the preaching of His Word.

God knew the condition of Nineveh and the number of persons who would hear and be saved once His preacher preached. What God knew that Jonah didn't was that his message would be received with gladness as the people of Nineveh were doomed unless they heard the Word of God from His preacher. They expressed their true repentance by their humility to God in fasting and wearing sack cloth as their clothing during this period. The people of Jonah's day had cultivated hearts and they were ready to receive the Word of God from His preacher. The results were a spiritual revival.

What does this say for the preacher who preaches God's Word? Souls are saved, more believers are born into the family of God and a spiritual revival is witness as the Christian Community share the good news of the gospel of Christ. Jesus came to free man from the bondage of sin.

Preachers preach in obedience to God's call.

Another thought on obeying God's call is that He calls each believer to some form of ministry and our response indicates our obedience and willingness to obey God. Jonah teaches an important lesson of disobedience and what happens when God has commissioned/called us to service-there is no escaping Him or His mission He has prepared us for. Also, God knows who will hear His Word and respond favorably and who will not. It is famously quoted that if no man speak for God that He will have the rocks to cry out. I would not want to stand before God during my service record reading and hear Him say I called you to speak for me and you refused. What I want to hear Him say is "Good and faithful servant a job well done." ***What about you?***

All are not called by God to preach as Jonah, but all are called to witness Christ the world over. More importantly, all believers have a testimony to tell others what God has done in your life---He saved you from sin because some obedience servant spoke a Word for the Lord.

It is noteworthy to reflect on some OT patriarchs, who obeyed God without hesitations-Abraham, Noah and Enoch just to name a few as they trusted God with blind faith and they were rewarded. Moses like Jonah objected at first to God's call, but became a great leader for the nation of Israel.

Obey God's call-He has the way prepared.

Mar 8

Wait On The Lord: Psalm 130

I wait for the Lord, my soul doth wait, and in His word do I hope

When reading this psalm it can be viewed as a psalm of distress when the writer was calling out to the Lord from the very depths of his soul asking the Lord to hear his voice and give his plea an attentive ear. What struck me most was that during the writer's plea he acknowledged that if "the Lord should mark his iniquities the question was then who shall stand?" This is an important question for all to ask of themselves because there is no one who will be able to stand and face God if He were to execute justice as it demands. But the beautiful part about this psalm as well as our plea to God is that His mercy reins supreme and His forgiveness is present through the blood stain banner of Jesus Christ.

Therefore, all who believe in the Lord can say like the Psalmist "I will wait for the Lord, my soul doth wait and in his word do I hope." This verse make a profound statement that brings into view ones faith in God and His deliverance is assured and all our hope lies in Him. Psalm 27:14 encourages all to "Wait on the Lord be of good courage, and he shall strengthen thine heart: Wait I say on the Lord."

Verse 8 provides the answer to an implied question of why wait on the Lord, because there is redemption in waiting on the Lord.
Wait on God He is our deliverer!

The Faithful God: Deuteronomy 7:9

Know therefore that the Lord thy God, He is God, the faithful God, which keepeth covenant and mercy with them that love Him and keep His commandments to a thousand generations.

What is faithful? Faithful can be defined as truth worthy, dependable, reliable, and an assurance. The above adjectives give a clear picture of God and His character as it relates to man and man's ability to trust God.

Throughout the history of man God has shown His faithfulness and trustworthiness as He is the creator and sustainer of all that exists. Our scripture text gives another reminder of God's faithfulness toward His people. Our scripture setting is directed toward the nation of Israel but is applicable to all humanity.

This verse goes on to tell of God keeping His covenant and displaying His mercy to all who love Him and keep His commandments as this is a relationship that is designed to last forever-generations to come. Another point in this number of psalm is that it speaks to the blessing of good health and a country's military victories/success one receives for being obedient to God's commandments. In essence, this psalm makes a strong case of putting God first in everything that we do as He is faithful to His promises.

Reflecting on God's faithfulness and His many acts of faithfulness are too numerous to count. It is noteworthy to say that God cannot lie and His word is true and can be counted on to be fulfilled. Case in point, He promised a Savior, Jesus came. God promised salvation it was granted through Jesus Christ for all who believe in Him.

Our faith rests in a faithful God!

Mar 10

Israel's Redeemer: Isaiah 48:12-22

Hearken unto Me, O Jacob, and Israel my called; I am He; I am the first, I also am the last.

Our scripture chapter deals with the obstinate Israel as they were a people who professed to follow God but in reality they had broken their covenant relationship with God and were rejecting the truth of His Word. They had a form of religion but were living unrighteous lives before God as well as denying Him His rightful place in their lives. This is seen as hypocrisy which is very much frowned upon by Jesus Himself as well as OT prophets denounced this kind of living.

God through His prophets warned Israel of worshiping graven images and idolatrous living and the consequences that were sure to follow if they failed to repent. God also warned Israel that He would use a wicked king and nation to punish Israel for her disobedience to His commandments.

What did Israel do? They keep on with their wicked ways which paved the way for the need of a redeemer to buy back their freedom from sin as well as all un-saved (v.16). Verse 20 makes a declaration for the Jews living in captivity as God would use Cyrus's decree to return them to their homeland. See how God works, He used a wicked king to lead them into captivity and another king to free them—a type of redeemer. The true redeemer is Jesus Christ who came to redeem man from sin.

Sin was the cause for humanity needing a redeemer—God in His divine love provided His Son.

Approach God In Confidence: 1 John 5:14

And this is the confidence that we have in Him, that, if we ask anything according to His will, He heareth us.

If the question were raised, How are we to approach God? The answer should be with confidence as our faith in Him assures us that He hears and will answer our prayers/requests. Verse 13 provides an answer as it relates to what and in whom we believe which states in part, that if "You believe on the name of the Son of God; that ye may know that ye have eternal life." As this is the confidence all believers should have with the full knowledge that according to His will whatever we ask in sincere prayer will be granted.

How else can we have this confidence? This is gained through living holy lives before God and when our prayers/lives are presented to Him we have the necessary confidence because of our right standing with Him. Also, we can know what God's will is for our lives through scripture and revelation from the Holy Spirit. 1 John 3:22 substantiates having the ability to approach God in confidence is by keeping His commandments and doing what is right in the eye sight of God.

An effective prayer life is essential to our daily walk with God as it is His desire to commune with us daily as this breeds a committed and devout disciple of Christ. Another thought is that the closer our relationship with God the brighter our light shines for Him in a sin darkened world.

Approach God in confidence He is listening!

Habitation In God: Ephesians 3:19-21

And to know the love of Christ, which passeth all knowledge, that ye might be filled with all the fullness of God.

Habitation can be defined as a dwelling place; in today's discussion we will discuss the believer dwelling in the safety of God through the indwelling Holy Spirit who resides in each of us. Another point of view of habitating in God is being grounded in His love through Christ Jesus, which can be expressed metaphorically as a tree with deep roots embedded in the soil or a building with a solid foundation. With that being said, believers' foundation is Christ Himself as all we ever hope to become is based on God's love and the Holy Spirit is our soil who provides the nutrients for the believer's growth.

Verse 16 of our discussion chapter makes a profound statement as it relates to having our inner man strengthened by the Spirit. It means to have our inner spirits and His Spirit aligned so that our souls will be under the directions and influence of the Holy Spirit that will enable all believers to manifest His powers to a greater degree.

Therefore, abiding in God has a threefold purpose, which are (a) the manifestation of Christ's presence in the believer's heart. (b) The full comprehension of Christ's love for all believers. (c) That the indwelling of God and His presence engulfs all believers until all believers reflect the character of Jesus Christ our Lord.

In conclusion, being embedded in the love of God carries many blessing as we show forth His love to the world.

Live safely in the love of God.

Believers And The Godhead in Unity: Ephesians 4:1-6

From whom the whole body fitly joined together and compacted by that which every joint supplieth, according to the effectual working in the measure of every part, maketh increase of the body unto the edifying of itself in love.

What does unity means? The word "unity" means to be on one accord or operate as one. The question that comes to mind is what does it mean by believers and the Godhead being in unity? It just as the Godhead operates coequally as one, believers must operate totally under the direction and guidance of the Holy Spirit thus making believers in harmony with the Godhead doing the will of the Father as all members of the Godhead are one—God.

Believers have this unity by believing the truth and have received Christ as Lord as proclaimed by the OT and NT prophets as well as apostles and modern day preachers/teachers. This unity is not gained through human effort or any organization but by living holy before God as all believers are called generations who have been set apart from the world.

Verses 5-6 drives home the point of being in unity with the Godhead, which states, "there is one Lord, one faith and one baptism, One God and Father of all, who is above all, and through all and in you all." What all this means is that Jesus Christ is the perfect and only redeemer/mediator for humanity and there will be no other redeemer to come, and there is no "unity of the Spirit" apart from affirming that Jesus is Lord.

Accepting Jesus as Lord, believers have "unity in the Spirit"—God.

In The Household Of God: Ephesians 2:11-17

Wherefore remember, that ye being in time passed Gentiles in the flesh, who are called Uncircumcision by that which is called the Circumcision in the flesh made by hands.

Our scripture text setting is Paul talking to the Gentiles Ephesus and the practices that were practiced on them. These principles hold true for non believers who have not accepted Christ as their personal Savior. Example, circumcision is the removal of the foreskin on males, while on a spiritual plane it is the removal of the foreskin of the unbeliever's heart. Spiritual circumcision occurs when the non-believer hears and believes the Word of God, and then their hearts are pricked and are opened to Christ's saving powers. Paul goes on to say that Gentiles and all non-believers who are without Christ have no hope of the covenant promise of salvation, and Christ appeared far off without hope. But with Christ's shed blood non-believers are no longer alienated and without hope only if they believe and with their belief are born into the household of faith in God.

Some of the blessings of being in the household of faith is salvation, spending eternity with the Father, and all who believe are no longer an enemy of God as we have been reconciled through the blood of Jesus Christ. Non-believers are brought into the household of faith through the teaching and preaching of God's Word and the individual having the necessary faith to accept what was heard/taught/preached as the truth. In addition to preaching/teaching believers are to exercise their God given gifts to edify the body of Christ through daily living so non-believers can and will see Christ manifested in our daily lives. This can and will be accomplished by obeying the great commission given by Christ Himself as recorded in Matthew 28:19-20, which is to make other disciples.

Additional benefits of being members of the household of faith is that we as believers are adopted sons of God as this too comes through our faith in Jesus Christ and accepting Him as Lord of our lives. Another thought on being the sons of God is that believers are constantly putting to death the misdeeds of the flesh which means that believes are being lead and guided by the Holy Spirit. This in-turn makes all believers children of God. Other blessings of being in the household of faith or adopted sons of God are that believers become heirs to God's kingdom. **What a glorious blessing?**

Romans 8:17 talks about being children of God which leads to becoming "heirs of God and joint-heirs with Christ" and with this distinction believers suffer with Christ as he suffered for all humanity. A believer's suffering with and for Christ is the consequences of his/her relationship with Him.

It is noteworthy to say that all believers were at one point alienated from God or possessed an uncircumcised heart before spiritual ears and eyes were open to the truth and the joyous hope of spending eternity with our creator, the one who sustains all humanity from beginning to the end. Daily Bible reading and meditating on God's Word keeps all believers fresh and in tune with God and prevents spiritual decay.

Glorify God as we are members of the royal family—the Godhead.

My Lord And My God: John 20:28

And Thomas answered and saith unto Him, my Lord and my God.

Thomas doubted that Jesus had risen as promised until he witnessed first hand by touching Jesus for himself and his belief was overwhelming that he addressed Jesus as "My Lord and My God" as this signifies reverence and honor while recognizing that Jesus is Lord and God all in one.

To authenticate that Jesus is Lord and God, scripture attributes several names to Him, in verse 20 He is called God, and Matthew 5:25 He is the Son of God, Revelation 1:17 He is the first and last, and Revelation 1:8 He is alpha and omega, and Revelation 22:13 He is the beginning and end, while in Hosea 11:9 He is the Holy One and Psalm 24:8-10 He is the Lord of glory and Lord of all. There are numerous scriptures outlining the divine worship given to Jesus as Lord who is worthy of all adoration in our worship and prayers.

To further authenticate the Lordship of Christ there are divine offices assigned to Him and some are (a) creator of the universe (John 1:3), (b) the sustainer of all things (Colossians 1:17), (c) the forgiver of sin (Mark 2:5-10), (d) the bestower of resurrection of life, (e) the judge of all people, and (f) the giver of salvation.

Given all that we know about Jesus and His deity He is worthy of the titles, worship, honor and praises given by all believers.

He is Lord of my life evermore.

Mar 16

Share In God's Blessings: 1 Samuel 30:21-31

...Ye shall not do so, my brethren, with that which the Lord hath given us, who hath preserved us, and delivered the company that came against us into our hand.

Today's discussion focuses on David's victories in battle and how he shared with those who were not in battle as his feelings were that they participated just by caring for the needs and belongings of those in battle. This principle is the guiding force behind missionaries who are supported by those left behind. The missionaries are doing the Will of God while being obedient to the Great Commission as recorded in Matthew 28:19-80 and Mark 16:15-20.

Believers participating in support services and or roles in the work of God will share in His blessing and heavenly rewards. Support workers provide support with prayer as well as material goods and supplies. This is prevalent in many churches and missionary organizations that have missionaries in foreign countries preaching, teaching and sharing God's Word with others as well as the many other forms of ministry such as providing basic essentials for life. All believers can and do participate in kingdom building in one form or another.

It is note worthy to say that it is wonderful to know that we as believers will share in God's blessing for (1) believing in His Son Jesus, (2) praying and loving one another as commanded, (3) aiding or caring for the underprivileged/needy because God Himself showed concern for the poor and needy and we are to do likewise. (4) There are blessings in giving because when giving we emulate God.

Blessings and rewards await kingdom builders--believers.

Fruits Of Repentance: Matthew 3:8

Bring forth therefore fruits meet for repentance.

If the question were raised, What are signs of true repentance? A tree is known by the fruit its bears and the same principle applies for believers who say they are children of God. With that being said, then the world will know God's children from Satan's by the fruit they bear, and the fruit is evidenced by the lives believers live. True repentance and conversion is seen in lives that live for Christ and forsake sin by refusing to conform to the world's lifestyle.

Galatians 5:22-23 records the fruit of the spirit as love, joy, peace, longsuffering, gentleness, goodness, faith, meekness and temperance. One gains these attributes by truly turning from the old way of life and a total commitment to God and His righteousness. Why this is so is because once the decision is made to follow Christ we become new creatures in Christ and the old sinful nature has been buried in the blood of Jesus.

How do repentant believers maintain their fruit bearing status? This is achieved through daily Bible reading and meditating on God's Word while yielding to the Holy Spirit. Furthermore, daily Bible reading promotes a close fellowship with God which promotes even greater fruit bearing.

Repentance yields God-like fruits.

Mar 18

An Everlasting Oath: 1 Samuel 20:30-42

And Jonathan said to David, Go in peace, forasmuch as we have sworn both of us in the name of the Lord, saying, The Lord be between me and thy seed for ever, And he arose and departed; and Jonathan went into the city.

Today's discussion setting takes place with David and his very best friend Jonathan who was the son of King Saul who had made it his mission to kill David. Jonathan and David were closer than some brothers and they made an everlasting oath that he would not disclose David's whereabouts to his father. King Saul's anger against David was the reason for David being on the run for his life, but thinks to God, he had a friend and ally in Jonathan who took risky measures to secure David's safety.

Several thoughts come to mind from reading this scripture text, (1) often times we encounter others who have a dislike and or hatred for us and we don't know the reason. (2) Living according to the Will of God He always has an ally to protect His chosen people. (3) On a spiritual plain, God made an everlasting oath/covenant with His people that He would be our God and we would be His people. Also, God wants His people to have no other God before Him---rightly so because He is our creator and sustainer. Most important, what He gave in His plan of salvation.

What does God ask in return of His covenant relationship? God wants a close fellowship with His people, who will live holy before Him and keep His commandments.

David and Jonathan's oath is the same in principle between man and God.

My Brother's Keeper: Romans 14:13-23

Let us not therefore judge one another any more; but judge this rather, that no man put a stumbling block or an occasion to fall in his brother's way.

I have often heard people say that I am not my brother's keeper, but today's scripture paints a different picture of causing our brother to fall and what we are to do to keep from being a stumbling bock for our brother.

Verse 13 encourages us to reframe from judging our brother, but instead offer encouraging words and or positive motivating advice. To judge or hinder ones progress is un-Christ like, but if and when the occasion arises for us to correct our brother we are to do so in love, humility and with sincere concern for our brother's well-being and spiritual growth.

I have encountered and heard some people who eat only certain kinds of meat because of their beliefs or conditions; needless to say salvation is based on our belief in Jesus Christ. However, I am not condemning those who do not eat certain food, rather when I am in their presence I ask if what I eat offends them (v.19), and if it does then I refrain. It is my desire to be a spiritual guide for my brother or sister and edify the body of Christ.

It is written that the strong is to bear the affirmatives of the weak; this in itself is caring for our brother/sister---being their keeper.

Being our brother's keeper is in line with the second commandment, because we love ourselves, then we are to love our brothers/sisters.

Mar 20

"Continue ye in my Love": John 15:9-17

And as the Father hath loved Me, so have I loved you; continue ye in my love.

The setting for today's discussion is Jesus talking to His disciples concerning love and how they and all believers are to love, which is in the same manner that His father loved Him and Jesus loved all mankind (v.9). Jesus further explained the intimacy of this love relationship that is to exist between Him and all believers as this love lifestyle is one of holiness and devotion to God. This is made possible by God Himself through the Holy Spirit. God demonstrated this love by giving His Son Jesus as the sacrificial lamb as He–Jesus was to give His life for humanity. **What love!**

How do we remain in God's love? Believers remain in God's love by pursuing an intimate relationship and being in communion with Him through daily prayers and Bible reading as well as obeying His commands as Christ obeyed His Father---God all in love.

Verse 16 makes a profound statement in that Jesus reminds all who chose whom; He chose us as oppose to man choosing God. Also, this verse states why we were chosen in that we are to bear fruit that is productive for kingdom building---making other disciples. Being that Christ chose us out of love, then we are commanded to love others and Him. Be obedient---love as God loved.

Lord I thank You for Your love, Lord help me to love all humanity as You loved all in Jesus name. Amen!

"Thy God Shall Be My God": Ruth 1:1-9, 16

And Ruth said, Intreat me not to leave thee, or to return from following after thee; for whither thou goest, I will go, and where thou lodgest, I will lodge; thy people shall be my people, and thy God shall be my God.

The story of Ruth and her mother-in-law Naomi is one of love and the power of God and His divine plan of salvation for all mankind. As the story goes Naomi and her family moved from their native hometown of Bethe-lejem-judah and moved to a country called Moab with her husband and two sons. While there Naomi's husband and two sons died--the sons had taken foreign wives and upon their deaths the three ladies had no means of support. Naomi decided to return to her home country knowing that her cousin Boaz was a wealthy man and would look after her. Naomi asked her two daughter-in-laws to return to their families, Oprah followed the advice given, but Ruth remained and put her faith in Naomi's God and His power to deliver. Additionally, Ruth's love for Naomi was greater than just a mother-in-law it was as a mother and daughter, flesh and blood.

From the union of Ruth and Naomi to Ruth and Boaz to the birth of Jesse the grandfather of David, this is the lineage of Jesus Christ. Matthew 1:1 traces Jesus' lineage beginning with Abraham. What we have here is God the Father fulfilling His promise of the Messiah who would come from the lineage of David. This promise took forty-two generations, but was kept just the same. The birth of Jesus Christ had been prophesied many years before His birth.

The love depicted in this story of Ruth, Naomi and God, as God knew from the beginning of time that He would use the persons depicted in this story as part of His master plan of salvation—as well as knowing when and where the lives of these persons would interact and how---now that's God. The greatest love depicted here is that of God in preparing His Son our Savior-Jesus Christ who would give His life for all mankind.

It is noteworthy to say that Ruth's faith is on display in this story as she believed in the one and true God who gives all life and sustains all that exits—He is the creator of all. No doubt that Naomi had told Ruth about her God and His power enabled her to believe---that's the power of God's Word.

Most important, while reflecting on this powerful story one can see the divine hand of God directing the events that would make way for His deliverer—Jesus Christ. It has been written and said many times that true love requires action---God put His love in action.

This begs the question, can we say like Ruth, "thy God shall be my God and thy people shall be my people (believers)?

An Exhortation to Love: Romans 12:9-18

Let love be without dismminulation. Abhor that which is evil; cleave to that which is good.

In Paul's letter to the Roman believers he is encouraging all to "let love be without dissimulation, Abhor that which is evil, cleave to that which is good. Be kindly affectionate one to another with brotherly love." What do these verses mean? The meaning of these verses is that Christians are to love righteousness but they are to hate or dislike evil and be devoted to Christ and His moral standards. Christ has commanded all believers to love his/her brother and sister as He first loved all. Our brotherly love includes caring for others needs/welfare, spiritual growth, as well as having sympathy during their time of sorrow and or troubles.

Another meaning derived from these verses is that Christians are commanded to love in a much greater and special way regardless of religious beliefs and or persuasions. True believers are to love those who only profess Christ and this can be determined by examining their obedience to Christ and their loyalty to God and His holy Word (John 5:24; 8:3). Also, true Christian love is never to compromise God's holiness as we must exemplify God's agape love--self-giving.

It can be concluded then that true love triumphs all as shown by God and His Son Jesus Christ. All believers must show our vertical and horizontal love---for God and others.

Let us love all mankind---God did!

Mar 23

Called To Be Saints: Romans 1:7-9

To all that be in Rome, beloved of God, called to be saints; Grace to you and peace from God our Father, and the Lord Jesus Christ.

What is the meaning of called to be saints? First, to be called means that believers have been called by God to do a special service. Another way of saying it is believers have been set apart or sanctified/consecrated to live in true holiness for God. Second, the basic idea or term behind being called saints is the separation from sin to God. Another term for saint is "God's holy ones," or "God's separated ones." Saints of God are viewed as being led and sanctified by the Holy Spirit (Romans 8:14; 1 Corinthians 6:11; 2 Thessalonians 2:13; 1 Peter 1:2). Third, the common Biblical term " saints" signifies two important points (a) that all believers conform to God's way of righteousness (Ephesians 5:3), and (b) saints realize that holiness carries an internal reality that all believers belong to Christ (1 Corinthians 1:30).

The question now becomes what does the term "saint" imply? The term "saint" does not imply absolute perfection, but an ethical righteousness of an unblemished character that is demonstrated through our obedience, purity and blamelessness which was set in order through Christ's blood.

Some of the blessings of being "saints" or set apart people is that all believers have had a holy encounter with God after his/her initial salvation as well as having the Holy Spirit aiding the believer in maintaining his/her intimacy with God.

It delights God for Him to transform sinners to saints so He will have a perfect bride for His Son—Christ.

Live As God Commands: James 2:8-13

If ye fulfill the royal law according to the scripture, Thou shalt love thy neighbour as thyself, ye do well:

In today's discussion we see James is encouraging all believers to live according to God's command which is to "love thy neighbor as thyself", in doing so all believers will do well because as God shows no favoritism and neither should we. James also warns for all who show favoritism is guilty of committing a sin and will be judged by God. What James is really saying is that true believers must treat everyone the same as Christ set the perfect example; while here on earth Christ treated everyone the same, case in point if there was a need He met the person's need regardless of situation or background, and prior to coming to earth He died for all humanity—believers and non-believers alike.

Another point to James' encouragement is that it is uncommon to find someone who mistreats or harms them self, therefore, if we love ourselves then why not love others the same. This command is motivated by love which stems from God and His love for He is love. Furthermore, the command to love is a direct command from Christ Himself. The question is often raised how can you say you love God whom you have never seen but fail to love your brother whom you see daily? John states that there is no true in the person. This is because for all who disobey the love command is in essence disobeying God.

Love everybody, even sinners, and live according to God's command.

Mar 25

Faith Evidenced By Works: James 2:14-17

What doth it profit, my brethren, though a man say he hath faith, and have not works? can faith save him?

James is addressing the issue of one's faith that is evidenced by their works and faith without works is dead. What James is really addressing is the problem that many churches are faced with many in their congregations are those who profess true faith, but show no evidence of their faith by participating in any ministry, kingdom building or devotion to Christ. Many congregations refer to these members as bench members. Also, James refers to faith as being essential to the point that it is active and enduring until it models the believer's very existence and or character. Ones character is who you are---a faithful child of God----evidenced by our works.

In verse 17 James states that faith without works is dead, because true faith manifests itself in total obedience to God and shows compassion to the underprivileged in our society. Believers who profess true faith will emulate God in expressing our concern for the poor and needy (underprivileged). God Himself expressed His concern for the poor and needy by expressing Himself as (a) their refuge (Psalm 14:6; Isaiah 25:4); (b) their help (Psalm 40:17; 70:5), (c) their deliverer (1 Samuel 2:8; Psalm 12:5; 34:6;35:10; 113:7), and (d) their provider (Psalm 10:14; 68:10; 132:15). God's caring theme is the common thread in both the OT and NT and was witnessed by the many acts of compassion by Jesus during His earthly ministry.

The true believer's works will speak to their faith.

Blessings For All: Isaiah 56:3-8

The Lord God which gathered the outcasts of Israel saith, Yet will I gather others to Him, besides those that are gathered unto Him.

In our scripture text where the Lord includes all humanity in His blessing as some were looked upon as being foreigners, but upon accepting the Lord as Savior then they too were included in the blessings of salvation.

When the promised Messiah—Jesus Christ died for the sins of the world it was inclusive regardless of ethnic background, physical and one's disabilities, and or social status as God loves and accepts all as His children. Another school of thought on receiving salvation and the blessing that comes with it is that the new believers then have the same rights and privileges in the Christian/covenant community as all others. With God there is no respect of person—meaning that there is no favoritism with God among believers.

The question now becomes what is required to be included in the household of faith? Faith is the necessary commodity to be included in the household of faith as God isn't looking for one's physical condition but the condition of the heart; because the heart is where all emotions and transformation begins. Reflect on the physical conditions of the many that were healed by Jesus during His earthly ministry. The persons healed by Jesus supplied the faith and their backgrounds were diverse as many were outside the covenant community---after meeting Jesus a transformation occurred. Many went away shouting and praising God---Mary Magdalene and the blind man who received his sight.

What a blessing!

Faith And Grace: Ephesians 2:8

For by grace are ye saved through faith; and that not of yourselves; it is the gift of God.

What is faith and grace as they relate to our salvation? According to scripture faith is our belief in Jesus Christ as God's Son and faith is a requirement for receiving God's free gift of salvation. Faith is our belief in the crucified and resurrected Christ as well as being obedient to Him, living according to His Will and having a repentant heart as this will parlay into our trust and love for God as He first loved us. Faith in Jesus Christ brings the believer into a right relationship with God and exempts all believers from God's oncoming wrath (Romans 1:18; 8:1). Faith is the essential ingredient to all believers' salvation to receive the blessings that come with salvation—eternal life. Lastly, through our faith and acceptance into God's family we have the indwelling Holy Spirit, who leads, guides, teaches, and protects us.

Let's look at grace and see how the two intertwine; grace is being given what we do not deserve and justice is being given what we deserve which was God's punishment of His wrath, but in God's mercy He spared humanity of what we deserved. **What a gracious God!**

Grace is also seen as God giving His best to restore a broke fellowship with humanity and this was through the shed blood of Jesus Christ. **What love!**

God gives a portion of His grace to unbelievers so they too can believe in Jesus Christ and be saved.

Faith ---belief—grace--mercy.

Blessed And Accepted: Ruth 2:5-13; 3:9-11

"The Lord recompense thy work, and a full reward be given thee of the Lord God of Israel, under whose wings thou art come to trust."

This verse makes a profound declaration of God's love and reward for all who trust in Him. As the verse states that God does not over look the work of His people who trust in Him and this is seen in the book of Ruth as it talks about Ruth and her trust of the God of Israel. Another declaration of this verse is that despite of the spiritual apostasy that existed during Ruth and Naomi's time and even today, God always rewards those who remain faithful to Him. This verse makes plain God's provision and providence for His faithful believers. Both Abraham and Ruth exhibited great faith in God whereas Abraham left his country and traveled to an unknown land so did Ruth, she knew only Naomi her mother-in-law.

At one point during Naomi's adversity she felt that God was against her because of her difficulties, this proved to be untrue. Job came to this point during his suffering he too was rewarded for his steadfastness. This is a valuable lesson for believers today who encounter adversities. Sometimes God uses or allows adversities to test our faith and trust in Him. Like Job and Naomi we too will be rewarded for our steadfastness.

Both Ruth and Naomi were handsomely rewarded for their trust in God; remember Ruth was a Moabite woman who came to love and trust God and Naomi was a faithful worshipper of God. Both women journeyed back to Naomi's home country believing and trusting God to provide for them as they had no husband to do so. The Bible records many faithful who exhibited great faith and trust in God and they were handsomely rewarded.

Faithful believers rewards can be viewed as his/her blessings. Example, Ruth and Naomi were blessed because God revealed to them through His actions that he had not forsaken them; food was provided. This re-established Naomi's faith that God was still caring for her and solidified Ruth's faith in Naomi's God of Israel as being the true and living God.

Ruth was accepted first by Naomi's people and by God because of His divine plan. What does this say for modern day believers? Believers today have the assurances that if the believer trust in God with all his/her being, then blessed rewards lie ahead Another thought on being accepted is that believers must first accept Jesus as Lord, and then blessing of eternal life is guaranteed. As well as the promise of God's provisional care as recorded in Psalm 23:1 and Philippians 4:19. There are blessings from being accepted in the family of God based on accepting His Son.

Ruth and Naomi played an integrate part of the lineage of Christ; we are blessed to be co-heirs with Christ. Believers are blessed and highly favored!

A Prayer To God: Psalm 5

Give ear to my words, o Lord, consider my meditation. Hearken unto the voice of my cry, my King, and my God; for unto thee will I pray.

In this psalm we see the author; David praying to God for deliverance by hearing his voice. He was calling on God early in the morning with confidence that God would hear his voice. David had purposed in his heart the following in this psalm and they were (a) that he was going to be persistent in his prayer to God, (b) that he could not live without his daily morning prayer to God. (c) He prayed with expectations of an answer from God. (d) Throughout the day, David looked for signs that God was at work in his life. (e) David's daily prayers renewed his relationship with God.

What do David's actions say about all believers' prayer life? First, it is essential for all believers to have a fervent prayer life. Second, it is good practice to begin our day with God and end our day by thanking God for His many blessings through our daily walk with him. Third, have confidence in our prayers to God as He hears and rewards a repentant heart. Fourth, God wants and values a fellowship with all His children. Fifth, believers are to pray for others as well as ourselves and lastly, thank God for His Holy Spirit. Prayers are our communication with God as they enhance our relationship with God.

The ACTS of prayer is adoration, confession, thanksgiving and supplication. Pray!

Mar 30

The Saints Arose: Matthew 27:52

And the graves were opened and many bodies of saints which slept arose.

Today's scripture deals with some of the events that occurred at Jesus' death; this verse talks about the graves opening and the saints that were sleep arose. This verse carries prophetic implications to the time when Jesus returns and all the dead in Christ will rise with glorified bodies. Believers' resurrection is guaranteed in Christ's resurrection as His resurrection assures all believers victory over sin and death.

According to scripture body resurrection is essential because the body is required to reunite with the spirit as the body is essential to the total human personality and through Christ's resurrection represents the whole person; at death the two become separated. At resurrection, the believer's body will become like that of Christ's resurrected body—glorified. Also, having a resurrected body means that the believer's body has been modified to enter the new heaven and earth which is spending eternity with God.

Another thought on the saints rising from the graves are the ones who died before Christ's first coming and those who died during His earthly ministry but believed in His coming and that He was the promised Messiah. As these saints died looking forward to the cross and believers who die after are looking back on the cross and Christ's atoning work. *As those saints arose knowing what was to come during Christ's second coming so will believers today---all saints will arise in that day to be with Christ.*

Persecuted for Righteousness: Matthew 5:10

Blessed are they which are persecuted for righteousness' sake; for theirs is the kingdom of heaven.

Our scripture text is taken from Jesus' sermon on the mountain that contains God's principles on righteousness which is what all Christians are to live by. For today's discussion we will look at Christians being persecuted for righteousness and what it means to be persecuted and the blessing/happiness that come with being persecuted for Christ's sake. Persecution is to suffer adversity because of one's beliefs, principles or way of life. There will come a day when all believers will suffer for being identified with Christ and His righteousness. Christian persecution will become the norm in society as overall society will refuse to hear "What thus saith the Lord" and will certainly turn a blind eye to His righteousness.

What are believers to do in the midst of their suffering? Believers are to rejoice (v.12) because (1) God rewards those who suffer for His sake and imparts His blessings. (2) Believers must rejoice in our suffering because Christ suffered and overcame all temptations, sin and death. (3) Believers must know that they will become unpopular, will be criticized, rejected and humiliated all for the sake of being identified with Christ. (4) Believers must never compromise on God's principles and standards as His Word and principles will never change. (5) Lastly, believers must remember that they are the salt (v.13) of the earth and have promises of the kingdom of heaven and its rewards.

"Blessed are they which are persecuted for righteousness' sake for theirs is the kingdom of heaven."

Christ Saves

Praying For Persecution And Deliverance
Psalm 69:16-20, 29-33

Hear me, O Lord; for thy lovingkindness is good; turn unto me according to the multitude of thy tender mercies.

The Psalmist is praying to God for Him to pass judgment on all who oppose Him and were afflicting pain and suffering on God's people-the righteous. What does this say about true believers and their concern for others? All believers have the love of God in their hearts and have a dreadful distaste for sin and those who commit sin especially when God's people are being oppressed. It is noteworthy to say there are times when some profess to love God, but seek to prosper at the hands of the less fortunate; this is not of God because He loves and treats all mankind the same. This was evidenced with Jesus and His earthly ministry as He performed no background checks on the ones He delivered from their afflictions.

Another point to this discussion is that the Psalmist was very shameful for the conduct of the people and their actions inflicting oppression on the less fortunate. He was so distressed until he asked God to remove "them from the book of the living." Also, during the Psalmist's prayer he prayed for deliverance for himself as well as others. The Psalmist knew that when praises and prayers of the righteous go up blessings come down. The Psalmist expressed a sincere desire to please God and recognized that praising God was far better than offering sacrifices of bullocks and ox.

The Psalmist had enough faith in God for deliverance of the persecuted from their affliction.

Pray and expect deliverance.

Jesus Predicts His Betrayal: John 13:21-30

...Verily, verily, I say unto you, that one of you shall betray me.

Jesus being God in the flesh knew all things and at this setting He knew that Judas was going to betray Him. It was during their last meal together that Jesus made His startling announcement. This puzzled some of His disciples until they began to ask "who is it"? Jesus gave them the answer but they still didn't know that Judas was the one. When Jesus gave the sop to Judas, He told Judas to go quickly and do His business—betray Him. Some scholars believe this was Jesus' final plea for Judas to repent –have a change of heart. Judas' betrayal was prophecy being fulfilled.

What does this say for believers who compromise on what appears as a harmless sin? All believers must be careful of what appears on the surface as harmless or innocent is the first step in Satan taking full control of ones life. Judas was a close disciple of Jesus --- the treasure where he had full access to the money and if Judas needed something he could have ask Jesus for permission to use the amount for the need.

Another school of thought on Judas' betrayal of Jesus is that he grew cold in his fellowship with the Lord. Could this have been prevented by telling Satan no at his first attempt on Judas? Judas' action serves as a stern reminder for all believers today in our walk and fellowship with the Lord.

Daily Bible reading blocks Satan's attacks.

Apr 3

Seeing The Resurrected Lord: John 20: 11-18

But Mary stood without at the sepulchre weeping; and as she wept, she stopped down, and looked into the sepulchre.

Much has been written about Jesus and His resurrection and who was the first to see Him. Mary Magdalene was the first to the grave early Sunday morning to anoint Jesus' body, but was surprised when she found an empty grave. Mary's actions speak to her love and devotion to Jesus as well as some doubt that He had risen as promised. Verse 2 speaks to Mary's doubt as she ran to Peter and the other disciples of Jesus stating that "they have taken away the Lord out of the sepulcher, we know not where they have laid him." Some doubt of His disciples can be surmised by their actions while disregarding the evidence of His resurrection. Verse 9 supplies the answer, but Jesus had told His disciples that He would rise again in three days. **Lord, help their unbelief!**

As Mary stood weeping for Jesus fearing the worst, He appeared and ask "Why weepest thou? Whom seekest thou? In layman's terms, why are you crying, who are you looking for? In other words, Jesus was saying to Mary and all who doubted His resurrection, "stop crying, I am right here."

Mary and the disciples' doubt turned to joy and praise. This is what happens when non-believers as well as believers with doubt accept Jesus as our risen Lord and Savior. All believers like Mary Magdalene can shout for joy because Jesus conquered sin and death.

All will see the resurrected Jesus one day!

From Pain To Joy: John 16:16-20

A little while, and ye shall not see me, and again, a little while ye shall see me, because I go to the Father.

The setting for today's topical discussion is after Jesus' resurrection and He was making ready to return to His Father. He took time out to teach His disciples of the coming Holy Spirit, but they failed in their understanding. Jesus was telling His disciples that for the Holy Spirit to come He must leave was the meaning of the statement "A little while, and ye shall not see me: and again, a little while, and ye shall see me, because I go to the Father (v.16).

The coming Holy Spirit will guide believers in all truth for He is God in the third person. The Holy Spirit and His convicting work is not only for the non-believers, but for believers and the church to teach, correct and guide them into truth (Matthew 18:15, 1 Timothy 5:20; Revelation 3:19). Also, the Holy Spirit speaks to believers concerning sin, the righteousness of Christ and the judgment of evil. Lastly, the Holy Spirit works within the believers to produce a Christ-like holy life as well as being a comforter.

Given the ministry and works of the Holy Spirit and Jesus telling His disciples that He was going away, but they and all believers as well were not going to be left alone without some guidance. It is humanly accepted that when a love one leaves for us to be sad and weary at their departure. Jesus' leaving His disciples was no exception. Jesus uses the analogy of a woman in childbirth pains and how she feels while going through this ordeal, but joy is forthcoming upon delivery. What Jesus meant was that His disciples would feel sorrowful at His departure, but once the Holy Spirit arrives there would be heartfelt joy as the Holy Spirit is God. The joy that is felt upon seeing Jesus no man can take that joy. All believers will experience this joy when we see Jesus face-to-face. ***What unspeakable joy!***

It is noteworthy to say that when Christ comes into your life and the Holy Spirit takes up residence there is such joy that the world did not give nor can it understand your joy. In the words of an OT prophet, "it is like fire shut up in my bones." This joy "put running in your feet, and clapping in your hands."

With that being said, the joy that all believers have in-store makes the pain and suffering in this life null and void. Another point of view; Christ Himself suffered pain all for the love of humanity and mankind spending eternity with Him. In that glorious day there will be endless joyful praise and worship.

Joy in Jesus are blessings abound.

Jesus' Love Command: John 13:31-35

A new commandment I give unto you, That ye love one another; as I have loved you, that ye also love one another.

Why would Jesus issue His command to love? Jesus issued this command because He is love and all believers are to emulate Jesus, and the perfect way is to love one another. Believers are to emulate Christ in that He gave His life for our sins because of His love for mankind and to have a loving fellowship with the Father. Also, loving one another Christians show their obedience and loyalty to God and His holy Word. Loving one another is the Christian trade mark of being a disciple of Christ.

The true essence of love is seen in John 3:16 because it set forth some assurances for all mankind. John 3:16 set forth that God's love embraces all mankind as well as speaking to the following facts:
- (a) God "gave" His Son as an offering for sin, and this was predicated on love.
- (b) In faith and love mankind must "believe" that Christ is God's Son.
- (c) All who believe "shall not perish", as this is our assurance of escaping God's wrath in judgment day.
- (d) "Everlasting life" is another assurance given by God out of love where all believers will spend eternity.

Given the love exhibited by God and His Son Jesus Christ, is it too much to love one another? The answer is no, being in the family of God we are love as He is love.

The world knows us by our love.

Apr 6

Earthly Or Heavenly Treasures Which Do You Chose?
Matthew 6:19-24

Lay not up for yourselves treasures upon earth, where moth and rust doth corrupt, and where thieves break through and steal.

Our discussion question begs an answer as it relates to ones priorities as to where we want to build treasures. Scripture encourages against laying up earthly treasures where moth and rust can destroy ones earthly wealth. In verse 20, it encourages all to place ones top priority on gaining heavenly rewards because where ever ones treasures are is where the heart is (v.21).

Verse 24 makes it very clear that one cannot serve God and mammon at the same time, for we will either turn away from God and love our money more or vice versa. Mammon is defined as money or ones valuable possessions. The question now becomes what danger is there in placing high value on money or possessions? The danger is that those who have money or wealthy values will place their trust and faith in their money or possessions. Wealthy people tend to expect security and happiness in their wealth, in reality true security and happiness is found in God our creator. The danger in accumulated wealth is that it can dominate ones total being and ignores God's kingdom to the point He is no longer first in their lives.

This is not to say that this writer or discussion is against having wealth, just encouraging the wealthy to remember God and His righteous standards. Lastly, in choosing God, one can then have all the riches the world has to offer.

Choose wisely.

Apr 7

Our Responsibility Toward Others: Romans 13:8-10

Owe no man anything, but to love one another; for he that loveth another hath fulfilled the law.

Our discussion topic outlines our responsibility toward others in that verse 8 speaks of owing no man anything, which means that all believers are to have no unpaid debts. However, believers are not prohibited from borrowing in time of need, but it does speak of unnecessary debt and having an indifferent attitude as it relates to repaying our debts (Psalm 37:21). A word of caution when borrowing it is wise to use reputable sources as to prevent usury in any form.

Now that we have discussed believers' responsibilities as they relate to borrowing, let's look at our responsibilities from a Biblical plane. The debt of love is one of no release as love will cause all to love our neighbors as thyself and refrain from committing any harm as outlined in verse 9. All believers are commanded to love by Christ Himself as His love was on display at Calvary and God's love was manifested in Jesus Christ.

Believers' responsibilities toward others in that if our brother/sister is in need we are to aid in every way we can. Believers are to pray for their brother/sisters constantly The Lord has always expressed His concern for the poor and needy or under privileged. During these expressions, God outlines His provisional care for the needy in both the OT and NT as His people are expected to give generously.

What is our responsibility? It is to love all first then provide aid/give second.

The Good Samaritan: Luke 10:29-37

Which now of these three, thinkest thou, was neighbour unto him that fell among the thieves?

Who is a good Samaritan? A good Samaritan is anyone who provides help to those in need regardless of their background or heritage. Our scripture text paints a vivid picture of a good Samaritan.

The parable of the good Samaritan teaches an important lesson on love and compassion as all followers of Christ must exhibit. This is true because (a) believers who truly profess Christ must show a resemblance of Christ in love and deed. (b) Love without compassion is suspect; because Christ in His love showed compassion on all in need. (c) To say that we love God and do not love others is hypocritical. (d) A true vertical (God) relationship results in a horizontal relationship--loving and doing good to others.

If the question were raised, what causes Christians/believers to take on the role of a good Samaritan? Christians/believers are good Samaritans because of the new life in Christ and in obedience to Him that produces this love, compassion and mercy toward others especially those in need. It is noteworthy to say that the Holy Spirit is at work in the lives of believers who obey His guidance that produces softened hearts.

Being a good Samaritan can be giving aid to persons regardless of location or distances. Seeing the magnitude of this country and individuals aiding those in need exemplifies the good Samaritan spirit which is a godly principle.

Being a good Samaritan is effortless when done in love.

Apr 9

God's Law Of Love: Luke 6:27-42

But I say unto you which hear, Love your enemies, do good to them which hate you.

The definition of the words in our subject text is law, it is a set of rules or guidelines set forth to be followed and in this scenario God set forth His laws of love which governs all believers. Love is an action word that expresses compassion. Throughout biblical history love is expressed in many acts of kindness as this love is representative of God's agape love.

In giving His law of love God begins by saying "Love your enemies, do good to them which hate you." What does this mean? It means that we are to show genuine concern for their good and eternal salvation. We are to pray for the evil doer asking the Holy Spirit to soften his/her heart and repent so that the person may come to Christ and join the faith community.

Another of God's laws of love is that we are to turn the other cheek when struck on one cheek. This does not mean that one is to be beaten without protecting oneself. God did not intend for believers to become a human punching bag, just show kindness for our evil brother/sister.

Lastly, God raises the question, what good is it to love those who love you, but the true test of godly love is showing love to those who hate and or misused you. It is noteworthy to say that to love our enemies is accomplished through the indwelling Holy Spirit.

God gave and showed love to all mankind.

Promise Of The Comforter: John 14: 16-17

And I will pray the Father, and He shall give you another Comforter, that He may abide with you for ever.

Today's topical discussion focuses on a conversation Jesus is having with His disciples regarding the coming of the Comforter—the Holy Spirit. The Holy Spirit abides in each believer and Jesus informed His disciples that the Comforter—Spirit would abide with them forever and on the Day of Pentecost He came giving power and many souls were saved that day. After the coming of the Holy Spirit, the disciples performed many miracles and the gospel of Christ spread tremendously.

If the question were raised, did the Holy Spirit-Comforter come as promised? In John 20:22 speaks of Jesus instructing His disciples to receive the Holy Spirit as this occurred on resurrection day and is separate from the baptism of the Holy Spirit that came on Pentecost. In this scenario Jesus breathed on the disciples and at that moment He entered and began to live in the disciples.

If the question were raised, what will the Comforter do once He gets here? The Comforter—the Holy Spirit---"the Spirit of truth as He is the Spirit of Jesus who is truth as He testifies of the truth, teaches the truth, exposes all untruths and guides the believer into all truths" (LSPB). The Holy Spirit counsels only those who are willing to abide by the truth and all who worship must do so "in spirit and in truth"(4:24).

Jesus-God kept His promise of the Holy Spirit—our Comforter who dwells in every believer.

Apr 11

Believers Separated From The World
1 John 2:9-11, 15-17

Love not the world, neither the things that are in the world. If any man love the world, the love of the Father is not in him.

Why is it necessary for believers to separate themselves from the World? Believers must separate themselves from the world as they are now children of God who is light. Being children of God we are no longer held hostage by Satan and sin for we have been ransomed out of this world by Christ's death and have been made new creatures by Him. We are justified—made right before God the Father meaning we are a holy nation, of a royal priesthood, and a set aside people.

Believers' are separated from the world is because the war that has been raging since Satan was thrown out of heaven. This war is between God and Satan, and Satan is controlling the vast systems of this age. A vast majority of what is occurring in today's world is controlled by Satan and his evil tactics as he is determined to destroy God and His people and the world that God created. Ephesians 6:10-18 provides our weapons for combating Satan and his evil attacks on this world. Many of those weapons are defensive in nature and the Bible is the only offensive weapon necessary to attack Satan for it gives a detail outline for godly living that will dispel the evil and immorality that is currently taking place.

It is noteworthy to point out that the world and the true church are two distinct groups of people. According to John 12:31 the world is currently under Satan's dominion; what this means is that Satan and all he stands for was defeated at the cross by Jesus Christ (Colossians 2:15) and his final banishment will occur when he is thrown into the lake of fire (Revelation 20:10). Needless to say that Satan is still active in this present world as its ruler (John 14:3; 16:11; 2 Corinthians 4:4; Ephesians 2:2). Satan appears successful at this present time because Satan uses things in the world against the church and Christ; with this in mind he knows his time is short and he has no win with God who created him. Needless to say being in friendship with the world is being an enemy with God because as shown Satan and God are at odds (1 John 2"15-16; James 4:4).

Therefore, believers are strangers/pilgrims in this world as we are a called-out people from the world (John15:19), as believers have been exhorted to no longer conform to the world (Romans 12:2), nor are we are to love the world (1 John 2:15), believers are to die to the world (Galatians 6:14) as believers we died with Christ and have been delivered from the world (Hebrews 1:9). With that being said, believers, loving the world defiles our fellowship with God and can be viewed as spiritual adultery it can/will lead to spiritual destruction Matthew 6:24; Luke 16:13). This speaks to Jesus' teaching on serving two masters, money/the world and God; it can't be done. Let this writer point that the term "world" does not mean the beautiful trees, mountains, forest and etc that God created, but instead the systems that operate in God's created realms.

It can be concluded then that believers are separated from the world because of the sanctification process that has occurred between God and His people. Sanctification requires believers maintaining an on-going love relationship with God and this is accomplished with the help of the Holy Spirit.

Apr 12

"Justified By Faith": Romans 5:1-11

Therefore, being justified by faith, we have peace with God through our Lord Jesus Christ.

Being justified means being made right with God through our belief (faith) in Jesus Christ, and in doing so we have peace/shalom with God our creator. Today's scripture provides insight to the benefits of being justified in Christ, and they are:
- a) We have the grace of God which is His righteousness that has been imparted to us through Christ Jesus.
- b) Our hope for the future is in Christ as through His death on the cross have made all provisions for our eternal salvation.
- c) Our assurance is our guarantee of our destiny which is seeing our Savior face-to face.
- d) Our perseverance is our steadfastness while on life's journey and our commitment to serve God and live holy lives before Him and men so they will see Christ manifested in our daily lives.
- e) We have the love of God manifested toward us—we respond to Him in love for His grace and mercy.
- f) Believers have the indwelling Holy Spirit to guide, teach, direct and protect from all manner of harm.
- g) All believers who have accepted Jesus Christ as their personal Savior have salvation as this was His plan for becoming God-man to take on the sins of the world. As salvation shields all believers from the coming wrath of God
- h) Through Jesus; death, burial and resurrection we have been reconciled back to God, thus restoring the broken fellowship between man and God.
- i) All believers have salvation through the presence of Jesus Christ who lives in each through the Holy Spirit.
- j) Lastly, all believers' joy in God has been restored.

Many blessings from being justified by God.

Apr 13

The Father Bore Witness Of Jesus: John 5:37-47

And the Father Himself, which hast sent Me, hath borne witness of Me. Ye have neither heard His words at any time, nor seen His shape.

Today's lesson focus is on Jesus' conversation regarding His identity and His Father's witness to the fact that He was truly God's Son and by what authority He had to do the works that was done. Jesus talks about John the Baptist bearing witness to Him, but was nothing in comparison to the witness by His Father. This occurred at Jesus' baptism in the Jordan River when the Godhead appeared together. As John bore witness to the truth which was Jesus was God's Son the promised Messiah who came to take away the sins of the world.

What Jesus was actually telling His audience is that "here you have the Son of God in the flesh preaching repentance and baptism in the Holy Spirit and you are refusing to hear and believe." I have been sent by my Father as I do all things through Him and by His Will, because I can do nothing in and of myself." This question comes to mind, if you fail to believe the true source, then who will you believe? To believe, one must have the love of God in them and accept Him and His Son for who they are one the provider of salvation and one the giver of salvation.

Just as God the Father bore witness of His Son, so can believers through faith and seeing with their spiritual eyes.
Christ our Savior---witness Him for He is worthy-God did.

Fulfill The Law: Matthew 5:17-20

Think not that I am come to destroy the law, or the prophets; I am not come to destroy, but to fulfill.

In today's discussion we will discuss the fulfilling of the law and what it means to all Christians. Jesus plainly states in verse 17 that He didn't "come to destroy the law or prophets, but to fulfill." What does that mean? It was not Christ's intention or mission to destroy or abolish any of the OT laws and revelation, but to see them accomplished in the lives of all believers (Romans 3:31; 8:4). What was prophesied in the OT was brought to life in the NT through Jesus Christ and can be seen in the following manner:
   a) Believers are obligated to keep the ethical and moral principles outlined in the OT as well as those of the apostles and Christ Himself.
   b) We as believers must view the moral code for all believes who have been saved and are living in obedience to Christ.
   c) Believers live in obedience to God and His morals through our faith in Jesus Christ as He is the sovereign law giver.
   d) Being freed from the bondage of sin, believers now are under the "law of Christ" (1 Corinthians 9:21).

We are now under the law of grace and are obligated to live accordingly as Christ through the Holy Spirit makes it possible for all believers to obey and keep God's sovereign laws as they are based on His righteousness not some legal system of mandates.

Believers have victory in Jesus Christ.

Parable Of The Lighted Candle: Luke 11: 33-36

No man, when he hath lighted a candle, putteth it in a secret place, neither under a bushel, but on a candlestick, that they which come in may see the light.

It has been documented that a parable is a earthly story with a heavenly meaning; in this discussion, we see Jesus talking about the eye as the light of the whole body using a lighted candle as the point of reference to begin the discussion. Jesus asks a profound implied question by stating that "no man would light a candle and put it under a bushel, but on a candlestick, that they which come in may see the light" (v.23).

What light is Jesus referring? Jesus is referring to the light of ones lifestyle as He is referring to the eye as the means by which the whole body receives light to direct his/her path because without proper eyesight one lives in total darkness. On a spiritual plane, when ones spiritual eye—attitudes, motives and desires are God centered, then when the person hears God's Word it then lights their hearts which produces godly fruit as recorded in Galatians 5:22-23 and salvation.

Another school of thought on our spiritual eyes is that believers are to let our light shine before God so men will see our good works and in doing so present the opportunity for others to come to Christ. Also, believers are the lighted candles in a sin darkened world, and how believers are to shine in this world is through witness---lifestyles and verbal preaching and teaching Christ.

Lit candles are Christ's spiritual eyes.

Apr 16

"You shall Be Free Indeed": John 8:31-47

If the Son therefore; shall make you free, ye shall be free indeed.

In our scripture text we see Jesus conversing with His Jewish believers that He is far superior to Abraham and if they continue to abide in His Word they would be free because they will know the truth which will set them free. This applies to all believers who accept Jesus as Lord and Savior.

Humanity's knowledge gives him knowledge of many things, but the truth that can and will set men free from sin's destruction and Satan's domination is that Jesus' truth brings salvation. It is noteworthy to say the truth that saves comes only from God and does not originate from some humanistic wisdom, as God's saving truth comes only "by His Spirit" (1 Corinthians 2:10).

If the question were raised, What about being "free indeed"? Being free indeed is total freedom from the bondage of sin where the unbeliever lives as a slave to sin, Satan and his dominating forces while lacking the ability to break free. Believers on the other hand have been freed from Satan's clutches and salvation as provided by Christ Himself and the Holy Spirit as a helper to aid in the believer remaining free from sin and its temptations. The world will know all who have been set free because of the brightness of God's glory shinning in each believer. Lastly, being free from sin is like breathing a breath of fresh air or a ray of sunshine entering ones life.

Believe and be set free—then shout glory halleluiah!

Apr 17

Strengthen The Inner Man: Ephesians 3:16-19

That He would grant you, according to the riches of His glory, to be strengthened with might by His Spirit in the inner man.

Who is the inner man? The inner man is the spirit man of all mankind because when man was created God breathed the breath of life into man, thus he became a living soul. Also, the inner man is the driving force behind man's thoughts, emotions, feelings and all comprehensions. The inner man is either controlled by the Holy Spirit---God or Satan, and when controlled by the Holy Spirit all humanity have the power, will and determination to live according to God's Will. This is the primary reason for the Holy Spirit which is to strengthen the inner man so that man's spirit will be energized, influenced, and aligned with God's Spirit.

Strengthening the inner man is threefold, and they are (a) Christ's presence is established in the hearts of man (vv.16-17), as this is where everything originates. (b) So that believers/Christians will have a solid foundation as our deepest desire is to love God and live for Him is accomplished. (c) All believers be filled with the fullness of God—the Holy Spirit. Therefore, being strengthen--the inner man, all believers can and will manifest the manifold presence of God.

Strengthening the inner man carries positive results as man and God have a loving relationship, which is what God desires. By daily communing with God this relationship grows stronger—in the words of Paul there is no separating us from the love of God.

Believers, align your spirit with God's spirit for strength.

Apr 18

The Great Commission: Matthew 28:19-20

Go ye therefore, and teach all nations, baptizing them in the name of the Father, and of the Son, and the Holy Ghost.

Looking at the Great Commission we have three directives issued by Christ Himself and those are (a) go, (b) teach and (c) baptize. This is the commission of all Christ's followers for all generations as this is the goal, responsibility and the mission and or commissioning of every church.

The "go" directive as it relates to the church and it congregation is to go into all nations/world and preach the gospel of Christ according to the NT revelation and the apostles. Christ intends for every person to hear the Word. In the "go", includes the primary responsibility of the church of sending missionaries into every nation (Acts 13:1-4).

The true church is founded on the Christ-inspired infallible revelation of the first apostles. Why the apostles because they were the eye witness of Christ's death, burial and resurrection, this makes them the foundation by which Christ is preached. Furthermore, the NT apostle were the original messengers, witnesses and authorized representatives of the risen Christ, as the Holy Ghost came upon them at Pentecost (Acts 1:8). First the apostles waited for the promise and were filled with the Holy Ghost (Acts 1:4) and on the day of Pentecost Jesus baptized with the Holy Ghost.

The "teach"/preach directive of the gospel is centered on "repentance and the remission (forgiveness) of sins" (Luke 24:47). This is because without repentance there can be no forgiveness of sin simply because the person haven't truly turned from their old ways or accepted Jesus Christ for who He really is and His saving power.

It is noteworthy to say that going and teaching is not simply to make converts but to make disciples/students of Christ. Neither is going and teaching is just to increase the church membership, but on discipleship which is for the converts to separate themselves from the world and its immoral. Thus the new disciples have totally committed

their hearts, souls and minds to do the Will of God. It is noteworthy to say that Christ's command on reaching the lost souls of men and women is not merely Christianizing society but true discipleship.
    Obey the great commission.

Apr 19

God's Provisional Care: Psalm 65:1-8

Today's topical discussion reflects on God's provisional care for all creation, but more importantly, His care for humanity. God's care is from three aspects, and they are (a) preservation, (b) His providence and human suffering, and (c) man's relationship to His providence. In each component of His care we see that God in His divine wisdom made all the necessary provisions for humanity's every need and situation we may encounter.

God made provision for all creation as He did not abandon His creation/the world. This can be seen in His preservation as recorded in the words of King David's Psalm 36:3, which states "Thy righteousness is like the great mountains; thy judgments are a great deep: O Lord, thou perservest man and beast." There is a plethora of other scriptures that speak of God's provisional care. Philippians 4:19 talks about god supplying all man's need according to His riches and glory through Christ Jesus (partial paraphrase).

Regarding human suffering and God's care, can be summed up by saying that God never instigates suffering, but from time to time He allows it, directs it, and overrules it to accomplish His redemptive purpose and Will, but know that all things work together for the good of those who love the Lord (Matthew 2:13; Romans 8:28).

Regarding our relationship to his providence, His care extends to both the righteous and unrighteous. He directs the affairs of the church and individuals who serve Him and ministers to other people in His name (Acts 18:9-10; 23: 11; 26:15-18; 27:22-24).

What a blessing to be in God's care.

All Nations Worshipping God: Psalm 86:8-13

All nations whom thou hast made shall come and worship before thee, o Lord, and shall glorify thy name.

The Psalmist recognizing God and His awesome power as the one true and living God, he makes a profound declaration by stating "All nations whom thou hast made shall come and worship before thee, O Lord; and shall glorify thy name." This speaks to the fact that there are many nations and or individuals who fail to recognize God as the Almighty creator of everything that is both seen and unseen, but in the days to come as the Psalmist of other Bible writers (Paul) have stated that "every knee shall bow to me and every tongue shall confess to God" (Isaiah 45:23; Romans 14:11; Philippians 2:10-1),..."that Jesus Christ is Lord, to the glory of God the Father." What this means is that every person may not turn to the Lord in true repentance in his/her lifetime, but all people one day will voluntarily or involuntarily bow before Christ and confess that He is Lord. Another point of view is that in society there are many gods who people worship, but in due time all will worship the true and living God.

During this time all who come to worship God will do so in spirit and truth and with a sincere heart as all humanity will have come to recognize that the other gods have no saving power.

These questions come to mind, do you know God as the only God worthy of worship and praise? How do you worship God? Worship Him—He is worthy.

Apr 21

Triumph In God's Kingdom: Isaiah 2:1-4

And many of the people shall go and say, Come ye, and let us go up to the mountain of the Lord, to the house of the God of Jacob; and He will teach us of His ways, and we will walk in His paths; for out of Zion shall go forth the law, and the word the Lord from Jerusalem.

The word "triumph" denotes victory and in today's discussion we will focus on the Lord's return to earth to establish God's kingdom. The prophet Isaiah talks about a time when God's rule will be established over in every nation as all evil, injustices and any and all rebellion that is currently directed against God and His law will have come to an end and righteousness will reign forever.

The "all nations" (v.2) includes both Jews and Gentiles will worship and serve the Lord with gladness as this reflects the Lord's purpose for both Israel and the entire human race. This will be fulfilled by Jesus Christ Himself who will execute justice and righteousness on all (9:1-7; 11:3-5).

Verse 3 gives insight to the condition of man during the end times as all will be willing to be taught God's ways and to walk in His paths. This verse is in-line with the Great Commission recorded in Matthew 28:19-20 as those who proclaim the gospel message of Christ do so with extreme care and sincerity as this represents the infallible Word of God. More importantly, all humanity both saved and unsaved need to hear the true word of God from those anointed by the Holy Spirit.

God's Kingdom is victorious because the truth will have been proclaimed the world over and many will come to know and worship Him.

Victory! Victory! God gave me the victory. Victory is mined today!

Apr 22

"Great And Marvelous Are Thy Works"
Revelation 15:3-4

And they sin the song of Moses the servant of God, and the song of the Lamb, saying, Great and marvelous are thy works, Lord God Almighty; just and true are thy ways, thou King of saints.

When one considers mighty works of God and His awesome powers then our subject phrase takes on new meaning.
    Let's reflect on some of the mighty works of God, first, He created all seen and unseen out of nothing. God said let there be and the universe came into existence. Second, God created all plant and animal life with a distant nature to survive and to know the seasons of the year. Third, God created both night and day by separating the two. Fourth, God created man in His liken and image and breathed the breath of life into man at which man became a living soul. God put part of Himself into man so man could love like God and the two have a close fellowship. Fifth, God gave man dominion over all creation. Sixth, God sustains all His creation. Lastly, God made provisions for all mans needs as well as all of His creation. The seasons know exactly when to change, the sun and moon as well as all heavenly bodies operate on schedule under God's command and control.
    In regards to man and God's love for him a plan for the two to spend eternity together was implemented through the shed blood of Jesus Christ and all who believe on Him shall be saved. God's love is so great until He is prepared and will defeat Satan and his army in the great battle of Armageddon and all who have been faithful to the Lord will reign with Him.
    Marvelous are thy name worthy to be praise---glory in the highest!

Apr 23

A Place Of Honor: Luke 14:7-14

When thou art bidden of any man to a wedding, sit not down in the highest room; lest a ore honorable man than thou be bidden of him.

In our scripture text Jesus is teaching on places of position or what man perceives as a place of honor, as Jesus uses the parable of the wedding party and where certain guests are invited to sit. Typically honored guest are invited to sit at the head of the table or other places to be recognized, but what Jesus was trying to get over to His audience was anyone who exalts him or herself will be put to shame by God in the future kingdom as the two honored positions oppose each other.

See! God loves all mankind the same, He does not place one above the other. What God honored most is humility and true servanthood and not by self-assertiveness, as this type of person is concerned with self and receiving the praise and honor from man---this praise is all that will be rewarded.

Jesus provided the perfect example of honor as He sought no honor for Himself, but only to do the will of His Father. Jesus humbled Himself and came to earth to be limited by human limitation and to suffer all manner of ill-treatments---a disgraceful death at Calvary. Did He deserve such treatment? No, because of love He did it anyway.

True honor is humility while serving others, because a humble person have the right view of self, others and God. What is your place of honor-humility or exaltation?

Apr 24

An Invitation To The Great Feast: Luke 14:15-24

And sent His servant at supper time to say to them that were bidden, Come; for all things are now ready.

Today's lesson study is another of Jesus parabolic teaching, and this parable looks at the salvation invitation that is being extended to mankind. This parable speaks of a man making a great feast/meal and inviting many guests, however his invited guest replied that they would attend but as the feast time was near, they had a change of heart and made excuses. This is indicative of many in today's society who say they will do something and then recant their decision.

On a spiritual plane, salvation came to the Jews first and they rejected it. Then salvation was made available to the Gentile nations and they accepted. This is seen in the second invitation that was sent by God. God instructed His servants to go into the highways and hedges, and compel them to come until His house/kingdom is filled (partial paraphrase). It has been said that when the Word of God is proclaimed and those who refuse to hear and adhere, then God will have the rocks to cry out. It is profitable that man adheres to God's Word rather than be replaced by rocks.

Another school of thought on the "Great Feast" is spending eternity with God and the heavenly angels is a feast of endless worship and praise as there will be no more suffering, dying or tears of sorrow to shed. Everything will be one great spiritual house party.

Will you be there?

Apr 25

Seek The Lord: Jeremiah 29:12-13

And ye shall seek Me, and find Me, when ye shall search for me with all your heart.

The prophet Jeremiah was writing to the Jewish captives providing hope of answered prayers that when they go into prayer it should be done in sincerity and with a repentant heart. God reminds the captives/Israel that while in captivity "I visited you and performed my good word toward you, causing you to return to this place"—their home land. God further reminds Israel that He knew their thoughts, whether good or evil, He knows everything. God asked the nation to seek Him with sincerity, in doing so they would find Him because He would hear and answer their prayers. More importantly, God told His people that He would bring them back to the place where they were taken from. In other words He would restore Israel as this applies to all who have turned from God.

In retrospect, "seek the Lord" can be viewed as an invitation that parallels Luke 14:15-24 where God is inviting all to accept salvation. Two reasons for this revelation is that God has always been there for man and it was man that turned from God. Therefore, it is man who must seek God and ask for forgiveness. It was Israel's sinful ways that resulted in them being in captivity for seventy years, and when man is out of fellowship with God he then is being held captive by sin and Satan. Man must sincerely pray to God for His hand of mercy.

It is time for all men to admit, confess and seek/ask for forgiveness and be saved. Seek the Lord—He is near.

Apr 26

Parabolic Teaching Using Ten Virgins
Matthew 25: 1-13

Then shall the kingdom of heaven be likened unto tem virgins, which took their lamps, and went forth to meet the bridegroom.

Today's discussion is a very familiar passage of scripture as Jesus uses this parable for everyone to take an in-depth look at their own spiritual condition. The wise in this lesson represents those believers who recognize their condition and rely on the Holy Spirit to aid them to be in fellowship with God regardless of the time of His return. The wise virgins have the faith of Christ's return and are determined to be ready when He comes if He delays; His delay is giving the unsaved time to repent. The foolish virgins lack the perseverance to remain steadfast in the Lord. He can return at an unexpected time, but Christ's return is guaranteed as this is a prophecy yet to be fulfilled.

These questions come to mind, Who will be wise and Who will be foolish? Will the church be prepared for Christ's return? Luke 18:8 implies that a large segment of the church will be unprepared when Christ returns. Verses 8-13, Christ makes it very clear that He will not wait until the church/believers are ready when he comes, as this is seen in the dialogue of the bridegroom coming and the door being shut on the foolish virgins.

The lessons learned are (a) perseverance in faith is necessary; (b) oil in our text represents true faith, righteousness, and the abiding presence of the Holy Spirit.

Be wise remain faithful and persevere to the end—Christ is coming!

Little And Much: Luke 16:10-12

He that is faithful in that which is least is faithful also in much, and he that is unjust in the least is unjust also in much.

In one of my weekly discussions I talked about expressions of gratitude. This discussion takes on the same flavor of appreciation of what God has blessed you with. Regardless of what we have is what God wants for us at that particular time and our responses reflect our gratitude and stewardship.

As reflected in our topic discussion text if you have not been faithful over little (least), then how can we expect to be blessed with even greater things/blessing? It is noteworthy to say whatever we have are blessings from God and should be treated as such. Also, God has granted blessings/possessions to each of us according to our faithfulness, stewardship and gratitude as our outward expressions of thankfulness stems from the heart and brings into focus our relationship with God and self; this depicts our reverential humility of His blessings.

Our blessings with little or a lot can be viewed from several perspectives, and some are (a) His presence with us, (b) God working in and through us to bring about good, (c) His blessings playing an integral part in our ministries, and we must look to Jesus for His blessing in our families, works as well as ministries, (d) they are conditional based upon our responses of obedience or disobedience where in disobedience cursing could follow.

In short, all our blessings come from the Lord---little or much. Be thankful and manage them well---this is our faithfulness.

Faithful Stewards: 1 Corinthians 4:1-5

Let a man so account of us, as of the ministers of Christ; and stewards of the mysteries of God. Moreover it is required in stewards, that a man be found faithful.

What is a steward? The definition of steward is one who manages goods, and or responsibilities. How one manages those responsibilities and or goods is known as his/her stewardship. Believers are to be faithful stewards while managing God's work and the monetary things that he has placed in our care.

Our scripture verses speak about being faithful stewards over the ministries that God has blessed us with. What does this mean? It means that all believers who remain faithful to God and His kingdom building have renounced all worldliness and are not walking in craftiness which is being blinded by Satan and his deceitful tactics. Also, being steadfast to God's Word and His works believers are rightly dividing he word of truth (2 Timothy 2:15) by constantly studying God's Word and being filled with the Holy Spirit. Believers constantly studying God's Word become doers of the word and it is spread to all lost souls as this is the Great Commission given by Christ Himself (Matthew 28:19-20). Through the power of the Holy Spirit believers have the power to do great and mighty works in the name of the Lord.

Believers' faithfulness in their stewardship as Christ is preached souls are saved as this can be attributed to believers love for Christ and His gospel message as well as obedience to Him. Ten believers' lights shine brightly in a sin darkened.

Faithful stewards are committed manager of delivering the truth about God's Word.

Apr 29

Christ The Firstborn Of Everything: Colossians 1:15-23

Who is the image of the invisible God, the firstborn of every creature.

What does it mean by the phrase "Christ the first born of everything/creature? This means that Christ is the Son of God as He was present during the creation process. This makes Him the ruler and heir of all creation as the eternal Son of God (v.18; Hebrews 1:3).

Verse 16 clarifies the meaning of the phrase by stating "For by him were all things created, that are in heaven and that are in earth, visible and invisible, whether they be thorns, or dominions, or principalities, or powers; all things were created by him and for him." Verse 17 further answers the question by saying that "all things were created for him and by him all things consist." To give further authentication of Christ being the firstborn of everything, Paul makes it very plain by saying "in him....all fullness dwell," which means all that is represented in the Godhead rests in Christ (Colossians 2:9; Hebrews 1:8).

Another look at Christ being the firstborn of everything is by stating that He is the firstborn from the dead, which means that Christ was the first to rise with a mortal and spiritual body (1 Corinthians 15:20). It is Christ who reconciled humanity and everything in the universe was brought in unity and harmony under Christ (vv. 16-18). Also, it was Christ who bridged the gap between mankind and God the Father.

Christ was the only one found worthy to die for the sins of the world while remaining sinless.

Apr 30

Who is Christ?: John 1:1-8; Colossians 1: 19-20

In the beginning was the Word, and the Word was God. The same was in the beginning with God. All things were made by Him; and without Him was not any thing made that was made.

Today's topical discussion will answer the question by stating that Christ is the incarnated Word of God, which means the Word of God became flesh/human being(man). He was preexistent with God. Christ is the eternal second person in the Godhead; existing from eternity to eternity. Christ is the second person in the Godhead who is equal to God the Father, but distinct from God the Father.

It was through Christ that God created the world and all exist in Him. Christ was in the beginning with God and not created by God. Christ is humanity's propitiator, meaning Christ died in man's place. He is man's redeemer as man has the opportunity to be freed from sin and its bondage. Christ is the Savior of the world and all who believe in Him shall have everlasting life (John 3:16). It is Christ who embodies true life because in Him all life exists and He is the light of the world.

Christ is the begotten of the Father, meaning He has God as His Father and Mary as His earthly mother; the two are His true parents.

It is through Christ that truth and grace are available to the fullest extent (Roman 5:17-21). It is Christ who gives thirst quenching water---the Holy Spirit and it is Christ who baptizes all believers in the Holy Spirit. Christ is the head of the church ---His bride.

Christ is all and all!

A Christ Centered Community

Laboring And Suffering For Christ And His Message
Colossians 1:24-29

Who now rejoicing in my suffering for you, and fill up that which is behind of the affliction of Christ in my flesh for His body's sake, which is the church.

What does it mean to labor for something? In common terms it means to work diligently at accomplishing a desired goal. Suffering on the other hand is to experience adversities. In our scripture text, Paul was expressing his joy in suffering and his labor for Christ as Christ continues to labor and suffer for His followers as we as believers carry His gospel message to others in obedience to the Great Commission.

The question now becomes why must we suffer as we carry the gospel message of Christ? Believers will experience suffering as followers of Christ because the world is opposed to His message and ministry. Therefore, Satan will and does use every tactic in his efforts to hinder kingdom building. Therefore, believers must remain steadfast in their commitment to Christ, His message and kingdom building. Believers are to come ready for battle as this is a spiritual warfare and believers are to be suited with the "Whole Armour of God" (Ephesians 4:11-18). Notice in our suit of armour, the Bible is our only offensive weapon with which to attack Satan on his turf through daily reading and meditating on God's Word." It is noteworthy to say that the more we read and remain in fellowship with God, the Holy Spirit is ever present in our lives giving believers the necessary strength to labor and suffer for Christ and His message.

Laboring and suffering for Christ is minute considering what He has done for all humanity.

May 1

The Fruit of Your Labor: Colossians 1: 1-14

Which is come unto you, as it is in all the world; and bringeth forth fruit, as it doth also in you, since the day ye heard of it, and knew the grace of God is truth.

When one speaks of fruit what comes to mind is that fruit that is eatable, however in our scripture text it is the results of ones labor to or for something or someone.

Therefore, biblically speaking the fruit of Christ's labor was to bring salvation to all who believe in and accept Him as his or her personal Savior. Also, during Christ's earthly ministry the fruit of His labor was to authenticate His deity as God's Son and with the many miracles He performed the results were that many believed and were saved. More importantly, many became His followers and in turn saved others through their testimony of their encounter with Jesus. Case in point, the woman at the well through her encounter with Jesus and testimony a whole town was saved; then there was the blind man who ran and told all he met about Jesus and what He had done for him—opened his blind eyes both spiritual and physical. **What a fruit bearing testimony?**

How can we fail to remember Mary Magdalene whom Jesus cast out several demons. Mary was in the company of women who were first to discover Jesus' resurrection on that glorious Sunday morning. Mary Magdalene became a devout follower of Jesus.

The following questions come to mind, Have you had a Jesus encounter and what changes has it brought? What is your testimony? Does the world see you as a different person? Can you run and tell everybody you meet that there is a man healing? He healed my sin-sick soul and now I am free to tell the world about Him-Jesus? The results of your Jesus encounter is a new beginning as there should be a commitment to the Great Command and Great Commission (Matthew 28:19-20), which is to make other disciples of Christ the world over.

In obedience to the Great Command and Commission all believers are to love as Christ loved—to the point of the cross and in our commission we are to witness Christ as we are to season the world with our testimony. **What is your testimony?** Does the world know you as a Christ follower? Is your light shinning bright enough to dispel the darkness in your area? Believers are to live so that men may see Christ in you. The question now becomes, are you living godly lives as required by God? As believers are in the world, but not of this world, which means believers are to be separated from the world as it opposes God and His righteousness.

A tree is known by the fruit it bears-believers are known by the fruit we bear—our lifestyles-true Christians or worldly Christians.

God's Wisdom Verses Worldly Wisdom
1 Corinthians 1:20-31

For after that in the wisdom of God, it pleased God by the foolishness of preaching to save them that believe.

What is wisdom? Wisdom is the wise use of knowledge. With that being said, then true wisdom comes from God as it contains His holiness and righteousness, which is imparted to all receptive hearts and minds. God's wisdom reveals who He is and His desire for a relationship with mankind; predicated upon His love. It is noteworthy to say that godly wisdom reveals our brotherly love for one another and godly living in honor and respect to God and His Sovereignty as well as His standards and values.

The question now becomes, What is worldly wisdom? Worldly wisdom is the wisdom of man that promotes human self-sufficiency and makes humanity the highest authority; it disregards the supremacy of God our creator. Another thought on worldly wisdom is that it is in direct opposite of God's Wisdom and His standards/morals. With man anything goes. Case in point, man's wisdom comprises or refutes the gospel message of the cross, the creation theory, the Virgin birth of Jesus Christ and His resurrection on the third day---Sunday morning. Additionally, man's wisdom compromises the institution of marriages between man and woman that God instituted many years ago. Lastly, man's wisdom is predicated on his philosophy, science and or his own thinking as to what he perceives to be right and just.

God's wisdom ---wise and righteous choices—man's wisdom is foolish and humanistic. Which do you choose? God or man!

May 4

True Wisdom Is A Gift From God: 1 Corinthians 2:6-14

Howbeit we speak wisdom among them that are perfect; yet not the wisdom of this world, nor of the princes of this world, that come to nought.

Yesterday we discussed the differences between God and man's wisdom in determining the better choice of the two. Today we will discuss true wisdom as a gift from God and the benefits it carries.

Paul in his message to the Corinthian church was expounding on the gift of true wisdom and by what authority he preached Christ. God gives specific gifts to His leaders in the church to edify the Body of Christ—His church and through these gifts God imparts His wisdom through the Holy Spirit because there is one Lord and one salvation. When preached all who hear and believe will know the truth. There is only one truth—God's truth. Paul explains to the Corinthian church that he did not come in his own wisdom or Excellency of speech, but in the wisdom of God through the Holy Spirit who gives the power to do great things for the Lord.

Some of the benefits of true wisdom are that it reveals through the Holy Spirit God's truth for all humanity, the benefits of salvation, the presence of the indwelling Holy Spirit and His functions and that the Bible is God's Word written by divinely inspired men of God. Lastly, true wisdom is one of the greatest gifts given by God. Solomon asked for wisdom, which God granted and Solomon became the wisest man in the world.

Accept God's wisdom as blessings and truth abounds. What a gift?

The Power Of The Gospel: 1 Corinthians 2:1-5

And my speech and my preaching was not with enticing words of men's wisdom, but in demonstration of the Spirit and of power.

What is the gospel? The term gospel is commonly known as the good news of Christ which includes His birth, death, burial and resurrection. There is power in the message because it requires a spiritual mind to comprehend Jesus as a spiritual being yet human—God-man who was conceived by the Holy Spirit and born of a woman—the Virgin Mary. Jesus came to earth with the sole purpose of dying for humanity's sins. His death bridged the spiritual divide between man and God. While Jesus was hanging on the cross suffering excruciating pain for hours all of nature went out of control. The earth acted as if it was drunk, the sun and moon were blinded by God the Father and midnight came at high noon. This was God's way of refusing to look on sin.

The burial component of the gospel is that Jesus had warned His disciples that He had no place to lay His head; He was buried in a borrowed tomb; the shouting part is Resurrection Sunday when Jesus got up from the grave and "declared all power both in heaven and earth is in my hands."

The gospel is to be preached to all nations as it has the power to save lost souls, heal broken hearts and free the captives from the prison of sin. The gospel of Christ has and will continue to be preached; men will hear and be saved.

May 6

"Oneness In Christ": Romans 12:3-8

For as we have many members in one body, and all members have not the same office. So we, being many, are one body in Christ, and every one member one of another.

What is the meaning of the phrase "oneness in Christ"? This phrase carries several connotations; (a) all believers have a renewed mind and have accepted the perfect will of God to lead and live holy lives as directed by the Holy Spirit (v.2). (b) All believers have become members of the body of Christ each having a different gift to edify the body of Christ. The body of Christ works on the same principle as the physical body and members of the Godhead; God the Father, God the Son and God the Holy Spirit---one God.

Some of those members are prophecy, pastoring, teaching and evangelizing, just as the physical body is made up of eyes, nose, legs, arms and one head. From a spiritual point of view, each believer with his or her gift constitutes the body of Christ. Therefore, all believers are on one accord with Christ as He is the head. Believers remain in oneness with Christ because we have the mind of Christ as revealed by the Holy Spirit.

Members of the body of Christ serve in their respective roles edifying the body through his or her service. Case in point, prophecy is foretelling what God has revealed of events to come. Pastors serve as the shepherd or head of a local congregation of believers just as Christ is the head of His church. Teachers explain/clarify and expound on God's Word as revealed to them by the Holy Spirit, and believers witness to others the world over.

Many members, but one in Christ!

The Mind Of Christ: 1 Corinthians 2:16

For who hath known the mind of the Lord, that He may instruct him? Be we have the mind of Christ.

How does one have the mind of Christ? Romans 12:2 give some insight into having the mind of Christ as there has been a transformation of ones life which begins in the mind and heart. First believers must accept Christ for who He is and what He has and continues to do in the lives of all mankind. Second, believers/mankind must be willing to be led by the Holy Spirit as He reveals all truths as it relates to God and His righteousness. Third, having the mind of Christ is knowing His will and Christ's redemptive plan and purpose (vv 9-10). His redemptive plan is to provide salvation for all, and His purpose is for all believers to be in fellowship with Him and spend eternity with the Father. Fourth, having the mind of Christ is seeing things as God does and adopting His morals and values. Lastly, having the mind of Christ believers are united with Christ having the bond of peace and united in the Spirit with Him as there is a constant desire to be in His presence.

Benefits from having the mind of Christ are an unbreakable bond that Satan cannot penetrate. Having the mind of Christ gives believers the desire and commitment of proclaiming His gospel message until every man, woman, boy or girl has the knowledge of Christ and a worldwide revival is the result.

Lastly, having the mind of Christ, believers are on a different plain—spiritual!

The Spiritual Man Verses The Natural Man
Colossians 2:11-19

In whom also ye are circumcised with the circumcision made without hands, in putting off the body of the sins of the flesh, by the circumcision of Christ.

Natural man is considered the sinful man prior to his or her acceptance of Jesus Christ and His saving power (John 3:16). The natural man is one who has not undergone circumcision at the hand of God. Whereas the spirit man is the person who has had the foreskin of his heart removed and is now in a covenant relationship with God. Believers in Christ have buried the natural/old man and were raised with Him as a new creature---the spirit man.

What is circumcision? Circumcision is the removal of the foreskin of male children's as this was a custom/practice of OT Israelites which represented a covenant relationship with God. While in the NT circumcision is seen as the believer undergoing a spiritual separation from the world and its ungodliness. This is putting off the body's sins of the flesh and its desires. In other words, circumcision represents a regenerated way of life, no more living in rebellion to God and His holiness as the sins of the heart have been removed.

Another school of thought on the spiritual man verses the natural man is that at conversion God performs a spiritual operation on man's heart. The stoniness in and around man's heart has been replaced with one of love and tenderness.

Lastly, the spirit man is superior to the natural man as the spirit man is controlled by the indwelling Holy Spirit.

May 9

Women And The Christian Home
Titus 2:4-5; Proverbs 31:10-31

That they may teach the young women to be sober, to love their husbands, to love their children.

In establishing the family structure God created woman to be a helpmeet for her husband. Woman was created using a rib from the man's side –Adam. It was never intended for a woman to be the head of the household. Woman was designed to be the nucleus of the household as she is to be soft, loving and possessing a quiet and gentle spirit. In the olden days the woman remained in the home and prepared for her family-husband and children. She taught them God's ways and His Word as she valued her family and the upbringing of the children. Women are regarded as the child's first teacher as she teaches her children the Reverence for God and respect for mankind early in the child's life. In today's society women have had to seek work outside the home compromising her wifely and motherly duties to the family.

Nevertheless, God has provided specific guidelines for the woman as it relates to her family, church and home. First, she is to love her husband, she is to obey him as in reverence to God. Second, she is to care for the children that God has entrusted her with as a service to the Lord. Third, women are to be a helpmeet and faithful companion to her husband. Fourth, women are to aid the father in training the children in godly character as recorded in Deuteronomy 6:7. Fifth, women are to use their God-given skills to provide for the needs of others--home and community. Seventh, women/mothers who seek to fulfill God's plan for their lives and their families must submit to the leading of the Holy Spirit and if it becomes necessary to seek employment outside the home, she must pray to God for the necessary means to fulfill her duties to her children and home first while maintaining good standings with her Christian Community.

It is noteworthy to highlight the preciousness of a Christian woman as she is looked upon as being virtuous as outlined in Proverbs

31:10-31. Her values are far beyond rubies as there is no monetary amount that can be placed on a virtuous Christian woman. She lives her life according to scripture in humble submission to God and her husband. She lovingly cares for her children as she will sacrifice herself for the good and welfare of her family. She works tireless and long hours ensuring that all is well with all under her watch. A Christian woman seeks no reputation for herself; she is highly recognized and known throughout the community as her works speak for her.

More importantly, Christian women recognize and understand the value of a Christian family-home as this perpetuates to the next generation of Christian women; so they too can carry on the Christian Family tradition.

Lastly, Christian women are worthy of all honor; marvelous are their works. A Christian woman teach her daughters in her home and the young women in her Christian Community—the church. Her method of teaching is by setting good examples for young women to see and follow as well as with kind words of encouragement and gentle corrections when warranted.

A virtuous Christian woman is a precious commodity.

May 10

Fellow Laborers In Christ: 1 Corinthians 3:5-9

Who then is Paul, and who is Apollos, but ministers by whom ye believed, even as the Lord gave to every man?

In Paul's writing to the Corinthians believers at Corinth he made some profound facts regarding believers working for Christ in His vineyard. He gave an example of how he and fellow laborer Apollos worked together building the kingdom of God. Paul preached, Apollos watered and God gave the increase. What Paul is saying is that Christ followers are to spread the Word and refrain from worrying about when the seed of your preaching, teaching and witnessing begin to bear fruit—persons come to Christ.

In obedience to the Great Commission all believers are to witness Christ regardless of territory or the person's condition. Following Christ's example He cast out demons and opened blind eyes and never performed a background check. Two things were at work, the person's faith in Jesus and His ability to heal and Christ's commitment to doing the will of His Father.

Another school of thought is that God's vineyard is in need of workers---people who will spread the gospel message of Christ, but the call for workers is even greater. Another thought on the cooperative spirit exhibited by Paul and Apollos is that all believers must display that we are united in Christ and His message. In the book of James chapter 3 which talks about true faith being evidenced by our works; meaning that we show our true faith by our works.

Our reward is heavenly when God says "good and faithful servant, job well done."

May 11

Believers Made perfect In Christ: Colossians 1:28

Whom we preach, warning every man, and teaching every man in all wisdom; that we may present every man perfect in Christ Jesus.

If the question were raised, how are believers made perfect in Christ? We could look no further than the sanctification process that occurred once we accepted Jesus as our personal Savior. Sanctification in itself is to make holy, to be set aside and or consecrated or separated from the world. This is so that all believers will have an intimate relationship with God and have the desire and ability to "love God with all thine heart, mind, and soul" (Matthew 22:37). Other attributes of being made perfect in Christ is believers are "made free from sin" (Romans 6:18), believers are "dead to sin" (Roman 6:2), believers are "servants to righteousness and holiness" (Romans 6:19), believers can "keep His commands" (1 John 3:22), and believers "have overcome the world" (1 John 5:4).

More importantly, the above attributes are works of the Holy Spirit through salvation in Christ as He delivers each believer from the bondage of sin and its power. Therefore, believers being made perfect in Christ gives all believers an ethnical righteousness of an unblemished character that is to demonstrate obedience and love for a holy God.

Believers receive sanctification by faith in God and in union with Christ in His death and resurrection as all believers died to sin with Christ on the cross and were raised with Him on Resurrection morning.

Believers working toward complete perfection in Christ will occur during transformation from mortality to immortality; believers will remain a set aside people with the help of the Holy Spirit and constant communication with God.

Believers Sufficient In Christ: Colossians 2-8-15

Beware lest any man spoil you through philosophy and vain deceit, after the tradition of men, after the rudiments of the world, and not after Christ.

The word "sufficient" carries a connotation of having just enough of what is needed or being made complete. With that being said, then all who have accepted Jesus Christ as his/her personal have just enough as Christ provides all our needs in God's provisional care as recorded in Psalm 23 and Philippians 4:19.

Our scripture text encourages us to refrain from getting caught up in human philosophy and its vain deceit because man's philosophy is traditional based while Christ is truth and righteousness. The two teachings are diametrically opposed to each other. The philosophy of humanism teaches that mankind and all that exists happened by chance, while the truth is that all humanity and creation are the works of God and the Godhead—God the Father, God the Son and God the Holy Spirit. With God nothing happens by chance, mankind is not an after thought, but a special creation of God as all humanity has a part of God within us.

Verse 10 solidifies the teaching that all "are complete in Him- Christ who is the head of all principality and power." This includes both the invisible and visible that mankind may require. Believers are sufficient in Christ, as our God and Savior left nothing to chance in that He saves us, regenerates us, justifies, and sanctifies us all to His glory. Given that Christ is all knowing, all seeing and loving the question becomes, ***What's the fuss? You have Christ—He's enough!***

Christ The Center Of True Christian Living
Colossians 3:1-17

Set your affection on things above, not on thing on the earth. For ye are dead, and your life is hid with Christ in God.

The word "Christian" means to be Christ-like, then all true believers have dedicated themselves to be more like Christ and His righteousness as Christ is to be our primary focus as oppose to the world and its unrighteousness.

The question now becomes, why must believers make Christ his/her primary focus? Because all believers have been clothed with His life and character in that we as believers died with Him and rose with Him and through the power of the Holy Spirit have conquered sin. Therefore, believers are to live as Christ lived in total obedience to His Father, we as believers should live to please God. Christ sought to make no reputation for Himself, we must do likewise.

Believers have the strength and power to live Christian lives by daily communication with God through prayer, Bible reading and yielding to the guidance of the Holy Spirit. It is noteworthy to say that the more we commune with God we align our will and ways to His. The world and its corrupt systems have no affect on believers as we have been called out of the world and set aside as a peculiar people, a royal priesthood called to carry His message and shine brightly for Him.

Lastly, true Christian living requires total commitment to Christ as He is the center and head of our lives. The world needs to see believers as being Christ-centered.

Living A Life Of Sacrifices: Romans 12:1-2

I beseech you therefore brethren, by the mercies of God, that ye present your bodies a living sacrifice, holy, acceptable unto God, which is your reasonable service.

What does it mean to live a life of sacrifices? Verse 1 provides the answer and this should be done in gratitude for what God has done for us because of His mercy. God and His grace provided salvation to all who believe at a tremendous cost to Him and His Son.

Our scripture verse has some profound facts that every believer must consider and they are (a) believers should be willing to offer our bodies as a living sacrifice to God as it should be our greatest desire to live holy lives and worship God with sincere devotion. (b) Believers' bodies are dead to sin and are the dwelling place for God's Spirit---the Holy Spirit. (c) Believers are to be instruments of righteousness so the world will know our family heritage.

Believers have the ability to present his/her body as a sacrifice unto God by being transformed which begins in the mind and accepting Jesus Christ as Lord and Savior. Transformations results in believers conforming to the will of God and His righteousness and are no longer dominated by this world and its present systems. The benefits of being transformed to God's will as a believer your values, visions and plans became different as the believer's values are Christ-centered. Lastly, each believer is encouraged to seek to know God's plans for his or her life.

Living a life of sacrifices is simply living for God and His righteousness.

May 15

The Christian Family: Colossians 3:18-25

Wives submit yourselves unto your husbands, as it is fit in the Lord. Husbands, love your wives and be not bitter against them. Children, obey your parents in all things; for this is well pleasing unto the Lord.

What constitutes a family? A family is defined as a clan or group of persons connected by blood and or marriage. God established the family with man, woman and the children. In modern day society the family is comprised of a single parent or two parents of the same sex and one as God established.

What does this say about our modern–day families? Are they blessed in the eye sight of God? Allow this writer to answer this way, marriage is an institution established by God with man as the head of the family, and wives as his loveable companion and in reverential submission to their husbands with the children obeying their parents. Husbands are to love their wives in reverence to God as He loved all humanity. Also, husbands are to refrain from being bitter towards their wives as this is not God's way.

Ephesians 5:21 talks about submitting yourself to one another as this is the mutual submission in Christ, it is the guiding principal and the core of all Christian Families. Submission is to be done in humility, gentleness, patience, love and respect for each family member. The wife's submission is done in love as this is her God given task to assist her husband, develop a quiet and gentle spirit and be a good mother to her children and home maker to her family (5:22).

It is the responsibility of the parents for their children's up bringing prepares them to live lives pleasing to God (Deuteronomy 6:7).

May 16

Believers Living As God's Chosen People
Colossians 3:12-17

Put on therefore, as the elect of God, holy and beloved, bowels of mercies, kindness, humbleness of mind, meekness, longsuffering;

What does it mean to live as God's chosen people? Verse 12 provides insight to what it means to live as chosen people of God, which is to say that believers have dressed themselves in peace, love, and truth; as these three attributes encompass characteristics of God.

It is noteworthy to say that believers being clothed in the attributes representative of God's character can and do forebear one another's burdens, and have a forgiving spirit as Christ forgave all as well as allowing "love to rule as it is the bond of perfection" (v.14). In regards to the peace characteristics are that believers have the "peace of God" ruling our hearts as God is a God of peace as all believers are in the body of Christ.

If the question were raised, how do believers put on the peace, love and truth of God? This task is achieved by allowing the Word of Christ to dwell in each believer by his or her daily Bible reading and meditating on the Word. By allowing the Word of Christ to dwell in each believer they become enriched in godly wisdom and the teaching of truth of God's Word as revealed by the Holy Spirit. Being endowed with God's truths gives each believer the ability to conduct themselves as outlined in verse 17, which is to live a life that is pleasing to God. One measurable way to ensure that our words and deeds are pleasing to God is by asking yourself some of the following questions: are my actions pleasing to God? Can what I am doing be done "in the name of Jesus"?

Other factors that identify believers as God's chosen people is being a holy nation, members of the royal priesthood of God as all believers have been sanctified by Christ Himself to do the Will of God and carry the message of the gospel to the entire world. Believers being of the royal priesthood and the holy nation of God, then all words and or actions must be representative of God's character. This can and will be witnessed by the believer's spoken words and lifestyle being that believers are a set aside people and are no longer subjected to this world and its corruptness. For believers have separated themselves from all worldliness and are light in this sin darkened world. We are to season the world through words and deeds. Lastly, believers living as God's chosen people, there has been a transformation of the heart/mind (Roman 12:1), and have committed his or herself to living holy lives unto God by presenting his/her body as a living sacrifice unto God which is through services rendered to God.

Believers, you are chosen by God to live for and to please Him, therefore, let Him be your focus for He is worthy of all that we have to give---a lifetime of service.

Believers Speak With Grace: Colossians 4:2-6

Let your speech be always with grace, seasoned with salt, that you may know how ye ought to answer every man.

Believers being in the family of God are to represent Him at all times with our lifestyles and speech. If the question were raised, how do our lifestyles and speech tell who we are? Godly lifestyles represent the holiness of God as His righteousness reflects the believer's intimacy with God. A godly lifestyle is one that has refrained from conforming to the quirks of society.

A believers' speech is one that is gracious, seasoned with pleasantries, served with winsome-cheerfulness and served on God's platter of love. Proverbs 15:26 talks about words of the pure (righteous) being pleasant and Ecclesiastes 10:12 talks about the graciousness of words spoken by the wise.

Believers speaking with God's grace do so for the good of edifying the body of Christ and the personal growth of the hearers. Also, believers speaking in God's grace speak the truth as it is God's truth. It is noteworthy to say when an occasion arises that requires correcting our fellowman it is done in grace and with the love of God, but with stern gracious words of wisdom.

When differences arise as they do reconciliatory words maintain unity among brothers and sisters as there is unity in Christ and God's truth is never compromised.

It can be concluded then that gracious words are words of wisdoms as believers are encouraged to hold firm to sound words in faith and love which is in Christ Jesus (1 Timothy 13); what is done (spoken) in and for Christ will last.

Doers Of The Word: James 1:17-22

..Be ye doers of the word, and not hearers only, deceiving your own selves.

What does it mean to become a doer of God's Word? Verses 22-23 provides the answer by stating "But be ye doers of the word, and not hearers only, deceiving your own self. For if any be a hearer of the word, and not a doer, he is like unto a man beholding his natural face in a glass." The meaning of these verses is that to hear the word and fail to adhere to it is null and void because God's Word has no effect on the hearer. There is power in God's Word and the hearer who listens with his/her spiritual ear, and then the "Word" brings about a change in the person. In the words of Ezekiel, God's Word is "like fire shut up in my bones," God's Word put running in your feet, clapping in your hands, singing in your heart; hearers of the word have to tell somebody about the goodness of the Lord.

James states (v.21) that once we hear the word we no longer are self deceivers because we as believers lay aside all unrighteousness and put on the righteousness of God by holy living according to the "Word" by it being engrafted/implanted in the hearer's very nature. Believers/ hearers of the word become new creatures in Christ and God's implanted Word brings all believers into his/her final salvation (Mathew 13:3-23; Romans 1:16; 1 Corinthians 15"2; Ephesians 1:13).

Be a doer not just a hearer.

May 19

Godly Behavior: James 4: 1-12

Speak no evil of another, brethren. He that speaketh evil of his brother, and judgeth his brother, speaketh evil of the law, and judgeth the law; but if thou judge the law, thou art not a doer of the law, but a judge.

Behavior is defined as "the conduct of an individual or a group, or the response of an individual, group or species in a particular environment" (Webster online Dictionary). With that being said, then ones godly behavior can be defined as believers/Christians response to God's Word both in our Christian setting and outside of the community of believers.

What are some godly behaviors exhibited by believers? Godly behaviors are seen in a believer's attitude toward the world as believers are no longer friends with the world. They hate or detest sin; believers resist being proud and boastful as believers have clothed themselves in humility and grace. Believers seek to draw nearer to God and are committed to doing His Will by humbly submitting to Him—the Holy Spirit. Believers draw near to God through our worship, praise and thanksgiving with the aid of the Holy Spirit. Believers put on more grace by truly confessing his/her sins and developing a pure heart with God's help.

Loving one another and seeking peace among the brethrens is godly behavior because the love command was issued by God as He is love and loves all. This question comes to mind; being children of God does the world see godly behavior or His holiness in our daily lives?

The world knows us by our conduct, therefore godly behavior tells the world that the Holy Spirit is at work in our lives and we are in the family of God.

A Praying Community: James 5:13-18

Is any sick among you? let him call for the elders of the church; and let them pray over him, anointing him with oil in the name of the Lord;

Let's look at our topical discussion by defining each word beginning with prayer, which is our communication with God as prayer is essential to all believers and their walk with God. Webster defines community as "a unified body of individuals."

Therefore, a praying community is one that has come together in prayer and has integrated prayer into their daily lives to the point that God walks in the cool of the garden of each community dweller's life. A popular scripture phrase is "prayers of the righteous availeth much" (James 5:16). This verse outlines the benefits from righteous prayers, and some are (a) prayers draw you nearer to God, (b) provides for a Spirit-filled life, (c) prayer brings power to respective ministries, (d) prayers builds up the prayer, (e) prayers give insight to God's provisional care, and (f) prayers give power to overcome Satan, and etc.

Who is the praying community? It is a baptized body of believers who have come together in the unified body of Christ dedicated to His message and ministry. A praying community consist of local congregations organized with Christ as its head which is further comprised of the individual Christian families. A praying community prays for the well-being of others whether it is for the sick and shut in or other adversities. Then the praying community prays for our society in general. A praying community recognizes the power of righteous prayers as they are sincere from the heart of the prayer.

A praying community is one of power.

May 21

A Loving Community: Philemon 1:7

For we have great joy and consolation in thy love, because the bowels of the saints are refreshed by thee, brother.

Our scripture text is taken from Paul's personal letter to the man named Philemon during his time of imprisonment at Rome. Philemon was a slave owner and church member of the Colossian church. Philemon's slave was Onesimus who escaped Rome for his freedom and through divine intervention made contact with Paul and the two became father and son in the ministry as Onesimus was a faithful and loyal servant to Paul and Christ. When the time came for Onesimus to be returned to Philemon Paul made several appeals on Onesimus' behalf, one of which was to receive him back as a brother in Christ (vv15-16) and stated that Onesimus was useful/profitable to him and could have the same profitability to Philemon if treated as a brother in Christ.

This story has some appealing love affects in that through Christ love supersedes all boundaries; all humanity owes a debt of gratitude to Christ for his immeasurable love. In regards to the Christian Community it displays immeasurable love for all while recognizing there is no respect of persons in God's eye sight. Verse 16 solidifies this fact when Paul states that Onesimus is no longer a slave but a beloved brother in Christ.

This question comes to mind, being a loving Christian community how do we receive and treat one who is less in social status? There is a saying that one must be careful how we treat others because we may be entertaining angels unaware?

May 22

A Covenant Community Of Believers: Genesis 17:7

And I will establish my covenant between me and thee and thy seed after thee in their generations for an everlasting covenant, to be a God unto thee, and to thy seed after thee.

According to The Student Bible Dictionary (P. 65) "a covenant is a mutual agreement between two persons or parties. The covenant between God and His people is unique because God alone sets the conditions."

Verse 7 states "And I will establish my covenant between me and thee and thy seed after thee and their generations for an everlasting covenant, to be a God unto thee, and they seed after thee." Here God sets the condition for which all other covenants are based. God tells Abraham that He was going to be his God and all of Abraham's descents for ever. God binds Himself to His faithful people who remain faithful to Him and for doing so he would be their shield, and rewarder. Inclusive in this promise was His grace, His pardon, protection, guidance, love, goodness, His blessing and help.

Therefore, the community of believers has God's faithful promise to be all that mankind needs in return for their reciprocated love and faithfulness. It is noteworthy to say that the old covenant was written on stones and tablets based on the law, but the new covenant is based on grace through His Son Jesus Christ and is written in the hearts of man; as there is no excuse for not obeying God commands and being unfaithful to Him.

As a covenant community of believers we have God's promises and know what to expect from Him, can He say the same? Yes Lord!

May 23

God's Love For His People
Romans 8:31-39; I John 4:8-16

He that spared not His own Son, but delivered Hi up for us all, how shall He not with Him also freely give us all things.

If the definition of love was provided it would include, "a strong affection for one another arising out of kinship or personal ties. Affection based on admiration, benevolence or common interest, a person's adoration for God, a fatherly concern of God for mankind" (Webster online Dictionary).

When speaking of God's love for mankind it talks of His agape love which depicts the very nature of God as carried out by His acts of kindness toward man. God's love is at the heart of all Christian beliefs and is essential between the two—God and man. The epitome of God's love is outlined in John 3:16 as it includes all races, nations, saved and unsaved as well as a guaranteed promise made by God with the most astounding promise is eternal life. Another point of view regarding God's love is expressed in Christ's sacrificial death at Calvary (I John 4:10) as man's propitiator.

The question now becomes, who would willingly lay down his/her life for another without giving thought of some form of reciprocation and or provocation? The answer is only a resounding loving God because He is love. All believers who have accepted Christ as their personal Savior is the object of God's love and because of His love for His children and their disobedience causes chastisement, but done in love. According to Romans 8:31-39 which states "there is nothing that can separate believers from the love of God." Sin caused a spiritual divide which Christ restored with His death on the cross, but because of His love we have experienced His forgiveness and have had our sins pardoned. ***Love in action!***

Another act of God's love for His people is expressed in His provisional care in that He preserves His prized creation in caring for all man's needs as well as sustaining man from the beginning to the end---man's very existence is in God. In the midst of man's suffering,

God still provides. According to Matthew 5:45 which states God provisions extend to both the righteous and unrighteous. ***God's love!***

The question now becomes, in light of God's love for all humanity, what are man's/believers' expressions of gratitude? Christians' expressions of gratitude are in the form of adoration and thankfulness to God. Christians' steadfast faithfulness, humility and commitment to God and doing His Will as this is an expression of man's love for God. Another point of view is that Christians are in the family of God which brings about reciprocated love. The love relationship that exists between Christians and God, Christians have a different relationship with the world in that Christians have been regenerated, justified, and sanctified. Then there is the brotherly love exhibited by all Christians in obedience and in simulation of God's love. According to Galatians 5:13 love is expressed in the believer's service to his/her fellow-man. James 2:17-26 talks about love and faith by saying that faith that does not express itself in love is dead. Romans 12:9 talks about love is to be without hypocrisy—true love. Lastly, love is the bond/glue that unites all Christian virtues (Colossians 3:14).

It can be concluded then that love is, was and will always be an unbreakable bond between God and His people.

What love!

May 24

Be Content Where You Are: I Timothy 6:3-16

But godliness with contentment is great gain.

Today's topical discussion addresses the issue of contentment, which is to say that one is happy where they are in life. It is alright to strive to achieve accomplisments in life, but to make wealth the focus of our being is ungodly. Paul in this epistle was warning his audience—Young Timothy and the church at Ephesus to be content with the necessities of life such as food, water, clothing and shelter. Why, because God in His provisional care was careful to provide for all man's needs according to His riches (Philippians 4:19).

These words of encouragement were due in part to the many false teachers and their doctrines that equate great gains with godliness (v.5) as their teachings were that great gain/wealth was a sign of God's approval and blessing and what Paul stressed was "great gain" is "gain with contentment." Paul had stressed in an earlier writing that he knew how to be continent whether he had plenty or not and that he was satisfied whatever stage of life he was in; true contentment is found only in God.

Verse 8, Paul encourages believers that when financial crises arise and they will, we are to look to God and His provisional care as we continue to work, believing and trusting in God for deliverance. Additionally, we are to continue to give and serve God and refrain from the desire of being wealthy as "the love of money is the root of all evil" (v.10).

Being money driven carries the temptations that can and will redirect out focus from being Christ-centered to self-centeredness.

May 25

The Purpose Of Jesus Earthly Ministry
Luke 15:1-7

What man of you, having an hundred sheep, if he lose one of them, doth not leave the ninety and nine in the wilderness; and go after that which i lost, and until he find it?

For the next several days we will focus on Jesus earthly ministry and its purpose, which was to seek and save the lost. Luke 15 illustrates through Jesus' parabolic teaching His earthly ministry's purpose of saving lost as it is God's desire for all to be saved. In each parable when the lost is found/save heaven rejoices as it pleases God for sinners to repent. Scripture states that both God and heaven rejoice when one sinner repents, imagine the rejoicing that occurs when a multitude of sinners repent (vv 7, 10).

Also, Luke 15 depicts there is no amount of suffering and sacrifice that the Father and the Son placed on saving the lost; the redemption of sinners is paramount with God and expresses the heart of God. It is noteworthy to say that Luke 15 and its teachings on saving the lost speaks to the collaboration between God the Father and His Son Jesus and their unified process of freeing mankind from the bondage of sin, thus closing the gap that sin caused. It also expresses the desired intimacy desired by God with humanity.

Luke 15:4 begins Jesus' teaching on salvation with the parable of the lost sheep and what occurs when the lost is found. Just because ninety-nine sheep remain committed to God it does not minimize the importance of the "one".

All is important in the eye sight of God—saved and unsaved!

May 26

Parable Of The Lost Coin: Luke 15:8-16

Either what woman having then pieces of silver, if she lose one piece, doth not light a candle, and sweep the house, and seek diligently till she find it?

Jesus continuing His teachings regarding His mission of saving the lost uses the parable of the lost coin. In this parable Jesus tells the story of a woman having ten pieces of silver and loses one, and she beings to search diligently until the one that was lost is found. Once the coin is found the woman celebrates with her neighbors giving rise to the love and concern for the one lost coin as she did for the nine that remained in her presence.

The moral to this story is that regardless of the many that are saved and committed to following Christ, the lost is of no less importance to God and that His hand of forgiveness and love is ever present. Regarding the diligent search for the lost is indicative of Christ's open invitation for salvation regardless of the condition and or length of time being out of the ark of salvation the lost/sinner is still welcome in God's house.

When a sinner recognizes his/her lost condition and comes to Christ, heaven rejoices with such joy and gladness until it is viewed as the master's great feast. The words to the song Amazing Grace come to mind because in it the words are about being lost but now is found, blind but now I see…all because of God's amazing grace.

There is salvation in His grace, mercy in His grace, love in His grace and most of all sacrifices in His grace. GRACE is Amazing!

May 27

Parable Of The Lost Son: Luke 15: 11-21

...A certain man had two sons; And the younger of them said to his father, Father, give me the portion of goods that falleth to me, And he divided unto them his living.

This parable brings home the point of being lost and out of fellowship with God the Father and God the Son as Jesus uses people in this story. This story depicts a father having two sons one becomes discontent with his life and where he is in his life and desires to explore the other side of life. He made a request of his father to give him his portion of his heritage that he may live on his own. The father honored his son's request while praying that some day he would come to recognize true love and return home—which the son did.

This story has four lessons in it: (1) it teaches that Satan and his schemes are at work in the lives of believers at all times and believers must be aware of them and rely on the help of the Holy Spirit who will prevent us from falling prey. The lost must acknowledge his/her sin and humbly return to the Father (2) Paul's teachings on being content where you are and having the ability to be abound and abased, which is knowing how to be happy with all that God has blessed you with whether it is a lot or a little. (3)This lesson teaches that the grass always looks greener on the other side until you get there. (4) This lesson teaches that friends are with you while you are on your feet, but God is there all the time.

Stay with God---He will never leave you.

May 28

A Father's Forgiving Love: Luke 15:18

I will arise and go to my father, and will say unto him, Father, I have sinned against heaven, and before thee.

Yesterday the prodigal came to himself and confessed his sins while realizing that he was separated from his father and his love. This is true with all who are held captive by sin; whether it is through regression or having never accepted Christ as his/her personal Savior. One must admit that he or she is a sinner, confess his or her sins and then ask for forgiveness from the father which is a sign of humility.

Verse 20 depicts the love of God by portrayed as the father of the prodigal son in this story. Just as children's earthly parents continue to love all their children so does our heavenly Father.

There are four important lessons in this text, which are: (1) God's love and compassion for the lost is evidenced by his joyous reaction. (2) God's love for the wandering soul never ceases and He waits for their return. (3) When the lost return to God He is ready and willing to forgive, love them with full compassion and accept them into His family as His children. (4) God's joy over a returning sinner seen by the father in this story, which displays his love for his returning son.

Verse 24 talks about the conditions of sinners as they are spiritually separated from God and are considered dead; any life away from God, is a spiritual death; 1 Peter 2:25 parallels being lost to that of sheep who have gone astray.

Heaven Rejoicing Lost Soul Saved: Luke 15:20

And he arose, and came to his father; But when he was yet a great way off, his father saw him and had compassion, and ran, and fell on his neck, and kissed him.

Concluding our study on the mission of Jesus' earthly ministry as we have discussed it using three different parables depicting the joy that is felt when a lost soul comes to Jesus. Today's discussion focus is primarily on the celebration feast put on by the prodigal son's father when he saw his son coming from afar. The father ran and kissed his son because his prayers had been answered. He hopes that one day his child would return home. This is true with any Christian parents when a child goes astray. It is noteworthy to say that Christian parents pray the Holy Spirit's protection on their children as they go about their daily routines. This is because Satan is busy trying to cause harm to our precious gifts from God.

With regards to heaven rejoicing when a lost soul returns expresses the love, compassion, and care that God the Father has for all humanity and His desire for all mankind to be saved and enjoy the royalties that heaven has to offer. God the Father is grieved when a sheep—man goes astray and His invitation for a sinner's return remains open. Fellow Christians join heaven in rejoicing when a soul comes to Christ because the fellow believer understands the joy he/she felt when salvation came to their house. Hymns were sung, praises went up, and shouts for joy were heard and witnessed because a sinner is now saved.

Christians and all Heaven rejoice.

May 30

Saved But Still Lost: Luke 15:28-32

And he was angry, and would not go in, therefore, came his father out and intreated him. And he answering said to his father, lo, these many years do I serve thee, neither transgressed, I at any time thy commandments; and yet thou never gavest me a kid, that might make merry with my friends;

Today's discussion begs the question, how can one be saved but still lost? The core of the answer rest in the heart of the believer who says that they love God but fail to have true love for his or her brother or sister who is living life as a sheep gone astray. Christians are commanded to love all as Christ loved us all to the point of death on the cross and rose for all our justification. All who are out of fellowship have the opportunity to become members of God's family as it is God's desire that all humanity be saved. The question now becomes, how can one love God whom he has never seen but hate his or her fellowman? Scripture clearly states that this person is living a lie simply because true virtual love resonates in a horizontal position as well---meaning loving our fellowman. If heaven can rejoice over a lost soul being saved why can't you? Why can't a lost soul come to God and enjoy the sweet savor of God's grace? Christ told His audience that He didn't come for the saved but for those who were lost, and on another occasion Christ stated that the well does not need a physician.

The question now becomes, was the elder son in this story really saved? The elder son in this story represents the Pharisees of Jesus' day and many others who outwardly keep God's commands, but on the inside are self-centered, self-righteous and feel that no one is entitled but them as these people have a judgmental spirit. What does the scripture say about judging others? "Judge not for you shall be judged." Self-centered and self-righteous Christians lack the ability to love as God loves, therefore, as the elder son in this story could not rejoice over his brother's return neither do his kind of Christians. These kinds of Christians are repulsive to God; as God told the church at Laodicea that they were neither hot nor cold and He could "spue" them out of His mouth. A lukewarm church is one that professes Christ, but doesn't really know Him. Just as Christ warned the church at Laodicea about their condition so did the father in our scripture text as he told his elder son all that he had was his and his dedicated services has not and will not go unnoticed. Verse 32 explains to the son that is befitting for them to rejoice over one coming to Christ. The father is God addressing the heart condition that all saved must possess.

To be saved but still lost is lacking the heart of God which is one of love for all and to be Christ-centered instead of being self-centered. Christians are to be in total likening to Christ in that our love and giving is without measure. Therefore, when a spiritually dead soul is made alive in Christ celebrate with much joy as heaven is rejoicing.

Let's pray, Lord I rejoice in my fellowman who was once dead but is now alive and I join the heavenly praise in rejoicing.

May 31

The Handiworks Of God: Hebrews 1:10-12

..Thou, Lord, in the beginning hast laid the foundation of the earth; and the heavens are the works of thine hands;

Our topical discussion calls for reflecting on God and the awesomeness of His works/creation specifically man. Only the Supreme God could create something out of nothing. Genesis 1:1-24 when He created everything that both seen and unseen—heaven and earth. During God's creative process, He created man and animal on the sixth day, but more importantly man was created last not because man is an after thought but was created in love and with special care as God breathed the breath of life into man, thus man became a living soul. In breathing breath into man God put part of Himself into man thus man was created in the image and likeness of God.

Speaking of man in regard to God's handiworks, lets take an in-depth look at how wonderfully man is made and the twelve systems that make-up man in addition to the mind, body and soul of man--three in one. Those systems are: Digestive, Respiratory, Integumentary, Immune, Lymphatic, Muscular, Circulatory, Skeletal, Nervous, Endocrine, Excretory, and Reproductive system, not to mention the different parts of the outer man's body. It is in the mind and heart of man which gives us the ability to choose right from wrong, to accept and love God or reject Him. **What a wonderfully made man!**

A further look at God's handiwork is seen in the changing of the seasons as directed by God, flowers bloom in their appropriate seasons and reproduce as God designed, the balance of nature operates according to His will and the heavenly bodies rotate as designed by God.

God, marvelous are thy works!

A Redeemed Community

June 1

The Son Reveals The Father: Hebrews 1:1-4

..In these last days spoken unto us by His Son, whom He hath appointed heir of all things, by whom also He made the worlds.

Prior to Jesus' earthly visit to earth God the Father had spoken to His people through His prophets in many ways and places. God's revelation of Himself is noted when He told Moses to tell the Israelites "I am that I am", and Jeremiah and Ezekiel used parabolic and symbolic actions to graphically illustrate their messages to the people in their efforts to get the people to adhere to the Word of God. Jeremiah uses such parables as "the useless girdle" (13:1-1), "the potter and the clay" (18:1-11), "the two baskets of figs (24:1-10). Ezekiel's prophesy used mysterious visions, daring parables and weird symbolic actions as his method of revealing God. For example, in Ezekiel's writing the phrase "Then shall they know that I am God occurs 65 times with variations. Another phrase used by Ezekiel is "the glory of God." God Himself addresses Ezekiel as "son of man" and 'watchman."

Of all the prophets revelations of God none equals that of Jesus Christ as He is heir of all things and is in the image of God representing the brightness and glory of God-"His person." Jesus Christ is God's Son who "upholds all things by the power of His word" and His ability to purge the sins of man after which He went back to heaven and is now sitting at the right had of the Father (v.3).

Christ is the only source of man's salvation and mediator between man and God.

Christ the perfect revelation of God!

June 2

Jesus Superiority: Hebrews 1:4-12

Being made so much better than the angels, as He hath by inheritance obtained a more excellent name than they.

If the question were raised, how is Jesus superior? First, Jesus is God's Son and was with God in the beginning as stated in verse 5, Thou are my Son, this day I have begotten thee". In Psalm 2:8 we see God promising His Son Jesus a harvest of souls as His earthly mission was to save the lost souls of the world. John 1:14 talks about the Word becoming flesh. Second Jesus is the Word of God, both written and spoken. Third, in verse 6 which speaks of the angels worshipping the first begotten of the Father and on that day the heavenly host sang praises to the newborn King. Fourth, Jesus is the only person found who met all requirements to be man's propitiator. Fifth, Jesus' kingdom is the only one that will last forever. Seventh, Jesus is the only one who has the power to heal all manner of diseases, give sight to the blind, and raise the dead.

Jesus is superior to all because He is in all, knows all and sees all as well as being in the beginning with God, and is God. Jesus superiority garners our worship, praise and thanksgiving for what He has done in the lives of humanity/believers. Lastly there is no other name in heaven and earth whereby men can and will be saved if one calls on the name of Jesus.

Jesus means J-just, E-eternal/everlasting, S-savior, U-unchangeable and S-salvation.

Jesus Here From The Beginning: John 1:1-2

In the beginning was the Word, and the Word was with God, and the Word was God. The same was in the beginning with God.

As a point of clarification of Jesus being God we don't have to look any further than Genesis 1:1 which states "in the beginning God created the heaven and earth." Verse 26 supports that Jesus was with God the Father which states "let us." This is the plural form of the word "us' which indicates that Jesus and the Holy Spirit was present. Is this confusing? Yes, because one must believe in the Trinity/Triune God which is comprised of God the Father, God the Son-Jesus and God the Holy Spirit. God exists as one God, but in three distinct and identifiable but not separate persons, neither was God created or made, but existed from eternity as each member of the Godhead existed co-equally in being and with distinct attributes, power and glory.

Still further authentication of Jesus being present in the beginning is our scripture text where the gospel writer John presents Jesus as the personal Word of God. In 1 Corinthians 1:30 and Ephesians 3:10-11 presents Jesus as the wisdom of God while John 1:3-5, 14, 18 and Colossians 2:9 presents Jesus as the perfect revelation of the nature and person of God.

To state Jesus being present from the beginning is to say God the Father does not exist without God the Son and Holy Spirit, nor does Jesus, God the Son exists without God, the Father and the Holy Spirit as all are one operating in complete unity.

Jesus is God!

June 4

God's Son Full Of Grace And Truth: John 1:14-18

And the Word was made flesh, and dwelt among us, (and we beheld His glory, the glory as of the only begotten of the Father full of grace and truth).

There are several definitions for grace and some are, "favor (Genesis 6:8). It is God's free and undeserved love that never quits (Ephesians 2:8). Grace is the gift of God that comes as eternal life through Jesus Christ our Lord (Romans 6:23)". Student's Bible Dictionary (P. 106). Then there is the profound definition of grace as God's Righteousness at Christ's Expense. All definitions of grace paint a profound picture of God's love for mankind and the unity that exist between the Father and Son. This is because Jesus Christ-the Son willingly came to earth to be the human sacrifice in bridging the spiritual divide between man and God. This is love in action by God and His Son all who believe will have eternal life—salvation. It is noteworthy to say that salvation does not come by man's action, but by the Holy Spirit and Christ coming into the believer's life thus making all believers a new creature in Christ.

Through Christ grace and truth is available in its fullest extent according to Romans 5:17-21 to all mankind who believe. Then what is truth? Truth is an actual fact not what claims to be the truth or appears to be truth. Then God is the source of all truth and John 14:6 states that "Jesus is the way, the truth and the life".

This mean then that man's existence is grounded in Jesus Christ; Christ is the way to the Father and all life exists in Jesus.

June 5

The Priesthood Of Melchisedec: Hebrews 7:1-14

To whom also Abraham gave a tenth part of all; first being by interpretation King of righteousness, and after that also King of Salem which is, King of Peace.

If the question were raised, who was Melchisedec? Melchisedec was a Canaanite king of Salem and a priest of God (Genesis 14:18) as well as being a contemporary of Abraham who Abraham paid tithes to and was blessed by Melchisedec. As some writers (Hebrew) consider Melchisedec a type of Christ because he was both a king and a priest. Verse 3 states that he was without mother or father, but this does not mean he didn't have parents, but it does mean that there is no biblical record of his parents or genealogy. When Hebrew 6:20 phrase speaks of Jesus being made in the order of Melchisedec it means that Christ is before and greater than Abraham, Levi and the Levitical priests as all were human and were fallible/imperfect.

What similarities are there between Christ and Melchisedec? Both were kings and priests, both were of God and kings of righteousness and served the most high God--the one and true God. Melchisedec was a non-Israelite godly man like Job. Melchisedec was a type of Christ as he represented what Christ would be like in His priesthood as God set the stage for the coming of His Son Christ as man's ultimate high priest.

Christ being God made Him the high priest forever as there is no imperfection in Christ Jesus as He has the power to save man's sin-sick souls.

Christ As Our High Priest: Hebrews 7:15-22

(For those priests were made without an oath, but this with an oath by Him that said unto Him, The Lord sware and will not repent, Thou are a priest for ever after the order of Melchisedec:)

The term priest denotes one who speaks to God for the people or relates to God on the behalf of others or self (The Student Bible Dictionary P.192). In both the OT and NT the priest offered sacrifices to God for the people and entered the holiest of holy and met with God for the people. The priest also taught the people the law, but in the New Testament, Jesus Christ became the once and for all sacrifice through His shed blood on Calvary's cross. Through His shed blood Christ became our high priest and ritualistic sacrifices are no longer required.

In retrospect, the qualities of a priest are that he must be free of sin as he is the people's spokesperson and the one who must atone for man's sin. However, human priests lacked the ability to permanently remove man's sin and atonement was required yearly. What makes Jesus' priesthood different from that of a human priest is that Christ possessed several qualities as outlined in verse 28 and they are: (a) His holiness as Jesus was holy and without sin which made Him perfect to carry out what God demanded. (b) He was harmless as seen in His earthly life, He did no evil and was free of it as He came to uplift and heal the brokenhearted and the down trodden, free the captives and preached deliverance /gospel to the poor, and gave sight to the blind (Luke 4 :18 paraphrase). (c) Christ was undefiled meaning there were no character flaws with Him. (d) Christ was consecrated for evermore, which Jesus being God He was higher and completely devoted in His service to God the Father.

Christ's role as our high priest is one of a mediator for believers. Being that believers are of the royal priesthood of Christ we then become priests ourselves, but require Christ mediatory services to God the Father. Because of Christ's intercession believers enjoy the love, grace, presence and mercy of God. As He is there in the time of trouble, when we sin, become weak and to prevent us from backsliding if we yield to the guidance of the Holy Spirit. It is noteworthy to say that Christ will no continue as our mediator for those who refuse to forsake sin and have broken the fellowship bond with God. However, Christ does act as a mediator for all who have broken God's moral law but confess their sins and seek forgiveness.

With Christ as our high priest and mediator believers have benefits which are (a) Christ's priesthood is a permanent position one where He acts in sympathy to believers' temptation and trials. (b) Christ is in heaven permanently until he returns for His church and continues to make intercessions for the faithful believers. (c) Christ is in the presence of God where He bestows God's grace on believers. (d) Christ as our high priest and mediator, He mediated the new and better covenant which is written in the hearts of all believers and with this new covenant we have the promise of eternal inheritance.

Christ as our high priest is far superior to human priests because of the infallibility of man and His sacrificial death gives Him the right to serve a believers' high priest.

HALLELUJAH!

June 7

Christ As Our Intercessor: Hebrews 7:25-28

Wherefore He is able also to save them to the uttermost that come unto God by Him, seeing He ever liveth to make intercession for them.

The term intercessor mean is a person who acts as a go between, and to make intercession is to pray or make a pleading to someone on the behalf of another. In this scenario Christ is our go between to God the Father where He is making intercessions to God for man/believers. Romans 8:26-27, 34 states that Jesus and the Holy Spirit intercede for Christians and Christians are to intercede for one another (1 Timothy 2:1).

It is through Christ's ministry of intercession we as believers' experience God's love, His presence, mercy and grace in the time of trouble. Even in our weakest hour God is there because of the intercessory pleadings of Christ and the Holy Spirit.

It is noteworthy to say that Christ's intercession as our high priest is essential to our salvation in that all who come to God in faith receives the fullness of His grace in salvation. It is likewise to say without God's grace, mercy and help mediated through Christ's intercession, we would fall away from God and again be held captive to sin and its domination.

What a blessing it is to have a high priest who takes our heartfelt prayers and pleadings and make them acceptable to God for Him to grant favor on our behalf. ***What an intercessor!***

Christ's work on Calvary and being God's Son makes Him worthy to be our intercessor and it is through His continuous interceding believers are made right with God.

Jesus' Blood: Hebrews 9:14

How much more shall the blood of Christ, who through the eternal Spirit offered Himself without spot to God, purge your conscience from dead works to serve the living God.

Blood is essential to life in both animal and humanity's existence. Blood in the OT was the key element to sacrifices in the atonement for sin (Levitical 1:5; 3:2; 4:18). Likewise in the NT Christ's shed blood in His death on Calvary's cross is essential to paving the way to our salvation (Romans 5:9-10; Hebrews 9:12-14).

With that being said, let's look at some of the key points of Christ's blood being shed for humanity's salvation. (a) Christ's blood forgives sin for all who repent and believe in Him. (b) It is through Christ's blood that all believers' sins were ransomed from Satan and his evil powers (Acts 20:28; Ephesians 1:7; 1 Peter 1:18-19; Revelation 5:9; 12:11). (c) Christ's blood justifies all who believe in Him (Romans 3: 24-25). (d) Christ's blood cleanses all believers' consciences so that they may serve God without any guilt and in full assurances of their faith (9:14; 10:22; 13:18). (e) Christ's blood sanctifies all God's people and makes them right with Him (13:12; 1 John 1:7-10). (f) Christ's blood opens the way for believers to come directly to God through Christ to find grace, mercy, help and salvation (7:25; 10:19; Ephesians 2:13; 18). (g) Christ's blood is the guarantee of all the promises in the new covenant (10:29; 13:20; Matthew 26; 28; 1 Corinthians 11:25). (h) Lastly, Christ's blood is the saving; reconciling and purifying agent that appropriates believers so they can come to God through Christ Himself (7:25; 10:22; 1 John 1:7).

Jesus' Blood!

God Prepares His people For The New Covenant
Jeremiah 31:31-34; Hebrews 8:8-12

Behold, the days come, saith the Lord, that I will make a new covenant with the house of Israel and Judah: Not according to the covenant I made with their fathers in the days I took them by the hands, to bring them out of Egypt; which my covenant they break.....

The all Mighty God saw the need to establish a new covenant with His people because the old covenant was based on their ability to keep the law which was broken numerous times. Under the old covenant salvation and a right relationship with God came through a person's faith and obedience to God's laws. The old covenant was written on stones/tables which gave way for misplacement and etc. Whereas the new covenant would be written in the hearts of man where there is no chance to be misplaced. The new covenant would be internalized and personal to all. Under the old covenant it pointed to the gravity of sin and covered over sin whereas under the new covenant through Christ's blood it done away with sin. Also, under the old covenant it provided a way for the nation of Israel to come to God through faith, obedience and love. The old covenant foreshadowed the coming of the new covenant established by Christ Himself.

God setting the terms of each covenant we see that the new covenant is better because it is based on God's grace.
What love!

Christ Establish The New Testament: Hebrews 9:15

And for this cause He is the mediator of the new testament, that by means of death, for the redemption of the transgression that were under the first testament, the which are called might receive the promise of eternal inheritance.

If the question were raised, what is Christ's function in the New Testament? First, Jesus is the one who initiated and established the New Testament. Second, through Christ's blood the New Testament removes sin as opposed to covering sin over. Also, in the New Testament the believer has God's forgiveness of sin as His blood thoroughly purged sin. Third, the New Testament is a covenant of promise for all who believe in Jesus Christ and accept Him as their personal Savior. Fourth, Christ is all believers' permanent mediator and high priest, because He is God's Son there is no need for priest or animal blood sacrifices. Because Jesus sacrifice of Himself is far superior to animal sacrifices. Fifth, with the establishment of the New Testament it is complete and permanent as the Old Testament/covenant was incomplete and temporary as it required keeping the law and obedience to God.

It is noteworthy to say that because the Old Testament/covenant was rendered obsolete, the New Testament doesn't mean that God's Word is obsolete, but the Old Covenant points to the coming of Christ and the establishment of the new covenant. God's Word is the same as always and was given by God Himself and is His inspired Words.

With the establishment of the new covenant/Testament the age of grace was ushered in, because it was God's grace that He saw fit to send His only begotten Son into the world to be man's atonement.
What love?

The Plan Of Salvation: Romans 3:23; 6:23; 10:9-10

For all have sinned, and come short of the glory of God.

God created man to be in fellowship with Him and sin destroyed this loving relationship through Adam's disobedience in the Garden of Eden. Man's sins filled the earth. God destroyed it with water as He pronounced the whole world guilty both Jew and Gentiles. As none were found righteous in the eye sight of God as they had no fear of God. If there had been fear of God there would have been human reconciliation which led to God's guilty verdict (3:23).

However, God in His love for humanity provides the consequences of the choices we make (6:23). The question now becomes, which do you choose death or eternal life? Will we continue in sin and spend eternity separated from God our creator or accept God's gift of salvation and spend eternity with Him.

The question now becomes what steps must one take to have eternal life? First, admit that you are a sinner. Second, confess your sins to God. Third, ask for forgiveness and turn from your sinful ways and accept Jesus Christ as your personal Savior and be saved.

Romans 10:10 states "For with the heart of man believeth unto righteousness, and with the mouth confession is made unto salvation", What this means is everything begins in the heart of man whether good or evil.

Therefore, salvation is to all who accept Jesus in faith and His atoning work and God for His plan to reconcile man back to Himself.

June 12

Christ Our Redeemer: Hebrews 10:12-18

But this man, after He had offered one sacrifice for sins for ever, sat down on the right hand of God;

The term redeem means to buy back or to set free or to pay a price for something or someone (1 Chronicles 17:21, Galatians 3:13) and the redeemer is the one who makes the purchase or frees. In this scenario Jesus is our redeemer because He paid the price for humanity's sin with His precious blood. All who believe in Jesus have redemption because of Jesus—He paid the price. Man was found unworthy to pay his sin debt after God the Father pronounced all humanity guilty of sin.

If the question were raised, what were the necessary requirements to make a one-time sin sacrifice? The requirement was to be sinless, holy, and man as Jesus fulfilled all the requirements. He was sinless regardless of the sinful conditions during His earthly stay. Jesus was holy because He is God's Son as well as being God-man.

More importantly, after completing His earthly mission of restoring the fellowship between God the Father and man He went back to heaven and is now seated at the right hand of the Father making intercessions for us. ***What a redeemer!***

If continuously making intercession for us isn't enough, Jesus left the Holy Spirit to be our guide, teacher, protector, and to be our earthly intercessor. This shows the love of God and the Godhead that "I will not only redeem man but will provide for their safe keeping until they get to heaven." ***What love!***

Christ our redeemer--there is none other!

I am the Messiah: John 4:21-26

Jesus said unto her, I that speak unto thee am He.

The setting of today's discussion is during Jesus' earthly ministry. He was traveling and stopped in a city called Sychar where He met a Samarian woman at Jacob's well getting water in the middle of the day.

Christ initiated a conversation in order to save her and through her the entire town would be saved. The irony here is that Christ being God knew this woman would be at the well and her condition. Christ used water as His talking point to get her to salvation by stating that He was living water and all that drink of Him would thirst no more (paraphrased). The other talking point was Jesus asked the woman to get her husband which He knew she didn't have and was living in sin.

During their conversation the woman recognized Christ as being someone special with authority as she had heard of the promised Messiah but failed to recognize Jesus as the one. What does this say for us today? Will we recognize Jesus when He comes? Jesus may not be here in the same format—as a man, but He still comes to us in many disguises. Another question, upon Jesus' second return to earth will you be ready when He comes? Will you have your house (life) in order? Scripture tells us "that no man knows the hour when the Son of man cometh." Scripture also states that He "is coming like a thief and robber in the night." With that being said, it behooves all of us to be ever ready for His return and for those who are alive when He returns will be changed in a moment's notice (twinkling of an eye). Unlike the woman in our scripture text had heard of the promise God made of sending the Messiah but when Christ appeared many did not recognize or accept Him as the Messiah.

The latter part of Jesus' conversation with the Samaritan woman was regarding her worship service and the place of worship. Here again Jesus was compelled to enlighten the woman on true worship by explaining that God is a Spirit and all who worship Him must be done in spirit and in truth. Her failure to recognize Jesus as the promised Messiah led to Jesus' statement "I that speak unto thee am he." **What an awesome revelation?** Upon recognizing that she had met the Messiah, she went and witnessed to the entire town, they believed and were saved.

There are several lessons in this text and they are (1) God keeps His promises. (2) We are to be ready at all times because we know not the day or hour and we are to live expecting His return. Therefore, our house/lives must be one of righteousness. (3) When Christ comes into your life tell somebody as this woman did for we never know who needs saving. (4) We are to worship God in spirit and in truth for He is a spirit for Christ is the truth and we as believers are in union with Him.

Christ the Messiah came as promised---completed His salvation mission and now lives in each believer through His spirit—the Holy Spirit.

Christ As Our Testator: Hebrews 9:16

For where a testament is, there must also of necessary be the death of the testator.

The definition of the word "testator" is a person who leaves a will in force at death (Merriam-Webster School Dictionary P. 948). The testator in this case is Jesus Christ, and His will is for all to be saved. However in this case Jesus is alive and His desires for mankind remain the same as God's Word is man's roadmap to heaven and the Holy Spirit is our compass to get us there; man has no excuse if he misses heaven.

Jesus' will in testament reads as follows "For God so loved the world, that He gave His only begotten Son, that whosoever believeth in Him should not perish, but have everlasting life" (John 3:16). With that being said, all humanity knows that God has a plan for us; it is our decision to make. We have no sin debt to pay--Christ paid it all. We can spend lavishly in righteous living for God or wasteful and in rebellion separated from God. ***Which lifestyle do you choose?***

It is noteworthy to say in some instances when a will is left family members will contest the testator's intent, but with God there is no contesting because it is very clear His intentions---***all to be saved.***

Lastly, the question now becomes where else could one find a better testator than God's Son who left an indelible mark on all human life and with no doubts of His intentions.

Shout for joy His love and compassion reigns forever!

Act Of Forgiveness: Hebrews 10:15-18

And their sins and iniquities will I remember no more.

In writing this discussion, I reflected on an earlier article I had written titled, The Healing of Forgiveness" which deals with the many acts of forgiveness and the most notable one is God's forgiving humanity of their sins and Christ bearing the sins of the world on His shoulders. What is forgiveness? Forgiveness is a pardon or the act of forgiving—God did both through Christ's death on the cross. God's forgiving process was done out of love and to heal the brokenness that existed between God and man.

Many scriptures encourage forgiveness as all forgiveness is to simulate God's forgiveness because there is no harm or sin too great—only blasphemy and grieving the Holy Spirit is unforgivable. Ephesians 4:32 states, "And be ye kind one to another, tenderhearted, forgiving one another, even as God for Christ's sake hath forgiven you." The last phrase of this verse drives home the message about forgiveness; it captures why God sent His son to redeem man. The solidification of this point is found in Colossians 3:13c which states "Even as Christ forgave you, so also do ye." This tells me that just as Christ has forgiven each of us, we are to forgive each other. Luke 6:37 reminds us how we should handle unforgivable situations which reads, "Judge not, and ye shall not be judged: condemn not, and ye shall not be condemned: for give, and ye shall be forgiven."

Forgive, live and let live--God forgave all!

Christ Died For Our Sanctification: Hebrews 10:10-12

By the which will we are sanctified through the offering of the body of Jesus Christ once for all.

Sanctify means to set apart, to consecrate, or to be separated from the world in this scenario. Man's sanctification process took place through the death of Jesus Christ on the cross at Calvary. This was done so that all who believe in and accept Jesus as Lord would be separated from the world and have the ability to live holy lives unto God as we are to love God with all our hearts, souls and mind (1 Thessalonians 3:13).

All believers receive sanctification by faith (Acts 26:18) and in union with Christ in His death and resurrections (John 15:4-10; Romans 6:1-11; 1 Corinthians 1:30). Additionally, sanctification comes by the blood of Jesus Christ, the Word of God, and the regenerating and sanctifying work of the Holy Spirit. Sanctification comes by God and in collaboration with the willing hearts of all who believe and with the willingness of heart to humbly submit ones self to God and His will and with the Holy Spirit who aids in purifying believers from the filthiness of this world.

How do believers remain separated from the world in its filthiness while in the world? This is accomplished through prayer, yielding to the Holy Spirit, devoting our lives to a life of righteous living and remaining in intimate communion and fellowship with Christ and His truths while being sensitive to God's presence in our lives.

Sanctification is necessary because believers are holy ones as Christ's bride.

Saved and sanctified by His blood.

Christ's One Time Sacrifice: Hebrews 9:24-28

So Christ was once offered to bear the sins of many; and unto them that look for Him shall He appear the second time without sin unto salvation.

If the question were raised, What is the difference between Christ's sacrifice and the priests? The priest who ministered during the days of Israel's early history were men chosen by God and of the priesthood of Aaron. These men were born into sin by nature as sin had entered the world through Adam's disobedience to God. These earthly priests lacked the ability to take away sin, but instead offered animal sacrifices that were unblemished. The blood from animals was only a temporary provision or atonement for sin as this ritual was repeated each year. Before the priest could offer atonement for others sins he has to offer a bull as a sacrifice for his own sins, after which he would take two goats and cast lots to determine which would be offered as the sacrifice. Then the chosen goat would be killed and the blood would be sprinkled on the mercy seat of the ark between God and the law as the atonement.

The Most Holy Place represents heaven. The animal sacrifices and their blood pointed toward the more permanent sacrifice of Jesus Christ as He was both man and God who required no sin atonement because He was sinless and everything is fulfilled in Him. Animal sacrifices covered over sin, whereas Christ's blood removed sin. The scapegoat that was sent away bearing the sins of the nation typifies Christ who bore the sins of the world. Human blood was required to permanently remove sin so Christ became human to fulfill the demands of God's holiness and justice.

Thanks God for Jesus and His blood!

Man's Approach To God: Hebrews 10:19-21

Having therefore, brethren, boldness to enter into the holiest by the blood of Jesus.

How should man approach God? Christ's death on the cross removed the need for men (mankind) to go to the priest on his/her behalf. Good Friday during Christ's dying hours when the veil in the temple was torn from top to bottom made it possible for man to approach God for him/herself.

Verse 19 states that we/man have "the boldness to enter into the holiest by the blood of Jesus." Jesus is the high priest over the house of God (v.21), therefore, man is to come to God with sincerity and a pure heart having the faith and believing in His goodness (11:6).

If the question were raised, how do we draw near to God or approach Him? We draw near to or approach God in sincere prayer which establishes a close and intimate relationship with God through Christ Jesus. The sincerity of one's prayers and the honesty of faith are essential to ones relationship with God.

Coming to God through Jesus Christ one finds mercy, grace, help (v.1; 4:16; 7:19), salvation (v.14), and cleansing (v.22). Remember, Christ is our High priest and Mediator He knows what we need and desire before we approach God. His intercessory ministry places all who approach God in the right frame of mind for approaching our heavenly Father.

How do you approach God? Is it with boldness in faith? Christ paved the way with His shed blood.

Let us come boldly to the throne of God!

"Christ The Author and Finisher of Our Faith"
Hebrews 12:1-2

Looking unto Jesus the author and finisher of our faith; who for the joy that was set before Him endured the cross, despising the shame, and is set down at the right hand of the throne of God.

A Christian's life is likened to that of a runner as the race is not given to the swiftest, but to the one who endures to the end. Christians are to run this Christian race with patience and perseverance which is the ability to withstand all trials, temptation and snares that are sure to come our way. Christian runners must be aware of the ever present temptation to give in to sin and give up our quest for our golden crown that awaits us in heaven. Christ is in all believers and all who want to join the Christian race (non-believers) perfect example on endurance and perseverance.

Reflect with me on Christ's most stressful hour in the Garden of Gethsemane when He prayed to the Father to remove the bitter cup of the cross, but stated that if it was God's Will for Him to go to the cross then let it be done (Mark 14:36)--the rest is history.

Christ the author and finisher of our faith is the perfect example for Christians as He is our source of encouragement and faith. Our example of trusting God in every situation (temptation and suffering and overcoming), in our commitment in doing God's Will, our loyalty to God, our commitment to completing the work God has assigned to us, and our source of His grace, love and mercy.

Thank God Christ persevered to the end—He endured the cross we can complete our race.

June 20

Christ-like Humility: Philippians 2:1-4

Fulfill ye my joy, that ye be likeminded, having the same love, being of one accord, of one mind.

Humility is the absence of pride or freedom from pride. The person who possesses humility has the right view of God, self and others. Also, humility is not a weakness but a strong character that all Christians should possess as it is an essential commodity in our Christ likeness.

Other central components to possessing a Christ-like humility are (a) we as believers are apt to recognize our weakness, but rely on God because He is the source of our strength that gives us the ability to accomplish every mission given to us. (b) Having Christ-like humility we recognize that we are sinful apart from Christ and have nothing to boast in or about. (c) Having Christ-like humility we are totally dependent on God for our worth, fruitfulness and Christ's justified righteousness. (d) Having Christ-like humility gives us the ability to be humble toward one another. (e) Lastly, having Christ-like humility, God rejoices/delights in those who walk humbly before Him as He gives an increase of His grace.

What characteristics did Christ display in His humility? First, Christ is God's Son and is the very nature of God and was equal with God before and during His earthly stay, though He "thought it not robbery with God to be equal with God" (v.6). What this verse means is that Christ let go of His royalty, glory and privileges as deity in heaven to put on humanity so that all who believe might be saved. Second, Christ sought to make no reputation for Himself (v.7), meaning everything that He did was according to the Will of His Father. Another meaning to this verse is that Christ emptied Himself of His glory, His position, His rights, and the divine use of His attributes for mankind's salvation. In doing so Christ was subjected to human limitations, suffering, hatred, ill-treatment, being misunderstood—all for humanity. It is noteworthy to say that while in human form, Christ remained fully God, but He became a servant of man (v.7) so that He would have experienced all that man will experience in life. Third, Christ being made of low esteem in human form was exalted by God and one day every knee shall bow and every tongue confess that Jesus is Lord (vv 10-11). ***What an honor!*** Also, the name Jesus is the name whereby when called upon all men should be saved.

Another point to Jesus displaying His humility is His birth. Jesus had the ability to be born in royal splendor, but instead chose a manger---humility—low-esteem. He entered Jerusalem on a donkey—humility again of low-esteem and even dying the horrific death on the cross---humility to the end.

It is noteworthy to say that humility is a conditioning of God's favor (II Chronicles 7:14) and His supreme requirement (Micah 6:8) as God dwells with the humble (Isaiah 57:15).

Humility does not mean we as Christians are pushovers—neither was Christ, but instead we are letting the God in us shine through. In laymen's terms humility is strength under control.

Where are we in our state of humility?

June 21

God Disciplines His Children: Hebrews 12:5

And ye have forgotten the exhortation which speaketh unto you as unto children. My son, despise not thou the chastening of the Lord, nor faint when thou art rebuked of Him;

The word chastise means to instruct, discipline and punish to make better (Psalm 94:10; 1Kings 12:11-14; Luke 23:16; Hebrews 12:8). The word chastise is synonymous with discipline which both means a form of instructions. Discipline is God's teachings in the lives of His people; both formative and corrective (Job 36:10). This word appears only in the above stated scripture, but is woven throughout the NT with such words as "correction", "instructions", chastisement", "reproof", and nurture" (The Student Bible Dictionary P. 77).

In God's disciplining of His people is based on His love and concern for our well-being and its purpose is to bring about maturity and happiness. In addition to God disciplining His children is to prevent us from being condemned with the world, and that we may continue to live sanctified lives and share in His holiness. God also allows His children to suffer hardships and troubles as His method of discipline, but we are assured of His love. As we endure hardships God will lead us through them so we may grow from them and remain faithful to Him and in doing so we will remain His spiritual children.

It is noteworthy to say there are some self-imposed disciplines that all believers should possess and some are daily Bible reading, a fervent prayer life, and a dedicated service to the Lord. God's discipline works the same as earthly parents who discipline their children out of love and for their growth.

Discipline equals growth and love!

The Eternal Christ: Hebrews 13:8

Jesus Christ the same yesterday, and today, and for evermore.

The above scripture verse speaks to the eternity of Christ as He has no beginning and no ending as well as being unchanging or immutable (Malachi 3:6). This truth about our eternal Christ provides the necessary faith for all believers to remain steadfast in their love, devotion and commitment to Christ as we make the journey to heaven. This also means that Christ is not a figure from the past or someone who will be instrumental in our lives in the future, but instead Christ is active in the lives of all believers from the moment He is accepted in ones life as Lord. The truth about His agape love is the same as it was beginning with creation and remains intact even when we reach our heavenly home.

It is noteworthy to say Christ was in the beginning with God when God stepped out on nothing and said, "let us" or let there be", and whatever God spoke came into existence. The Eternal Christ is the embodiment of God the Father as He is God. He is an all knowing, everywhere and all seeing God. ***Glory to God!***

All believers should desire to spend an everlasting life with our Eternal Christ when our earthly tabernacle has ended as there will be unspeakable joy and a never ending worship service.

What a time that will be in the presence of the Lord!

June 23

Jesus The Master Teacher: Luke 20:1-8

And it came to pass, that on one of those days, as He taught the people in the temple, and preached the gospel, the chief priests and the scribes came upon Him with the elders.

During Jesus' earthly ministry He taught in many places, but His biggest challenges came from the religious leaders—priests, scribes and elders who questioned His authority to teach. This was due in large part to Jesus' style and truths with which He taught. Also, Jesus' teaching upset their status quo as His teachings were opening the blinded eyes of many of His hearers and followers. How did Jesus upset their status quo? Jesus condemned their evil practices that were being conducted in God's house. Many if not all tolerated and participated in such practices and Jesus came teaching the truth.

These religious leaders came to question by what authority Jesus had to teach such doctrines. This also pointed to their unworthiness' of such positions and their spiritual leadership as they were not upholding the righteousness of God.

Jesus being truth and God in the flesh could only teach the "truth" which is the Word of God as He is the spoken Word.

Another note on Jesus being the master teacher is that He taught mankind all things in many ways. Case in point on obedience He lived in total obedience to His Father and He remained faithful to the end. After being baptized in the Jordan River He relied on the Holy Spirit while being tempted by Satan in the wilderness for forty days. Christ's actions of obedience and relying on the power of the Holy Spirit are powerful lessons for all humanity.

Jesus-the master teacher!

June 24

Jesus The Healer: Mark 1:29-34

And He healed man that were sick of divers diseases, and cast out many devils, and suffered not the devils to speak, because they knew Him.

What comes to mind when we say being healed or a healer? Healing is to be made whole or a repaired brokenness. Therefore, the healer is the one who is doing the restoring to wholeness. Throughout Jesus' earthly ministry He healed many of diverse diseases. Our scripture text speaks of Jesus healing Simon Peter's mother-in-law from being sick with fever. As Jesus' fame spread of His ability to heal many came from far and near seeking His healing powers.

Regardless of the nature of ones sickness whether physical, emotional or spiritual Jesus healed; there were many where He cast out demons and the person was made whole again. It is noteworthy to say that after being healed by Jesus many would become devout followers of Jesus. Mary Magdalene became a devote follower of Christ so much so she was one of the first at His tomb on Sunday Morning and the first person He spoke to after His resurrection.

This question comes to mind, what physical, emotional or spiritual sickness or disease do you want Jesus to heal you of? Is there a spiritual sickness that needs healing? Jesus is the answer. If there is an emotional problem; take it to Jesus, He is a mind regulator and He mends all broken hearts. If you have a physical infirmity; give it to Jesus. When healed what is your reaction? Will you react like the leper and tell everyone you meet or forget to say "Thank You Jesus for my healing."

He is still healing!

June 25

God Is Our Refuge: Psalm 118:5-9

I called upon the Lord in distress; the Lord answered me, and set me in a large place.

The term refuge denotes a place of safety, protection or shelter; in our discussion we will look at God being our protection or shelter in a time of storm. If the question were raised what does God protect us from and how He does it? First, God in His provisional care made provisions for all man's needs this includes our safety. He provides for all necessities of life which includes bread, water, shelter, and healing regardless of the nature of healing.

When man encounters adversities, God is there in the presence of the Holy Spirit as stated in Psalm 23 which includes all protective elements. Verse 4 which states, "Yea, though I walk through the valley of the shadow of death, I will fear no evil, for thou art with me, thy rod and thy staff comfort me." Verse 5 speaks to the issue of God caring for all needs even in the midst of evil as these evil attacks are designed to destroy both life and soul, but there is refuge in the safety of God's love and mercy—so much so until the Holy Spirit overflows our cup with His grace. **What a mighty God!**

Our scripture text drives home the point of God being our refuge by stating that when one calls on the Lord He answers, because if the Lord is on your side, then there is nothing to fear. God is present to give strength and the ability to overcome any situation.

God our safety valve!

June 26

Obeying Godly Leaders: Hebrews 13:17

Obey them that have the rule over you, and submit yourselves for they watch for your souls, as they that must give account, that they may do it with joy, and not with grief; for that is unprofitable for you.

What is the significance of members of the household of faith obeying godly leaders? Godly leaders are anointed by God to perform ministry as each one has been called by Him. God called some to pastor, evangelize, preach, teach, prophesy and some to be apostles. The true significance of obeying godly leaders is based on a higher loyalty to God in obedience and faithfulness to Him. This is because believers have a one-to-one personal relationship with God which includes the truth and faithfulness to God's Word. Also, the visible church---baptized body of believers are to remain faithful to God and His written Word. The study of God's Word as recorded in II Timothy 2:15 come into view. Lastly, leaders themselves are to remain faithful to God, His Word and His mission for the church---Christ's bride. The church is to be the light seated on the hill calling sinners to salvation. Therefore, leaders are compelled to maintain a right standing with God.

The question now becomes what if the leader no longer follows God and His righteousness? If this occurs, then every believer should pray for a spiritual healing for that leader because Satan is seeking whom he can destroy and leaders are no exception. This is to be done in love as all believers are to imitate God and His love toward all. Also, each believer must remain in fellowship with God through continuous prayer and Bible study.

Let's pray for one another—leaders included.

"Search The Scriptures": Acts 17:10-12

These were more noble than those in Thessalonica, in that they received the word with all readiness of mind, and searched the scriptures daily, whether those things were so.

Today's discussion setting is in ancient Macedonia a city called Berea which is not Veria Greece. This was one of Paul's stops on his preaching tour/journeys and his congregation in Berea had the mind to search the scriptures to authenticate what Paul was preaching was actually the Word of God.

Verse 17 carries a profound message of relevancy as it relates to Christians hearers of others proclaiming the Word of God. It should be examined for validity and not taken at face value. All believers and or hearers are encouraged to thoroughly examine all explanations and or interpretations of scripture as this is to ensure that the proclaimers are expounding on the word of truth and its foundation-Christ. Proclaimers/preachers who preach God's Word make Bible students/hearers, but the word that is preached is to be Christ-centered and His infallible Word. It is noteworthy to say that Bible students who know God's Word for his or herself will not be fooled by every doctrine that comes along. This is because Bible students have done according to II Timothy 2:15 which states, "Study to shew thyself approved unto God, a workman that needeth not to be ashamed, rightly dividing the word of truth." Also, when studying and meditating on God's Word ask for divine interpretation so when the "Word" is being proclaimed either through preaching or teaching you will know if he/she is on point.

The question now becomes why must the NT church support the apostles' doctrines? The apostles were the original messengers, witnesses and authorized representatives of the crucified Christ and His resurrection. The early church apostles are the foundational stones of the church and their writings have been preserved for all times as they are the original and fundamental testimony to the gospel of Christ and will stand throughout the ages (KJV commentary). It is also noteworthy to say that all scriptures are given by the inspiration of God (II Timothy 3:16). Psalm 138:2 supports the fact that God's Word is divinely inspired because He exalts His Word and name above all else.

OT prophets were careful to say "Thus said the Lord" and Jesus Himself taught that scriptures are God's inspired Word in the smallest detail (Matthew 5:18). Jesus who is God stated that His Word is divinely inspired and all that He said came from His Father. God in His divine wisdom moved the scripture/Bible writer that they wrote as He instructed. Therefore, scriptures/the Bible is without error and should be obeyed and trusted as the final word of authority. Additionally, all doctrines, commentaries, interpretations, explanations and traditions must be judged and legitimized by scriptures (Deuteronomy 13:3). This is to nullify any and all false teacher/word proclaimers who may appear on the scene contradicting the true Word of God.

Therefore, knowing that scriptures are the true divinely inspired Word of God, they must be treasured, loved, and guarded by all believers.

Search the scriptures for they are "profitable for doctrine, for reproof, for correction, for instruction in righteousness"—then you will know for yourself.

Consequences of False Teachers: Galatians 1:6-9

But through we, or any angel from heaven, preach any other gospel unto you than that which we have preached unto you, let him be accursed.

During Paul's ministry he encountered false teachers attempting to pervert the gospel of Christ. In his effort for his followers to know the truth and be aware of these false teachers, Paul provided important facts for his followers to look for in these false teachers, some were that if such persons come teaching that salvation includes circumcision, observing the law and keeping Jewish holidays is not the gospel of Christ. Because the gospel of Christ teaches that salvation comes by grace through faith in Christ as Lord and Savior.

Paul laid out the consequences that befalls false teachers who teach any other gospel than that of Christ, and some of these persons will have his/her part taken from the book of life (Revelation 22:18-19). *Who wants to be taken out of the book of life?*

Other signs to discern false teachers are evidenced by their prayer lives. Do their lives manifest their love for God? Do they manifest fruit of the spirit? Do they hate iniquity and love righteousness? Do they honor Christ, and lead the church into sanctification? Are they seeking to save lost souls? Do they proclaim the gospel of Christ and the apostles? Do they deny Christ's deity and virgin birth? Do they teach that humanity is lost without Christ? Do they teach that Christ rose on the third day as promised? What are their teachings on heaven and hell? What are their teachings on Satan and demons as spiritual beings? Lastly, do they teach that Christ is coming back again?

False teachers are present—know the scripture.

June 29

Living To Please God: Galatians 1:10; 1 Thessalonians 2:4

..As we were allowed of God to be put in trust with the gospel, even so we speak; not as pleasing men, but God, which trieth our hearts.

What does it mean to live to please God? Living to please God means to move self out of the way as believers have nothing to boast about or glory in because all of the work has been done by God. He created us, He saved us, He sustains us and He sanctified us to have fellowship with Him. Therefore, all we are or ever hope to become we owe it all to God. Speaking of spiritual gifts likewise we owe them to God for His glorification, edification-the body of Christ and honor.

If the question were raised, how do we as believers and leaders please God at all times? Believers and leaders alike must preach, teach and stand on the inerrant Word of God and reframe from yielding to the temptation of doing what pleases others by saying or tolerating sin. By doing so our reputation and integrity as believers and or leaders will have been comprised and the world will not see the righteousness' of God manifested. What are we to do? All believers/leaders are to seek God's approval first by asking these questions, will this honor God and will He be pleased? The answers are found in the scriptures. Also, all believers can live to please God by knowing His Will and living accordingly as a fervent prayer life is essential.

Living to please God establishes an intimate relationship between God and the believers. The closer we become to Him the more like Him we become.

Notables Of Faith: Hebrews 11:4-7

By faith Noah, being warned of God of things not seen as yet, moved with fear, prepared an ark to the saving of his house; by which he condemned the world, and became heir of the righteousness which is by faith.

Scripture defines faith as "the substance of things hoped for, the evidence of things not seen" (v.11). Also, believers believe and "understand that the world is framed by the word of God, so that things which are seen were not made of things which do appear" (v.3).

With that being said our scripture text points out some patriarchs who took faith to heart and were bountifully blessed. Abel is looked upon as a true worshipper of God because he offered a more excellent sacrifice to God than his brother Cain (v.4a). It is recorded that Enoch walked closely with God (Genesis 5:24) and had a great intimacy with God until he did not experience death. Brother Noah by his faith staked his reputation on God's Word when he was told to build an ark because it was going to rain. By Noah's faith he was counted as righteous. God kept His promise 120 years later. Lastly, Abraham began a journey to a far country not knowing where he was going, but had enough faith that God would show him when the time came. Abraham became the father of many nations. **What faith!**

The above patriarchs are examples of the benefits of true faith and its rewards, which bring these questions to mind, When called by God what is our response? Do we take God at His word? Are we willing to stake our reputation on God's Word like Noah?

Faith is the key to many outcomes.

God's Covenant Community

July 1

The Renewed Covenant: II Kings 23: 1-3, 21-23

And the king went up into the house of the Lord, and all the men of Judah and all the inhabitants of Jerusalem with him, and the priest, and the prophets, and all the people, both small, and great; and he read in their ears all the words of the book of the covenant, which was found in the house of the Lord.

Josiah was a godly king and very young, only eight years old when he began his reign as king of Judah. He is said to be the last righteous king of Judah (22:1). At the age of 16, King Josiah began to seek the Lord (2 Chronicle 34:3) and history records that four years later he began to purge the nation of its idolatry that was rampart. Also, in II Kings 22:13 we see King Josiah sincerely desired to know the Lord and believed in his heart that a sincere return to the true and living God would prevent divine judgment upon Judah. It was through the prophetess Huldah that God promised divine judgment upon the nation.

Because Josiah's humility before the Lord he led Judah into a nationwide revival with the renewal of the covenant and a rededication to true worship of the Lord.

Our scripture text outlines King Josiah's commitment to renewing the nation's covenant vowels to the Lord. King Josiah read for the nation the covenant so there would be no excuse for the people's lack of knowledge, and then the king began to destroy all symbols of false worship regardless of their location.

The lesson learned here, is if leaders become spiritually depraved, then all believers are to read, study and meditate on God's Word, then worship and live according to God's Word. Our daily walk with God will keep us in a renewed covenant relationship with Him.

A renewed covenant is a rededication to God.

July 2

The Lord Remembers His Covenant
Psalm 105:1-12

He hath remembered His covenant for ever, the word which He commanded to a thousand generations.

The beginning of our scripture text, the Psalmist thanksgiving is being made to the Lord for His goodness and mercy as a praise of thanksgiving should be a main part of our communication with God. Verse 4 encourages us to seek the Lord and His strength as this assures us of God's presence and daily grace. It is noteworthy to say that in order to persevere in salvation and to live lives pleasing to God we need His presence through the Holy Spirit.

If the question were raised why seek the strength of and presence of the Lord? It is because of His marvelous and wondrous work in the lives of all mankind. More importantly, because God remembers His covenant that He made with Abraham and his seed that blessings abound forever. Verses 38-45, the psalmist recounts the acts of God's mercy toward His people and His covenant relationship with them as part of His promise to Abraham and Israel was the seed of Abraham; just as we are.

Additionally, biblical history records God remembering His covenant after the Great Flood and God promised never to destroy the earth with water again and He would put a rainbow in the sky as His remembrance.

Just as God remembers His covenant promise and kept them, what is our commitment to God as our expressions of gratitude for His goodness and mercy?

God promised us a Savior; He gave His only begotten Son-Jesus Christ.

Thou Art The God That Doest Wonders"
Psalm 77:14

Thou are the God that doest wonders; thou hast declared thy strength among the people.

When experiencing adversities in life it is good to reflect on the wonders of God, our creator One can't help but say Thank You God for Your goodness and mercy that endures for all generations. While in our reflective mode, we see God the creator of all as being fully capable of handling our situation, simply because He cares for our every need and desires to aid in our problems.

Additional reflective points are that it was God who saved a nation through one man Joseph. It was God who provided salvation through Jesus Christ. It is God who sends the rain in due season when and where it is needed and causes the seasons to change on schedule. It is God who holds all the stars of the universe in place and causes the sun to provide heat and light by day and the moon lights up the night skies. It is God who rings the chimes of our internal alarm clocks each morning and say "arise my child because this is a new day." It was God who parted the Red Sea for the nation of Israel and it was God who caused the River of Jordan to wall up while the Israelites crossed over. It is God who causes time to stand still on a moment's notice and spread time from eternity to eternity. ***What a God!***

A God of many wonders; worthy to be praised for evermore.

July 4

Remember Thy Creator: Ecclesiastes 12:1-7

"Remember now thy Creator in the days of thy youth, while the evil days come not, nor the years draw night, when thou shalt way, I have no pleasure in them."

Our scripture text (vv 1-7) deals with the span of life and the occurrences therein, while the remaining chapter deals with the whole duty of man. In this chapter, Solomon issues a warning of how best to utilize our time as verses 3-7 paints a vivid picture of the aging process of the physical body and what happens at death. Solomon encourages all to remember God, our Creator during our youthful years while there is an abundance of energy that can be used for God and His kingdom building. Why is this? Because there will come a time as we age when there is less energy and we become slow in our walk and our eyesight becomes dim. Solomon uses the phrase "I have no pleasure in them" meaning in our old age we are content just to sit and watch as time passes on.

In verse 2, Solomon speaks of the brightness of the sun, moon and the stars are lit can be parallel to that of our youthful years as the sharpness of our eyesight. In our golden years our eyesight is not as sharp as during our youthful years. In verses 3-6, Solomon paints a vivid picture of human life with parabolic representations of the eight stages of human life. It is noteworthy to say these verses are indicative of a movie title "The Eight Stages of Life," which depicts human life from conception to death and the physical changes that occur in each stage.

More importantly, Solomon clarifies the final resting place for the physical and inner man in that the physical returns to dust where it came from while the spirit man returns to God who gave it (v.7). However, there is hope for all who live to see old age as the inner man can be renewed daily (II Corinthians 4:16). The question now becomes, how is the inner man renewed daily? This occurs through the infusion of Christ's life into our lives through the Holy Spirit. The Holy Spirit enables our minds, emotions and wills to be conformed to the likeness of Christ and His eternal purpose. What this really means is that even though our physical bodies are experiencing decay because of mortality; all who are in Christ have the rejuvenating spiritual waters of life that causes one to never grow old and when physical death does come we will be assured of eternal life where we will never grow old.

    A closing question, why is it important to remember God our Creator in our youth? It is good to know and remember God early in life as our physical life goes so does our spiritual life. Also, God is the essence of our being from beginning to end; therefore, He deserves the best we have to give and our best years.

    Lastly, God gave His best; why not give Him our best in return? Our best is "a reasonable service" to Him.

God Calls People For Special Service
Leviticus 8:1-13

And Moses did as the Lord commanded him; and the assembly was gathered together unto the door of the tabernacle of the congregation.

Today's discussion topic deals with the anointing of priests, Aaron and his sons to the priesthood by Moses under the direction of God. In the OT we know the importance and roles of the priests as they were to be godly persons who spoke to God for the people. The purpose of priest were to aid men and women draw near to God and bring them to forgiveness of their sins and salvation (Hebrew 7:24-25). How did priests bring the people close to God? The people were brought close to God by offering gifts and sacrifices to God for their sins. The priests taught Israel the law of God (Deuteronomy 33:8-10; Hebrews 5:1, 8:3; 9:7, 13). It is noteworthy to say that in the NT the office of priests were no longer needed as it was fulfilled in Christ as He is our high priest who replaced the imperfection of the OT priests who required cleansing themselves before they could make atonements for the people.

The OT is sprinkled with God calling people to special services in His kingdom building. Who can forget Elijah being called at an early age? There is Ezekiel preaching to the rebellious house of Israel. Remember Jonah who preached to Nineveh and the people believed. Another school of thought on God calling people for special services continues today as His kingdom building must continue. God gives different gifts according to His good pleasure all to the edification of the body of Christ—the Church.

Answer God's call to service.

July 6

Seek And Keep God's Commands: 1 Chronicle 28:8

Now therefore in the sight of all Israel the congregation of the Lord, and in the audience of our God; keep and seek for all the commandments of the lord your God; that ye may possess this good land, and leave it for an inheritance for your children after you for ever.

In today's discussion we see King David giving wise instructions to his son Solomon as he was to begin his reign as king of Israel. David is known for being a man after God's own heart and a mighty warrior. King David loved God with all his heart and when he committed a sin he willingly went to God in prayer asking for forgiveness.

Verse 4 expresses David's heart felt gratitude to God for being chosen king of Israel; this represents humility. In verse 5 David reminds Solomon that he was chosen by God to succeed him to the throne of Israel and it behooved him to keep and seek the Lord's commandments, because if he did then the Lord would be with him, but if Solomon forsook the Lord then God would "cast him off." It is noteworthy to say what David was giving Solomon were the conditions for establishing his kingdom. It was a life of obedience and faithfulness to God. History tells us that Solomon followed his father's instructions early in his kingdom, but later departed from God and was punished by God (I Kings 11:1).

The lesson for us today is to adhere to wise counsel, walk faithfully and humbly with God and remain steadfast to His ways; by doing so we can be assured of God's blessings as opposed to punishment.

All believers have the presence of the Holy Spirit to help us keep God's commandments.

July 7

Daniel Keep God's Covenant: Daniel 1:8-20

..Daniel purposed in his heart that he would not defile himself with the portion of the king's meat, nor with the wine he drank; therefore he requested of the prince of the eunuchs that he might not defile himself.

The setting of today's discussion is when Daniel was in captivity in Babylon and the moral climate was one of heathen and from the history of Daniel his teaching contradicts that of Babylon. It is believed that the food and wine that King Nebuchadnezzar served Daniel and his friends were from that which was offered as idol sacrifices. To eat such food would have disobeyed God's laws. Therefore, Daniel made up his mind to remain obedient to his teaching regarding the true and living God.

In keeping God's covenant resulted in Daniel and his friends suffering what would have been sure death if God was not in the plan to reward His faithful believers. David's friends were thrown in the fiery furnace, David was thrown in the lion's den, but in God's deliverance, David used the lions as his pillow and slept safe in the arms of Jesus. Likewise, the Hebrew boys trusted the God of their convictions who shielded them from the flames of the fire. ***Deliverance! Deliverance! Deliverance!***

Daniel's actions express several lessons for all believers and they are (a) remain faithful to God and keep His covenant if it means death. (b)Believe and trust God for deliverance. (c) Fear God rather than man for He is a deliverer. (d) Daniel's actions speaking to his childhood training in God (Deuteronomy 6:7).

Given Daniel's situation, ask yourself what would you have done? Trust God or bow to the king—the world?

July 8

Know God For His Mercifulness: Ephesians 2:4-5

But God, who is rich in mercy for His great love wherewith He loved us.

What is mercy? The Student Bible dictionary (P. 154) defines mercy as "compassion, love, sympathy, deep caring, forgiveness (Psalm 145:9; Ephesians 4-5), or giving or receiving care when it is not deserved. Mercy may withhold or ease expected punishment."

From our definition and scripture text we see the attributes of God as He has been and continues to be merciful to His people. All of God's mercy is undergirded by love, for He is love. How has God expressed His mercy? When we, mankind were enemy to God He reconciled us back to Him through His Son Jesus Christ with Christ's death on the cross. Both the Old and New Testament links mercy to God's covenant grace when justice was demanded mercy prevailed.

If the question were raised, how do we get to know God's mercy? Verse 7 provides the answer for knowing God's mercy as it came through the blood of Jesus Christ by God's grace which is His righteousness. Why? Because when we were lost in sin, God redeemed us, when we-mankind hated God, He loved us. God continues to shower humanity with His mercy by sending the elements that are essential to our earthly life and the indwelling Holy Spirit to nourish our spiritual lives all to His glory.

The mercifulness of God is manifested in our daily lives.

July 9

God Cares: 1 Peter 5:7

Casting all your care upon Him; for He careth for you.

If the question were raised, what does it mean to say that God cares? Our scripture verse makes a profound statement regarding the care from our heavenly father in that He ask that we cast all our cares upon Him, because He cares and wants to resolve any and all situations. Also, we know that God cares because in His providence He made provisions for every aspect of human life.

Throughout biblical history we have evidence of God caring for mankind in all that He did and most of all God wants an intimate relationship with humanity. Therefore, being the caring God that He is would not leave man out of His protective arms of safety.

Psalm 27:10 provides assurances of God caring which states "when my father and my mother forsake me, then the Lord will take me up." What this verse means is when our parents turn their backs on us we have the assurances that God will never leave nor forsake us.

It goes without saying for someone to give the best that they have is the ultimate display of love and care, because without love there is no care/concern. The word "care" is an expression of concern, or "being the object of ones watchful attention" (Merriam-Webster Dictionary (P.130). In this scenario all believers are the object of God's watchful attention, for He is the essence of our being from our beginning to end.

Give all concerns and anxieties to the Lord.

July 10

A Trustworthy God: Psalm 20:7

Some trust in chariots and some in horse, but we will remember the name of the Lord our God.

What is trust? The Student Bible Dictionary defines trust as the ability to depend on, put one's confidence in (Proverbs 3:5; II Corinthians 1:9), a confident hope (II Corinthians 1:10) a belief (I Thessalonians 2:4).

Now that we have defined the word "trust" let us search the scriptures for further clarification of trust Proverbs 3:5 encourages us to "trust in the Lord with all thine heart" which is the opposite of doubting God for His sustaining powers. Our trust in God is essential to our relationship with Him as it is based on Him being trustworthy. It is noteworthy to say that believers being children of God have the assurances of His love, devotion, and faithfulness to care for our every need (Matthew 10:31). God has proven His trustworthiness because every promise He made was kept. Also, God is intertwined in every aspect of our lives and is there to work out every difficult situation.

The second part of verse 5 encourages us from leaning to our own understanding as our understanding is limited at best and is subject to error because man is fallible as well as being limited in his knowledge of the future; whereas with God who knows all and sees all is better able to direct our path.

Man who leans to his or her understanding as this comes from the human mind it diminishes the human spirit. Another hindrance to leaning on ones own understanding is that it leads to self pride thus preventing spiritual growth. Rather than being wise in our own eyes we should trust God and acknowledge Him at all times and we will grow in wisdom and knowledge as well as knowing His will for our lives. To acknowledge God, we must accept God for who He is and what He has and continues to do in the lives of mankind. To know God is through our prayer lives and as promised He will "direct our paths" (v. 6) as well as daily scripture reading and meditating on His Word.

Psalm 37:3 also encourages us to "trust in the Lord, and do good, so shalt thou dwell in the land, and verily thou shalt be fed." This verse parallel I Peter 5:7 which speaks about God caring because He will take care of all our needs and situations. While trusting God we are to delight ourselves in God and He will give us the desires of our heart (37: 6). ***What a good God!***

What are some of the blessings from trusting God? Some of the blessing that come from trusting God are (a) answered prayers; (b) we are assured of a heavenly inheritance, (c) His sustaining help in the time of trouble, (d) His guidance, protection and presence (e) we are assured of righteous standards and (f) salvation.

The question now becomes, why fret when we have a trustworthy God? There is no need to worry, consider the lilies of the field; the fowls of the air, all their needs are met. God will do the same for you and me.

Trust God; He is worthy!

July 11

An All Seeing God: Job 34:21

For His eyes are upon the ways of man, and He seeth all his goings.

The story of Job depicts a righteous man who had lived according to God's statues and regardless of his situation he remained steadfast to his faith in God believing that God would see him through.

During Job's illness his three friends came to visit, and in their effort to cheer up Job they accused him of sin that he failed to admit. Elihu was adamant in beliefs of Job's sins, but Job in his righteousness remained steadfast in his conviction that he had walked upright in the eyesight of God. Job expressed that God knew his heart and would judge him accordingly. What Job knew is that God looks at man differently than man; man looks at the outer appearance while God sees the heart. The heart is where all actions, thoughts and feelings begin.

It is noteworthy to say that the God of all Creation sees all, knows all, hears all and can do all; therefore, nothing is hidden from God. It would be foolish to withhold committed sin because God knows our sins. Another thought on our all seeing God is that when Job's dilemma began, God knew Job would remain steadfast in his faith to Him. God asked Satan had he "considered my servant Job" (paraphrased). God knew that with His help Job would withstand the test of Satan's attacks. What does this say for you and I, God sees all of us and knows each of our limits.

There is no hiding place from God.

July 12

The Love Of God: 1 John 4:19

We love Him, because he first loved us.

The word love has been written about, talked about and preached about, but the love of God is the most demonstrated act of love recorded in man's history. We see love being expressed by God throughout the Bible. Some say that the Bible is one big love story of God expressing His love for humanity. John 3:16 sum's up God's love for humanity for there is no greater love than what is expressed by God.

If the question were raised, Why is love expressed with such magnitude? God expressed His love with such magnitude because He is love; it is His nature, and because of His love we share in His nature and forgiveness and are born of Him. Because of our love relationship with God we reap the bountiful harvest of His love and we are commanded to love others so they too can experience what we as God's children experience.

Another point of God's love is that once we as believers establish our vertical love relationship with God then we can share God's agape love with our fellowman, and then the world will know our family heritage. Love is one of the fruits of the Spirit (Galatians 5:22-23) and is evidence of the indwelling Holy Spirit.

It is noteworthy to say that we cannot love God whom we have never seen and fail to love our brothers and sister whom we see daily.
Only agape like love will stand the test of time!

Know The Lord: Isaiah 45:6

That they may know from the rising of he sun, and from the west, that there is none besides Me. I am the lord, and there is none else.

If the question were raised, How do we get to know the Lord? We can get to know the Lord through daily Bible reading, and meditating on His Word as recorded in scripture. Genesis records that from the beginning of time God has been in existence by stating "in the beginning God created heaven and earth" (v.1), and we hold that scripture as being the final authority and His written Word. Also, it is believed that only the true and living God of heaven could step out on nothing and create all that exist with the spoken word. God's creation includes nature, all human life, and all living creatures as well as unseen created matter. Another method of knowing God is to reflect on nature and its life cycle and how it changes on schedule and the beauty therein, then realize that only a God could do such magnificent and majestic wonders. If nature fails to arouse our knowledge of God, then reflect further on the heavenly bodies and the wonderful way they move about the sky. Then take a look at the balance of nature and the life cycle of man as well as the force of gravity that holds everything in its rightful place.

Since the beginning of time, God has poured out His Spirit on called persons to speak to humanity for Him, to give mankind personal knowledge of Him and to remind humanity what He has done and continues to do in the lives of mankind.
Know God!

July 14

The God Of Righteousness: Malachi 4:2

But unto you tat fear My name shall the Sun of righteousness arise with healing in His wings, and ye shall go forth, and grow up as calves of the stall.

What is righteousness? The Student Bible Dictionary (P. 202) defines "righteousness as the rightness by God's standards, His justice and fairness." All humanity is to match life with that of God's commandments, love and purposes. It is determined that all actions are based on love for God and a relationship with Him.

Isaiah 41:10 speaks of God's righteousness as it relates to the nation of Israel, they were blessed and protected when they obeyed His commandments and punished for their disobedience. This holds true for all humanity today.

II Corinthians 5:21 speaks to the righteousness of God not as a legal righteousness but the experiences we feel as believers in Christ. This is made possible when we become a new creation with a new character and morals that are founded upon our faith in Christ that flows from Him (Philippians 3:9). Also, the righteousness of God is experienced by all believers as we remain in union and fellowship with Christ. It is important to know that Christ took on humanity's sins so that God the Father could justly forgive sinners as Christ was the sinless human sacrifice. Therefore, God in His righteousness could not look on sin, but through His Son man is no longer an enemy of God; as Jesus Christ has made things right with God for us.

God's righteousness (morals and standards) is what all mankind will be judged for. He is the righteous judge. Be right!

Hear The Voice Of The Lord: John 10:1-27

To him the porter openeth, and the sheep hear His voice; and He calleth His own sheep by name, and leadeth them out.

Today's lesson deals with Christ as the good shepherd one who cares for the needs of his sheep. In doing so the sheep knows the voice of the shepherd-Christ and will not stray from the fold and become subject to harm-temptation.

First, Jesus began His comparison by comparing the true shepherd from false shepherds. Verse 1 Jesus explains that anyone who enters the sheepfold other than through the door is a thief and robber. Thieves and robbers enter the household only to steal and take what has been gained. In this scenario false shepherds rob believers of their faith in Christ and commitment to Him. Verse 10, Jesus makes it plain that He is "the door" and is the only entrance to salvation and He came to give life…"more abundantly." Another comparison Jesus makes is that the good shepherd will lay down his life for his sheep as opposed to that of a hireling/false shepherd, because when trouble arises the hireling will flee. Christ gave His life for believers—His sheep.

The last point of hearing the voice of God is that the sheep know the voice of their shepherd—true Christians and the shepherd knows his sheep; this is because of the deep devotion and personal relationship that exist between the two. Therefore, when the shepherd, Jesus Christ calls all true Christians will hear and answer the voice of the Lord.

Hear the voice of Jesus and follow Him. He is the good shepherd!

New Creatures In Christ: 2 Corinthians 5:17

Therefore if any man be in Christ, he is a new creature; old things are become new.

What does it mean to be new creatures in Christ? First, it means to be born again in the spirit as we no longer walk in the darkness of sin, but have accepted the atoning death and resurrection of Jesus Christ. Second, being a new creature in Christ we rose with Christ to a new life in Him as He rose for our justification. Third, all who have accepted Christ by faith now totally belongs to God and lives in a world where the Spirit rules (Romans 8:14), because Romans 8:14 states that "for as many as are led by the Spirit of God, they are the sons of God." This means that all believers have the assurance of salvation and are constantly putting to death the misdeeds of the flesh as we are led by the Spirit we will walk in the Spirit (Galatians 5:25). The fourth meaning of being a new creature in Christ is that in walking in the Spirit we have yielded all control of our lives to the Holy Spirit.

Other attributes of being new creatures in Christ and being led by the Holy Spirit, are that living a spirit-filled life, believers are in harmony with the scriptures, believers no longer have sinful desires, and concerned with the consequences that sin brings. Additionally, believers strive to live righteous lives before God as He has set the standard for righteousness.

New creatures in Christ enjoy an everlasting peace with God.

"Give Thanks Unto The Lord"
1 Chronicles 16:8-11, 34

O give thanks unto the Lord; for He is good; for His mercy endureth for ever.

If the question were raised, Why "give thanks unto the Lord"? Giving thanks to the God is to admit and recognize who God is and what He has and continues to do for all creation and especially in the lives of all humanity. In this chapter of 1 Chronicles, the writer highlights David's gratitude to the Lord for deliverance; David was a mighty warrior who had fought and won many battles. Therefore, David recognized where his strength came from and was obliged to give thanks unto the Lord and encouraged Israel to do likewise. David also remembered the Lord's covenant promises that He would be with His people and God has been faithful and kept His promises throughout history. The faithfulness of God and His holiness renders Him worthy of thanksgiving, praises and honor.

The question now becomes how do we give thanks to the Lord or express our gratitude? Expressions of thanks and gratitude to God is through praise and worship with singing psalms and hymns of praise to His holy name for His grace and mercy. Also, believers are to give of themselves sacrificially to the Lord as recorded in Romans 12:1.

It is noteworthy to say that God accepts true worship that reflects the heart of the worshiper as it expresses the worshiper's sincere desire to be near the Lord and in fellowship as well as the worshiper's commitment to live a holy life before Him.

Praise and sincere worship express thanksgiving.

"The Earth Is The Lord": Psalm 24:1

The earth is the Lord, and the fullness thereof; the world, and they that dwell therein.

Our topic reveals the exclusivity of God's Sovereign ownership of all creation which includes both seen and unseen, and if there is any doubt about the creator of all things, then our scripture text removes all doubt. Why? Because it states, "The earth is the Lord's and the fullness thereof; the world, and they that dwell therein." It is noteworthy to say that this verse is relevant today as there are many in our society trying to deny the existence of the Sovereign God. Humanist are trying to convince many believers that man came into existence from some one-cell animal, then the question becomes where did the one-cell animal come from? Where and how did this vast universe come into existence? Who holds the heavenly bodies in place as well as mankind walking in an upright position while the earth rotates on its axis? Another question that comes to mind is who but God would know the perfect conditions that support all life whether plant, animal or man? Who but God could establish the life cycles for all life? Who but God would know about gravity and implement gravity during creation? If this writer had to supply an answer it would be only God who knows all and has existed from eternity as He has no beginning and no end; He is alpha and omega.

Since we have established through scripture that God is Sovereign and is the rightful owner of all creation this makes Him worthy of all praise, honor and worship. How must we worship a holy God? We must worship God with a clean hand and a pure heart (v.4), which means that our hands must be free of all sin and the "pure heart" is one that has the right motives and goals which is to have a close relationship with God. Also, a "pure heart" is one that possesses an inward holiness which will be manifested in holy living.

Allow me to discuss briefly God and His sovereignty at it relates to His care for His beloved created man. God provides for all man's needs regardless of his or her beliefs and or accepting Him for who His is. While man was separated from God, He loved us so much so that He gave His best to reconcile humanity back to Him. ***Love! Love!***

God also provides ways in which man can know Him and receive the blessing from being in fellowship with Him. How does He do this? God spoke through the prophets, he spoke through the law and then He spoke to humanity through His Son Jesus Christ. Most important, God sent the Holy Spirit to dwell in each believer as our guide, teacher and protector. Why is this so? Because He is Lord and owns all humanity as we were bought with a price. Furthermore, our scripture verse states His ownership.

It can be concluded that God is the rightful owner and creator of all that exists; therefore when humanist say there is no God, ask them how did the world come into existence? Through God!

Stand Still: Exodus 14:13

And Moses said unto the people, Fear ye not, Stand still, and see the salvation of the Lord, which He will shew to you today; for the Egyptians whom ye have seen today, ye shall see them again no more for ever.

The setting of today's discussion takes place with the Israelites nearing the Red Sea and Pharaoh's army fast approaching with no place for the Israelites to go. The Israelites saw their situation as hopeless and appeared as they were doomed to die at the hands of Pharaoh. The people cried out to Moses their leader who cried out to God for deliverance. Moses' faith in God told Israel to "Fear ye not, stand still, and see the salvation of the Lord." Verse 14 explains why we as believers like the Israelites are not to fear and just "stand still."

Verses 13 and 14 give assurances that God our mighty warrior as He has never lost a battle for all His people who walk with Him in faith. Another thought is that standing still requires faith, and patience from us as believers. We must have faith enough to trust God in any and every situation because the "shall" is our guarantee, and then we must have the patience to wait for deliverance because His time is not our time. Like Israel's deliverance our deliverance is assured and timely.

Reflecting on God's deliverance of the young nation of Israel, then ask how many times has God delivered? Just as God delivered Israel, He will do the same for you and I today if we only "stand still" and know that we have victory in Him. Would a loving God who asks us of cast all our cares upon Him (1 Peter 5:7) if He were not going to fight your battles? ***Absolutely not!***

Walk In God's Ways: Psalm 1:1

Blessed is the man that walketh not in the counsel of the ungodly, nor standeth in the way of the sinners, nor sitteth in the seat of the scornful.

Psalm 1:1 speaks of the blessing for all who walk not in the counsel of the ungodly, but refrain from associating with sinners. This depicts the two kinds of people as our discussion title asks us to walk in God's ways.

All who walk in God's ways are the righteous as they seek to know and do the Will of God. How are we to know the Will of God so that we may walk in His ways? All believers are to study, meditate on God's Word, and then ask for divine interpretation of His Word. Also, believers are to commune with God daily through prayer as this builds an intimate relationship with God. All who walk in God's ways manifest their love, commitment, obedience, righteousness and their separation from all worldliness. Also, all who walk in God's ways have the indwelling Holy Spirit to aid in sustaining our walk in His ways and a constant renewing of our love for God.

Verse 3 assures all believers of the continued blessing from walking and being delighted in God's Laws that the writer equated the presence of the Holy Spirit to that of a" tree planted by the rivers of water." This means that water is wet and constantly moving, so is the Holy Spirit.

Walking in God's ways assures all believers of salvation through Jesus Christ and spending eternity with God.

Righteousness is walking in God's ways as blessings abound.

Strength In The Lord: Psalm 27:14

Wait on the Lord; be of good courage, and He shall strengthen thine heart; wait, I say, on the Lord.

What is strength? There are several passages of scripture that speak on strength and how man is to rely on God's strength because in our weakest moments we are strong in the Lord. If I, the writer were to provide a definition of strength it would be "strength is the ability to perform a certain task or to accomplish a goal." Merriam-Webster Dictionary agrees in principal with me, the writer's definition of strength.

With that being said, the writer, David of our scripture text is encouraging all to "be strong in the Lord, and he shall strengthen thine heart." how do we become strong in the Lord? First, we must know God for who He is, second, we must trust God for deliverance, and third, we must be patient and wait on Him. This gives us confidence in God for His trustworthiness has been proven time and again.

The consequences of failing to wait on God are that we become weary, worn and tired and then we faint, thus rendering us unable to complete our task or desired goal. In this scenario we are to live righteous lives before God and give Him the best of our service, which is the up building of His kingdom.

God is the source of our strength; therefore, we can do nothing of ourselves, but we can do all things through Christ who strengthens us (Philippians 4:13). Be strong in the Lord (Ephesians 6:10)!

July 22

Behold! The Wonders Of God: Habakkuk 1:5

Behold ye among the heathens, and regard, and wonder marvelously; for I will work a work in your days, which ye will not believe, though it be told you.

Habakkuk was a prophet who prophesied during 605-597 B.C, but what is different about Habakkuk's prophecy is that his was more of an exchange between him and God. Habakkuk wanted to know why God didn't do something about the evil that was rampant during his day. God answered the prophet by allowing a wicked nation Babylon to punish Judah. This confused Habakkuk, but he learned a valuable lesson in the end—to trust God and live by faith.

Our scripture verse brings clarity to Habakkuk's confusion in that God stated that He would display His work in such an awesome fashion that it would be unbelievable. What was going to be unbelievable was the astonishing judgment God would bring on Babylon.

There is a plethora of wonders worthy of beholding His awesome powers and works. Creation is one of many of God's wonders. Parting of the Red Sea is another. The miraculous Virgin birth of the promise Messiah—Jesus Christ and the grand announcement made by the heavenly host. If those weren't enough to say **Behold!** Then reflect on the awesome events that occurred during Jesus' dying hours on the cross.

Are God's awesome events being displayed today? Yes, who but God can take ash from a volcano from another country and disrupt air travel that affects many other countries world wide.

When God shows up He shows out on a grand scale every time. Behold! See the wonder of God.

God's Creative Works: Colossians 1:16

For by Him were all things created, that are in heaven, and that are in earth, visible and invisible, whether they be thrones, or dominions, or principalities, or powers; all things were created by Him, and for Him.

Continuing our discussion on God's wonders and His creative powers, today we will focus on Jesus Christ who is the first born of everything(v.15), and is the head of all and sustains all that exists. This is because by Him all things both visible and invisible were made by God (v.17). John 1:1 tells us that Jesus was in the beginning with God who became the Word of God. Therefore, Jesus being present with God during creation His works are present throughout the universe. It is safe to say that God spoke and Jesus carried out the command and the Holy Spirit is the one who moved over the deep (Genesis1:2). This tells us that all members of the Godhead were present during creation—Jesus Christ.

Let us look at some spiritual creative works of God, and some are Christ being the firstborn from the dead (v.18), because it was Christ who was the first to rise from the dead with a spiritual and immortal body (1 Corinthians 15:20). This signified what is to come for all believers as believers died with Christ and rose with Him. Jesus' resurrection, He became the head of the church. This is occurred on the day of Pentecost when the disciples received the Holy Spirit. Lastly, it was Jesus' blood on the cross that humanity, all who believe and everything in the universe was brought into unity and harmony under Christ (vv 16-18; 20); meaning Christ reconciled everything.

Imaginable and unimaginable is God's creative works.

July 24

Great Is The Lord: Nehemiah 4:14

And I looked, and rose up, and said unto the nobles, and to the rulers, and to the rest of the people, Be not ye afraid of them; remember the Lord, which is great and terrible, and fight for your brethren, your sons, and your daughters, your wives, and your houses.

Nehemiah was a man who loved his home country Israel and desired to return to rebuild a wall around the city. What is most notable about Nehemiah is that he was a praying man and trusted God. Upon receiving permission to return to his hometown to begin this monumental task he prayed and followed God's instructions. As the project began, haters began their plot to disrupt God's plan, but God in His greatness gave Nehemiah the insight on what to do.

In Nehemiah 2:19 we see how the enemy will try to disrupt God's kingdom, but Christians are to remain steadfast in the Lord as He will fight your battles only if you keep still. Just as Nehemiah and the Jews were committed to rebuilding the walls around the city of Jerusalem so must believers today remain faithful to God and His kingdom building. Nehemiah and the Jews are perfect examples of overcoming obstacles, when they were ridiculed they went into prayer, when discouragement and fear approached they were met with encouragement from godly leaders to continue in faith in God as they were dressed in the whole armour of God (Ephesians 6:10-18).

God's greatness is greater than Satan and his evil doers; therefore, prayer is a mighty weapon in this spiritual warfare. Nehemiah prayed and was successful, Jeremiah prayed and the walls of Jericho fell; with our sincere prayers we too will be successful.

How great is your Lord?

"Worthy Is The Lamb": Revelation 5:12

Saying with a loud voice, Worth is the Lamb that was slain to receive power, and riches, and wisdom, and strength, and honour, and glory, and blessing.

While marooned on the Isle of Patmos, John the Baptist wrote what he saw in the vision of the Lord and the events that are to occur. Our discussion text deals with the opening of the book and the Lamb who is found worthy to open the book that would reveal the seals, which discloses God's end-time judgments in the earth.

Today's focus is who is worthy to open the book, and to loose the seals (v. 2). The search was made and no man was found worthy to open the book neither in heaven, the earth, under the earth and this caused John to weep (v.3), but one of the elders instructed John to hold his peace, because there was one found worthy to open the book who came out of the tribe of Judah and the root of David. This promise was foretold as recorded in Genesis 49:9-10 as this refers to Jesus Christ who came out of the lineage of David and as David was from the tribe of Judah. Jesus Christ is the worthy Lamb of God to open the book as He is worthy because of His sacrificial death on the cross for all humanity. The purpose of His death was to take way the sins of the world (John 1:29). Christ's love and work for mankind renders Him worthy of all honor, praise, glory, and worship by all in heaven and earth because of His power, wisdom, strength, and wealth. More importantly, Christ is God's Son, therefore, He is worthy to take the book from God the Father and open the seals and disclose the content that reveals the future destiny of the earth and all mankind. Verse 9 make Christ's worthiness plain by stating, "Thou art worthy to take to book, and to open the seals thereof; for thou was slain, and hast redeemed us to God by thy blood out of every kindred, and tongue, and people, and nation."

It is noteworthy to say the love of God is on display because (a) man was created in the image and liken of God with the indwelling spirit of God in each of us. (b) Because of man's sin it required a human sacrifice to remove sin and its stain. (c) Here comes Jesus with forgiving in His blood reconciling man back to God. (d) Jesus went back to heaven where He is now making intercessions for us, but He left the Holy Spirit as our guide to get to heaven. ***What love!***

Given all that Christ has done for humanity and who He is these questions come to mind, do you find Him as the worthy Lamb of God? Will you praise Him like the angels and elders? Will you thank God the Father for lovingly giving His best to shed His precious blood for all humanity? Are you looking forward to one day seeing your Savior face-to-face?

Jesus Christ is the worthy Lamb of God who was slain from the foundation of the world.

He is worthy! He is worthy! He is worthy! Praise His holy name!

July 26

"Believe Jesus Is The Christ": 1 John 5:1

Whosoever believeth that Jesus is the Christ is born of God; and every one that loveth Him that begat loveth Him also that is begotten of Him

This and other epistles were written by the apostle John who was one of the original disciples of Jesus Christ. This epistle gives no specific targeted group of people that were the designed recipients of John's writings, but it is believed that John wrote this letter from his home in Ephesus to several of the congregation in the province of Asia. These churches experienced a similar problem with false teachers and John wanted to refute their teachings and have the congregation to believe the truth that Jesus is the Christ, and to encourage the congregations to pursue and remain in a life of holy fellowship with God as His truth, righteousness and holiness provides true joy. Also, faith in Christ will bring eternal life.

There are essentials that must be exercised by all and they are, (1) believe that Jesus is the Christ and that He is God's Son. (2) All must accept Him in faith, as faith is the key to all our beliefs. (3) It is through Jesus Christ that we have eternal life—salvation, and that Jesus is the way to God.

Benefits from believing that Jesus is the Christ and following Him are (a) believers are in union with Christ, (b) believers become new creatures in Christ as they are washed in the blood of Jesus; (c) believers have the indwelling Holy Spirit, (d) believers are sanctified, and justified in Christ, and (e) believers live in holy obedience to Christ with the aid of the Holy Spirit.

Believe!

July 27

God Hears: Psalm 86:1

Bow thine thy ear, O Lord hear me; for I am poor and needy.

This Psalm is a prayer for deliverance, David cried out to the Lord stating his condition and his desires from God. David was mindful to acknowledge the goodness of the Lord and in the midst of his afflictions and troubles David knew where his help came from and by humbly submitting himself to the Lord that he would get an answer.

The epitome of our prayers is to acknowledge that we can do nothing in and of ourselves and prayers to the Lord must be of sincerity, humility and with thanksgiving. God will hear and will answer our prayers because He cares for His people and through His providence He has made provisions for all our needs.

Several scriptures speak of God hearing the prayers of the righteous and answering their prayers. Case in point, when the nation of Israel cried out to God for deliverance from the bondage of Pharaoh, God heard and responded. Each time Moses prayed to the Lord God answered. While in prison Paul prayed; God heard and responded Peter and his followers prayed while he was in prison God heard and Peter was released.

II Chronicles 7:14 gives assurances of God hearing the cries of His people and His response. Humility, honesty and faith are essential components to answered prayers.

Jesus being God's Son would often steal away and pray to His Father, for He knew His Father heard His prayers.

Pray-God hears.

July 28

Hide The Word Of God In Your Heart
Deuteronomy 6:6-7

And these word, which I command thee this day, shall be in thine heart.

Yesterday we discussed heeding the Spirit of God; today's discussion gives insight to heeding the spirit of God by hiding His Word in you heart. Why is it important to have the Word of God hidden in ones heart? When the word is in the heart it becomes personal and removes all possibilities of being misplaced when written on stones or tablets. When God gave the Ten Commandments to Moses they were written on tablets and the people failed to keep them. The heart is the best place to keep or hide things/words and feeling because the heart is the center of all activity. Proverbs 4:23 explains the heart being the core of all activities.

Hiding the Word of God in our hearts, Christ is dwelling in each of us (Colossians 3:16), but His Word gets in the heart through daily Bible reading and meditating on the scriptures, and then abiding by what the "Word" has to say. It is noteworthy to say that it is God's desire for His Word to be hidden in the hearts of all believers (Psalm 119:11).

With regards to children they are to be taught the Word of God at an early and diligently. This is the responsibility of all parents to bring up their children with the knowledge of God. Spiritual instructions for our children are a command from God.

Reverence the Lord, hide His Word in your heart, and know Him for yourself.

God Commands Nature: Psalm 104:10
He sendeth the springs into the valleys, which run among the hills.

This number of Psalm is a hymn that deals with God's creative works of nature and His command of it. When reflecting on how God laid the foundation of the earth that it would remain forever (v.5), one must shout with joy of a great God.

This entire psalm outlines in reflective fashion the majestic ability of God to stretch forth all creation and then sustains all aspects of nature in its rightful place. As each verse gives descriptive analogies of each of God's creations and how wonderfully made all of His creations are. The Psalmist speaks to the wonders of God's command when the earth was covered with water and how He spoke and it obeyed and immediately receded to its proper place. How He uses the clouds as His chariot and the wings of the wind as His sidewalk. ***What a God!***

The Psalmist continues his vivid description of God's command of nature in stating the mountains, valley and even spring know their places as He strategically placed each. Every part of nature knows its purpose and fulfills that purpose as God designed and commanded. There was a perfect balance of harmony and nature, sin has marred His perfect creation, but when Christ returns harmony will be resorted.

God is the commander in chief.

Heed The Spirit Of God: Malachi 2:6

The law of truth was in His mouth, and iniquity was not found in His lips; He walked with me in peace and equity, and did turn many away from iniquity.

Malachi prophesied about 100 years after the first exiles had returned to their homeland Jerusalem and the priests had become corrupt. Priests are the leaders responsible for leading the people in spiritual morality. Priests are God's called leaders who are to exemplify the righteousness of God through the preached word and holy living. They are to adhere to the Spirit of God as priests are to go to God for the people. As many church leaders go astray, so does the congregation.

Our scripture verse depicts the moral standards by which God's called leaders are to abide by as they must first show love and respect for God. Second live honestly and righteously. Third, they are to preach and teach the true Word of God. This applies today for all of God's called leaders as they are responsible for rightly diving the word of truth (II Timothy 2:15), in both word and in deed according to His Word. This is because Christian leaders and Christians in general lives may be the only Bible others are reading. **Live holy!**

What does it mean to heed the Spirit of God? All believers both leaders and non-leaders adhere to what the Word of God is saying. It is imperative for all believers who have accepted Christ as his or her personal Savior to separate his or herself from the world, and have the indwelling Holy Spirit living inside who speaks to our consciousness of God's Will.

Listen, the Spirit of God is speaking.

July 31

Salvation In Jesus Christ: Matthew 19:24; James 3:5

.....I say unto you, it is easier for a camel to go through the eye of a needle than for a rich man to enter into the kingdom of God.

Today's discussion is focused on dealing with setting priorities as they relate to earthly and heavenly wealth, a rich young rule approached Jesus with the question, "What good thing shall I do, that I may have eternal life"? First, ones salvation is not based on being good and there is no amount of good that will earn salvation. Salvation is a gift from God through faith in Jesus Christ. All who are saved must accept Jesus as his or her personal Savior. James 3:5 tells us that it is not by the works of our righteousness that we have done but according to the mercy of God who saved us. The Holy Spirit takes us and washes us clean and makes us new creatures in Christ. It is noteworthy to say that if good works would save, then all under the OT law would have been saved because they would have had the ability to keep the law. **Not so!** It required Jesus Christ to keep and fulfill the law of God.

Second, when the young man was asked to depart with his possessions he left sad because his primary priorities were earthly wealth. Also, he wanted eternal life on his terms. Jesus made it plain that earthly possessions and good works are insufficient for eternal life (v.24). Matthew 6:33 encourages all to seek God and His righteousness first as this is our first priority and everything else will be added.

Rich or poor Jesus comes first!

God's Plan For His People

Aug 1

Outpouring Of God's Spirit: Joel 2: 28-29

And it shall come to pass afterward, that I will pour out my spirit upon all flesh; and your sons and your daughters shall prophesy, your old men shall dream dreams, your young men shall see visions.

The prophet Joel prophesied to Judah and Jerusalem. His prophetic ministry is believed to have occurred after the Jewish exiles had returned to Jerusalem and built the temple. During this time there was no king, only spiritual leaders—priests. Another belief is that Joel's prophecy occurred during the early days of King Joash. Regardless of the era of Joel's prophecy, his message was threefold, which were (a) to bring the people together in sacred assembly before the Lord. (b) Exhort the people into repentance and humbly return to God in worship which includes fasting, weeping, mourning and making intercessions for God's mercy. (c) He relayed God's prophetic message to His people when they sincerely repented and turned to Him He would pour out His Spirit on all flesh. **What a joy it is for walking with God?**

Specifically to our discussion text, we see that deliverance follows repentance (vv 18-27) as well as the promised outpouring of the Spirit (vv 28-29). To clearly answer our previous question joy for repentance and walking with God is outlined in verses 18-27 where God promises to provide an abundance of everything that is needed. For example, verse 24 makes the point which states "And the floors shall be full of wheat, and the fats shall overflow with wine and oil." In verse 25 God tells His people that not only will He overflow their supply, but He will restore what has been destroyed.

This brings us to the second part of God's promise to His people through the prophet Joel. This prophetic promise of the coming Holy Spirit is the manifestation of God's Spirit among His people and this promise was fulfilled on the day of Pentecost. This prophecy is an ongoing promise for all who accept Jesus Christ as their Lord and Savior as all believers can and should be filled with the Holy Spirit. Who is the Holy Spirit? The Holy Spirit is the third person in the

Godhead, who lives in each believer.

    In our scripture verse speaks about who God's Spirit will fall upon, "all flesh" and what will happen after receiving the Spirit of God. What will they do? Sons and daughters will prophesy, old men will dream, young men will see visions. Included in receiving the Spirit is laity, non leaders of the church. The question now becomes, what does this say for leaders and laity in the church? All who believe in Jesus Christ have the indwelling Holy Spirit and is commissioned by God to tell others about the goodness of the Lord (Matthew 28:19-20). The day of Pentecost is a perfect example of what does and will happen at the outpouring of the Holy Spirit and believers being filled with the Holy Spirit—lives are changed and souls are saved. What are the results? There will be a harvest of souls for salvation and God's kingdom increases. Other results of the outpouring of the Holy Spirit and His works are (a) He is the agent of sanctification, (b) He is the agent of service that empowers every believer for service and witness, and (c) He is the agent that incorporates every believer into the body of Christ; in doing so the church grows, believers lives are filled, worship is inspired, the mission of the church is directed, the church's righteousness is promoted, gifts are given according to His pleasures, and lastly, the gospel of Christ is guarded.

    God's Spirit lives in every believer.

Aug 2

A Call To Repentance: Joel 2: 11-17

Therefore also now, saith the Lord, turn ye even to Me, with all your heart, and with fasting, and with weeping, and with mourning. And rent your heart, and not your garments, and turn unto the Lord your God; for He is gracious and merciful, slow to anger, and of great kindness, and repenteth Him of the evil.

Discussed in an earlier writing the definition of "a call" was defined as being summoned. The verb form of the word "call" is to be invited to serve the Lord or become His follower.

In today's discussion, we see God calling the nation of Israel to repentance. Sin had caused a divide between God and His people. Through His prophet Joel God was asking Israel to return to Him and be blessed. This call extends to all who is out of the ark of salvation. The call for repentance did not begin with Joel, but was issued by God when Adam and Eve fell from grace with their disobedience to God. However, for one to return to God, the heart must be changed (contrite); meaning one must be sorry for his or her sins and admit his or her sins and be willing to change by confessing his or her sins, and then turn from a life of sin.

In God's call to repentance, His grace and mercy He shows compassion to forgive one for his or her sin. More importantly, His grace and mercy was played out with Christ's death on the cross for the sins of the world. What this means is that man does not have to pay his sin debt, just accept Jesus Christ as Lord and Savior.

The question now becomes, being a believer, have you accepted the call to service in God's kingdom building? Answer the call.

Aug 3

God's Pity Upon His People: Joel 2:17-26

Then will the Lord be jealous for His land, and pity His people.

If we were to define the term pity it would say "loving-kindness, concern, compassion" (Job 19; 21; Matthew 18:33, The Student Bible Dictionary P. 187). From the definition of the word pity, we see all the adjectives describing God for His people.

The question now becomes why was God's pity necessary? **Sin! Sin!** The nation of Israel had continually sinned against God and was punished repeatedly for it. Each generation grew more sinful as do many today, but the first chapter of Joel outlines the devastations that would plague the nation because of their sinful ways. This was the generation of the Israelites who had returned for captivity as a result of sin. Through it all God showed compassion for His people. However, in showing compassion God requires something of all, which is recorded in II Chronicles 7:14. God asks for humility, seek God in prayer and then turn from your wicked ways. God promised that He would hear them in doing so He would reverse His pronounced judgment, then He would heal their land and He would overflow them with His blessings of plenty (18-26).

The question that comes to mind is how does this principle apply in today's society? God's promises are sure and man today must do what is asked of him for we know God has never failed and will continue to keep His Word.

God's concern for His people is witnessed by the indwelling Holy Spirit who will teach us all things if we yield to His instructions.

Instructions From God: Psalm 32:8

I will instruct thee and teach thee in the way which thou shalt go; I will guide thee with mine eye.

What are instructions? Instructions are a set of commands, lessons, orders, and or rules in which to live by, or a manual or procedures that must be followed. For the purpose of this discussion we see God promising to provide a set of instructions for His people and the purpose of these instructions are ethical codes for humanity to live by.

In order for one to adhere to God's instructions one must have a willing and repentant heart, a heart that is teachable, trusting and obedient to His word. As each believer has come to trust God for whom He is and rejoices in His presence, and be willing to be led by His Spirit. What comes to mind are God's moral laws, the Ten Commandments which outline the relationship between man and Himself and man and his fellowman. Then there are the covenants God made with His people and if followed a beautiful relationship between the two is the result with overflowed blessings.

God is worthy to provide instructions to all humanity because He is the creator and sustainer of all that exist both visible and invisible and He knows all. Being that God is our creator and all knowing makes Him our teacher as He wrote the manual for our lives.

Therefore, adhere to God's instructions and live holy lives so that the world may see Him in all believers. God's manual for living is one of righteousness, prudence and obedience to an all wise God.

Obeying God: Deuteronomy 11:1-32

"Therefore, thou shalt love the Lord thy God, and keep his charge, and his statutes, and his judgments, and his commandments always. And know you this day: for I speak not with your children which have not known, and which have not see the chastisement of the Lord your god, his greatness, his mighty hand, and his stretched out arm."

The setting of this text is Moses reminding the children of Israel why it is prudent to obey God. First, the nation of Israel's new generation was reminded that they should love God and obey all that He asks them to do. Second, they were reminded why it was prudent to obeying God and this reminder was in the form of the many acts and miracles He performed in delivering Israel out of bondage to Pharaoh. During their wilderness journey, God fed them without any effort on their part and provided water from a rock and this prevented Israel from having to search for water in dry land—the desert. What was Israel's appreciation? Israel whined and complained which resulted in many dying in the wilderness. A journey that lasted forty years that was designed to last forty days---disobedience and rebellion.

What does this say for obeying God? Disobedience brings chastisement and curses while obedience brings blessings and a fruitful life. Verse 26 brings home the benefits from obeying God. The nation Israel is an example for modern day humanity and the results of each decision we make.

Obedience-blessings, disobedience-chastisement which do you chose?

Aug 6

Living A Holy Life Unto God
1 Thessalonians 3:13; 4:1-12

To the end He may stablish your hearts unblameable in holiness before God, even our Father, at the coming of our Lord Jesus Christ with all His saints.

If the question were raised, how do we live holy lives unto God? To live holy unto God is to obey His ordinances in total obedience and commitment to God. This also means that all who live holy lives are totally dependent on God and His righteousness so the world can see Christ manifested in our lives. Also, living holy lives means that all believers recognize that God's standards are the true measures of righteous living.

Furthermore, living holy lives unto God means that we as believers have separated ourselves from all worldliness and sin. This is because the world is an enemy toward God. Then too, believers are a set aside people, a royal priesthood, a holy nation who have been called out of the world. Believers are a called out people and in the family of God we as believers have been called to do a special service for God which is kingdom building; this is commonly referred to as winning souls for Christ.

Lastly, living holy lives unto God is obeying the great command of love for God is love as well as obeying the great commission issued by Jesus Christ. (Matthew 28:19-20). Most important, living holy lives means that all believers love God and live to please Him as this means believers are the church which is the bride of Christ who must be blameless when He returns.

Holy living is reflective of Christ. Live holy!

Salvation Through Jesus Christ
II Thessalonians 2:13-16

Now the Lord of peace Himself give you peace always by all means. The Lord be with you all.

What is salvation? Salvation is the brining of one safely from harm, or deliverance. Salvation is the deliverance from a life of sin to a life of righteousness which is through Jesus Christ. In the saving process man is redeemed through the blood of Jesus Christ which He shed on Calvary's cross. Then man is justified or acquitted of his sins or made right with God.

The question now becomes, why was man's redemption necessary? Redemption was necessary because of sin which caused a separation from God. Therefore, the divide that existed between man and God required repairing and Jesus Christ is the repairer, which renders Him the way to salvation and back to God our creator. It is noteworthy to say that our salvation is by God's grace which He freely gives through His Son Jesus Christ. However, man must accept the gift of salvation in faith believing that Jesus is God's Son who became the human sacrifice for all humanity.

If the question were raised what happened to those persons who died before Christ's coming? All who died in faith believing that God would deliver on His promise of sending a Savior and who believed would be saved. This principle applies to all believers, past, present and future as John 3:16 is essential to ones faith and with that belief the believer has several assurances of eternal life.

Salvation cannot be earned through our good works because Jesus paid it all.

Aug 8

Children Of God: 1 John 3:1-3, 9-11

Beloved, now are we the sons of God; and it doth not yet appear what we shall be; but we know that, when He shall appear, we shall be like Him; for we shall see Him as He is.

Being called a child of God is one of the highest honors that can be bestowed on a person as it carries with it several connations, which are (1) being a child of God is that the believer has been adopted as God's very own (Ephesians 1:5) which carries with it a privilege of honor and salvation. (2) Being called a child of God is undergirded by our faith in Jesus Christ as Lord and Savior and all believers have placed their trust in God. (3) Being children of God, we become heirs of God and all His riches and glory and co-heirs with Christ (Romans 8:16-17). (4) Being children of God, believers have the indwelling Holy Spirit in each of us as we are being led by God's Spirit. (5) Being children of God we live to please Him and are willing to be disciplined by Him for He is our father. (6) Being children of God we are conformed to the likeness of His Son Jesus Christ which is God's desire. Therefore, the world can see Christ in all believers. (7) Lastly, being children of God means that all believers have been saved and will spend eternity in the presence of God. **What a blessed privilege!**

It is noteworthy to say all humanity must chose between children of God or Satan. However, given the benefits from being in the family of God and that of Satan the choice is clear. What Satan is offering for being in his family is death, destruction and eternal separation from our creator. It is important to remember that Satan's mission is to disrupt the kingdom of God as this battle has been raging since he was thrown out of heaven for wanting to be equal and above God his creator.

God in His provisional care and wisdom made provisions for mankind to become sons of God and provided His Spirit to keep all believers in the family as well as His written Word to live by. His written Word provides clear instructions and the ability for all who believe to know His will. **What a caring Father!**

If the question were raised, How do we know our family members? Other family members are known by their righteous living and the manifestation of Christ in ones life. As all believers emulate God and His righteousness, it means that the believer has turned his or her back on sin and the world as this is a requirement from God. It is important to know that believers cannot say that they are children of God and continue in sin, then truth is not there and this person is living a life of hypocrisy and this is not of God; for God changes not, He is the same yesterday, today and will be the same tomorrow.

It can be concluded then that being a child of God is a forever life changing experience that lasts through eternity. "What a wonderful change since Jesus came into my life."

Aug 9

Chosen By God: 1 Peter 2:4

"To whom coming, as unto a living stone, disallowed indeed of men, but chosen of God, and precious."

Several questions come to mind when reading this verse, and they are who was first chosen by God that men rejected or disallowed? Christ is the living stone who was chosen by God from the foundation of the world to be the head of everything including the church. Why was Christ chosen by God? Christ was chosen by God because Christ was present with God during creation; Christ is the living Word of God for He is God in the second person. Christ was chosen because He was human and divine thus He remained sinless. Christ was chosen because He met all requirements to redeem man back to God the Father. Christ was chosen because He became man's high priest and is now in heaven making intercessions for all believers. Christ was chosen because He is the foundation for which all righteousness is found and built upon. Christ was chosen because He is the head of the church-His bride and upon His return His bride must be pure and holy.

Now that we have established who was chosen and why the choice, the question now becomes, what does this say for mankind? All who believe in Jesus Christ is chosen by God to be in fellowship with Him, to be a holy nation and the bride of Christ—the church.

God's chosen people blessed and highly favored!

Aug 10

Called For A Purpose: Exodus 3:4-10; Romans 8:28

Come now therefore, and I will send thee unto Pharaoh, that thou mayest bring forth my people the children of Israel out of Egypt...And we know that all things work together for good to them that love God, who are the called according to his purpose.

Today's discussion focus is on Moses being called by God to lead the children of Israel out of bondage. The Israelites cried out to God and the scene takes place with God calling Moses from a burning bush. God gave Moses instructions as to what his called assignment would be. Moses has witness first hand the pain and suffering afflicted upon the nation of Israel by Pharaoh. God choose leaders that best fit the designed purpose of God at that time.

At the end of Moses' leadership God had equipped Joshua to begin his leadership of leading the Israelites to the Promise Land. There are many other notables who answered God's call and some are Noah who answered when God told him to build an ark as this was God's method of saving a remnant to replenish the earth after the great flood. The twelve disciples answered the call when "Jesus said follow me." The apostle Paul answered the call after his encounter with Jesus and went on to become a great defender of the gospel. Many today are answering God's call to spread the gospel message of Christ.

All believers are called for a purpose.

Aug 11

Called Out Of Darkness: 1 Peter 2:9

But ye are a chosen generation, a royal priesthood, a holy nation, a peculiar people, that ye should shew forth the praises of him who hath called you out of darkness into his marvelous light.

Our scripture text explains why believers have been called out of darkness, as believers are a set aside people and have been called into the royal family of God. Being that believers are a set aside people believers are viewed as peculiar people to the world. This is because believers no longer conform to the world and its rules as believers' live in harmony with God and has been made a priest before God.

Being in the priesthood and called out of darkness, believers have direct access to God through Christ (3:18; John 14:6; Ephesians 2:18). Believers are obligated to live holy lives and to offer up spiritual sacrifices to God (vv 5, 9; 1:14-17). This includes being a living sacrifice of holy obedience to God (Romans 1:1-2). Believers are to offer petitions and sacrifices of praises to God (Psalm 50:14; Hebrews 13:15). Also, believers are to serve God with his or her whole heart and willing hands (1 Chronicles 28:9; Ephesians 5:1-2; Philippians 2:17). According to Hebrews 13:16, believers are to perform good deeds which include giving of our material goods/possessions to others (Romans 12:13). Lastly, believers' bodies are to be instruments of righteousness and believers are to pray intercessory prayers for others and one another.

Believers are called out of darkness to witness Christ.

Called To Be Sons Of God: 1 John 3:1

Behold what manner of love the Father hath bestowed upon us, that we should be called the sons of God: therefore the world knoweth us not, because it knew him not.

If the question were raised what does it mean to be called sons of God? Being called sons of God means that all believers have been adopted in Christ as His own which is the highest honor and privilege of our salvation (Ephesians 1:5; John 1:12; Galatians 4:7). This is because God is our heavenly Father; He created all mankind and gave His Son Jesus Christ as our redeemer. Therefore, being a child of God is the basis for our faith and trust in God (Matthew 6:25-34). As sons of God we have our hope of a glorious future—spending eternity with our Father. Then too being children/sons of God all believers become heirs of God and co-heirs with Christ (Romans 8:16-17; Galatians 4:7).

With that being said, God through His love and care has instilled His Spirit—the Holy Spirit who resides in each believer reminding him or her of just who they belong to. Therefore, being a child of God leads to the desire to be in intimate fellowship with the Father. More importantly, it is God's desire for all of His children to become more like Him as all believers represent the family of God.

It is noteworthy to say that being called sons of God carries an enormous blessing that the world could never give.

Aug 13

Called Into Fellowship With Christ: 1 Corinthians 1:9

God is faithful, by whom ye were called unto the fellowship of His Son Jesus Christ our Lord.

The term fellowship denotes a like-mindedness, communicates acceptance and it helps believers to grow in Christ. Fellowship also encourages sharing of the work of the church (II Corinthians 8:4). Another point to fellowship is that it denotes a family feeling and a partnership among Christians (Galatians 2:9).

With regards to fellowship with Christ it denotes that all believers are in the family of God, therefore, there is unity among Christians/believers and Christ as all share the mind of Christ. It is noteworthy to say that all believers share in Christ's death, burial and resurrection as we died with Him to sin and rose with Him to a new life of righteousness and holy living. Also, believers are committed to obeying the Great Commission as recorded in Matthew 28:19-20. Being in fellowship with Christ and fellow believers, we are eager to participate in worship services giving praises to His holy name. The joyousness of spiritual fellowship reverberates throughout our local congregation and into the community; in turn the community becomes a faithful community—**all through Christian fellowship**.

Scripture warns believers of the dangers of fellowshipping with unbelievers or wrongdoers. This is because unbelievers are not is fellowship with God and believers run the risk of harming his or her fellowship with Christ.

It can be concluded then that being called into fellowship with Christ is because believers have the mind of Christ and the desire to be with like-minded persons and in the presence of Christ.

Called To Be A Servant: Romans 1:1

Paul, a servant of Jesus Christ, called to be an apostle, separated unto the gospel of God.

Our scripture text outlines just who Paul was as he was an apostle, but most of all Paul was a servant to Jesus Christ just as all believers are servants to the most high God. The life of Paul describes what a true servant is as well as the life of Jesus Christ. Christ made it plain that a true servant is not to be served, but to serve others. Paul enslaved himself to Christ as he preached Christ throughout Asia Minor and established churches as he went. All believers are to exemplify true servant hood through a life of serving others as believers are committed to a life of Christ and His gospel message. Additionally, believers are a called people and have been gifted with a gift of his or her calling by God.

It is noteworthy to say that Christian servants are different from servants in worldly arenas. This is because the world sees things differently than those of Christians. Case in point, the greatest servant of Jesus Christ made no reputation for Himself, He rendered whatever service that was needed in that particular place and time. Christ made no grand announcement of His arrival. His works spoke volume for Him as the crowds grew and His fame spread of His good works of meeting the people's needs.

What does this say for you and I as today's servants? Serve to the glory of God and He will reward His servants.

Servants answer the call!

Aug 15

Called To Live By Faith: Romans 1:17

For thereby is the righteousness of God revealed from faith to faith; as it is written, The just shall live by faith.

What is faith? Faith is our belief, a trust (Habakkuk 2:4; Mark 11:22). Hebrews 11:1 records as "the substance of things hoped for, the evidence of things not seen." Verse 3 further explains faith by stating that it is "through faith we understand that the world was made (framed) by the Word of God." It is through our spiritual eye that we as believers see and believe that there is a God the one who created the heavens and the earth both seen and unseen. It is through faith that the heroes of the Bible moved on God's command and many times not knowing destination or outcome, but trusted God for a blessed end. Noah, Enoch, Abraham and Abel are notables who lived by faith.

Hebrews 10:38 states that "the just shall live by faith", which means the believer's faith is the foundation of his or her beliefs as this faith governs ones relationship with God the Father. It is through faith in Jesus Christ that all who believe are saved. It is through faith that the believer's spiritual realities lead to his or her righteousness which in turn causes the believer to seek God and His goodness. It is through faith the believer perseveres in the face of persecution and is willing to suffer for God and His righteousness. It is through faith the believer performs mighty acts of righteousness through the power of the Holy Spirit. It is through faith the believer hopes in one day seeing God our creator and Jesus Christ our Savior face to face. **What faith!** It is through faith that all believers can live holy and righteous lives that are pleasing to God. It is noteworthy to say that all who live by faith can and will have the Enoch like intimacy with God as God desired Enoch like relationship with His people.

If the question were raised, how can one develop such faith? Faith comes from completely trusting God for who He is and what He has done and continues to do in the lives of mankind. God is the essence of our being from beginning to end. It is in Christ Jesus that we live and breathe. More importantly, it is Christ Jesus that all believers have eternal life. Another thought on developing an unwavering faith is through prayer as prayer is an essential component in the lives of all believers. This is the believer's communication with God.

Another school of thought on developing unyielding faith in God is building a trust in God so that each time trial and tribulations of this world are encountered, believers cast all these situations on God—He cares. Believers must have the confidence in God knowing that if He brings you to a situation He will bring you through the situation. **Trust Him.**

Being that believers called to live by faith our victory is assured in Jesus Christ, therefore, all believers can boldly live for Christ as all are of the royal family of God.

Faith is the key to salvation--Believe.

Aug 16

"Called To Be Saints": Romans 1:7

To all that be in Rome, beloved of God, called to be saints; Grace to you and peace from God our Father, and the Lord Jesus Christ.

What does it mean to be called? First, a calling means that the called has been chosen by God for a special purpose to serve Him in a special way and to be in the royal family of God. Second, all believers have been invited to become followers of Christ—be Christians. Third, being called carries with it special blessings in that God looked beyond our faults and saw the good and our individual abilities to live for Him. Lastly, being called by God all believers are looked upon as saints of God as all believers have been adopted into the royal family of God.

Another connation on being called saints of God is that believers have been set apart from sin and the world and its wickedness to a life of righteousness and have been consecrated for service to God. If the question were raised, what services are believers to perform for God? All believers are to witness Christ the world over. All believers are to obey the great commission as recorded in Matthew 28:19-20 which believers are to teach, preach and baptize in the name of Jesus. Also, believers are to use their God given gifts to edify the body of Christ in preparation for Christ's return for His bride—**the church.**

Lastly, believers being called to be saints are all believers who have been washed in the blood of Jesus Christ and while here on earth to be a light in a sin darkened world.

Believing saints are saved, baptized in the Holy Ghost and Holy Ghost filled for God's purpose.

Aug 17

Called To God's Eternal Glory: 1 Peter 5:10

But the God of all grace, who hath called us unto his eternal glory by Christ Jesus, after that ye have suffered a while, make you perfect, stablish, strengthen, settle you.

The purpose of Peter's writing in 1st Peter was to give hope of a divine and eternal perspective of their lives while here on earth as many were facing opposition for living as Christians. Peter reminds believers suffering for Christ's sake that one day they will be richly rewarded by God as He has called all believers to His eternal glory.

Our chapter text outlines a Christian's life in God's care, as all believers have been called by God to His glory and yes believers may suffer for Christ's sake, but this too has a purpose and that purpose is to make all believers perfect in Christ, establish a union with Him. All believers will be strengthened through the indwelling Holy Spirit all through God's grace that is bound in Jesus Christ.

It is noteworthy to say that Peter also encouraged church leaders/elders to live holy lives before God's people and feed them the Word of God as they have been called in leadership roles. Therefore, leaders and laity are to live holy unto God because He called all believers to His eternal glory.

Glorify God in your calling and become more like Him.

Aug 18

Called To The Marriage Of The Lamb
Revelation 19:7-9

Let us be glad and rejoice, and give honour to him; for the marriage of the lamb is come, and his wife hath made herself ready.

The Lamb's marriage in this setting is Christ coming for His church-His bride which is comprised of baptized believers. The church will be already in heaven with Christ before He returns to earth as she will be taken to heaven during the Rapture. Christ's bride- the church is seen fully clothed in fine linen; dressed waiting for her husband—Jesus Christ. Also, all believing saints who died in Christ will return with Him after the Rapture and will rule with Him during His earthly kingdom here on earth.

What this constitutes is that all believers/saints will be fully clothed in righteousness and will have been delivered from all impurity that sin brings. It is noteworthy to say that all believers make up the true church of Christ as their bodies are the temple of God.

If the question were raised, Why the church is considered the bride of Christ? The church consists of a called body of believers and that no true church exists without the union with Christ and in spiritual fellowship. More importantly, the church as Christ's bride denotes the faithfulness and devotion of the church to Christ and the intimacy of Christ's love for the church. ***What a marriage!***

Will you be at the wedding of Christ and His bride—the church?

Aug 19

Worship Christ-The Lamb: Revelation 19:10

And I fell at his feet to worship him, And He said unto me, See thou do it not; I am thy fellowservant, and of thy brethren that have the testimony of Jesus; worship God; for the testimony of Jesus is the spirit of prophecy.

What is worship? Worship is an expression of praise, giving honor and glory to one who deserves such honor. In this scenario an expression of worship is expressed to Jesus Christ our Lord and Savior. True worship is done in spirit and in truth as God is a spirit and must be worshipped in such fashion.

What does it means to worship God in Spirit and in Truth? The term "In spirit" denotes the level at which true worship takes place and one must come to God with a sincere heart as directed by the Holy Spirit. Another element of worship is truth which is a characteristic of God, incarnated in Christ and intrinsic to the Holy Spirit and lies at the heart of the gospel as recorded in the NT. What this means is that worship must occur according to the truth of God the Father as revealed in the Son Jesus Christ and received by the Holy Spirit---the Godhead involved in true worship.

Worship has been explained and how it should be done, now let us discuss Christ worthiness of worship. First, He is the Savior of the world who was slain from the foundation of the world to man's Savior. Second, Christ is God's Son who was in the beginning with God during creation. Third, Christ became the Word of God who was born of a Virgin and lived sinless before man to be an example for man on righteous living to please God the Father. Lastly, Christ is the Lamb who took away the sins of the world.

Worship Him for He is worthy!

Stand Fast In Christ: 2 Thessalonians 2:15

Therefore, brethren, stand fast, and hold the traditions which ye have been taught, whether by word, or by our epistle.

In Paul's writing to the Thessalonian believers he provides instructions concerning the day of the Lord from different aspects on how to live and what to expect when Christ returns. In verse 3, Paul warns the Thessalonian believers the time would come when there would be a great falling away as he encourages them to refrain from being deceived by "the son of perdition"—the antichrist. The great falling away means that many will depart from the church and or profess any connections with the church because of deception. There will be both moral and theological apostasy during those days.

Therefore, in verse 13-17 Paul outlines his encouragements to the Thessalonian believers in their stand for Christ as only God and His righteousness will last. It is important for all believers both then and now to remember we have victory in Christ as this was won on Calvary's cross. Revelation 19:19-21 records the events of the war where Christ will defeat the antichrist and all the ungodly as this war will end quickly with the antichrist's destruction.

How must believers stand fast in Christ when sin is raging? Believes have the indwelling Holy Spirit to guide, aid and protect all who yield to Him in faith from Satan's demonic tactics. The believer's prayer life is vital on this Christian journey as believers are engaged in a spiritual warfare as all believers are to put on the whole armour of God (Ephesians 6:10-18).

Stand for Christ---victory is assured.

Christ's Return: 1 Thessalonians 5:1-11

For yourselves know perfectly that the day of the Lord so cometh as a thief in the night.

Again in Paul's writings to the Thessalonian believers regard the Day of the Lord and His return for his faithful. Previously Paul had spoken to the Thessalonian believers regarding the Rapture when the church will be taken out of the earth, but in our scripture it is referring to the time when God's final judgment on all who have rejected salvation in Christ. It is during this time period when the enemy of God will be overthrown. Scripture has that time occurring at the end of this age—**the church age**.

Verse 3 has this day occurring when mankind is hoping for peace and safety, the exact occurrence is at best a guess, but believers can be sure that "day" will not overtake them as a thief in the night. This is because believers have been appointed salvation and they will be watchful living in faith, love and righteousness to God through Jesus Christ (v.6). For this all believers will be spared God's wrath. Paul goes on to explain that Christ died for us and regardless of being physically alive or sleeping in our graves when Christ returns all believers will live with Him. Remember scripture tells us that the dead in Christ shall rise upon His return when He comes for His church.

Therefore, believers can take comfort in knowing that being in Christ we have been spared God's final judgment and will spend eternity with Him to rejoice for evermore (vv 11, 16).

Christ's return is certain, be ready when He comes.

Aug 22

God's Love: Psalm 89:1-8

I will sing of the mercies of the Lord for ever; with my mouth will I make known thy faithfulness to all generations.

God's love is expressed in His many acts that show love and His affection for all humanity. The entire Bible is an expression of God's love for humanity. Many have referred to the Bible as one big love story of God expressing His love for mankind.

If one were to recount or reflect on the many expressions of God's love one should begin in creation when man was created in the image and likeness of God and God breathed the breath of life into man. God placed part of Himself into man making him a living soul. God's expression did not stop there, He made provisions for all man's needs and stated very clearly that He would supply all your needs according to His riches and glory through His Son Christ Jesus (Philippians 4:19). God further stated that He did not want man to worry about anything and for him to cast all his cares upon Him (1 Peter 5:7). God served as the nation of Israel as their king and through their rebellious nature God still loved and remain faithful to His people. During their wilderness journey God led the nation of Israel as a cloud by day and a pillar of fire by night. He fed them with manna from heaven and water from a rock. God allowed their shoes to last their entire journey in the wilderness. When man sins became overbearing He still loved mankind and His loving kindness was expressed in His providing for man even while man was an enemy to God. In the words of an OT prophet which states I have drawn you with bands of love. God gave the law for man to live by and keep His statues, but man failed every time.

Despite man's sinfulness, God made provision for him to atone for his or her sins and return to God in sincerity. God established animal sacrifices to atone for man's sins, but was insufficient as animal sacrifices covered over sin and what was required was human sacrifice to do away with sin. Man lacked the ability to pay his sin debt, but God in His love provided the perfect human sacrifice---His

Son. Christ's shed blood on Calvary took away the sins of the world so that all who believe on His name shall be saved and be reunited with God the Father and live in holy union with the Godhead. **What love!**

Who would give all they have to pay a debt they did not owe? Only God would do such a thing all because of His love for humanity and His desire for a restored fellowship with mankind. This fellowship was broken with Adam's disobedience and restored through Christ's death. Lastly, it is God's love that all who believe have salvation and will spend eternity with Him where there will be everlasting peace, joy, worship and praises. The cares of this world will be gone forever.

There is no other love like God's love—agape. It is too wide to go around; too tall to go over; too deep to go under, we just have to come through the door—Jesus Christ.

Aug 23

The Faithfulness Of God: 1 Corinthians 4:9

For I think that God hath set forth us the apostles last, as it were appointed to death; for we are made special unto the world, and to angels, and to men.

The term faithful is defined as true (Proverbs 20:6), steady (Acts 16:15), and even the adjectives dependable and steadfast. Merriam-Webster School dictionary defines faithful as being "full of faith especially in God, steadfast in keeping promises or in fulfilling duties. Steady, firm, and dependable in allegiance or devotion (P. 318).

The common thread from the above definitions of faithful is dependability and the steadiness found in Acts 16:15 speaks of Lydia's conversion due to her faithfulness to God while providing support and service to Paul and his companions. Also, Lydia was a committed worshiper of the Lord.

With that being said we find many accounts of God's faithfulness to His people. God's faithfulness to His people He sent the Messiah—Jesus Christ as promised who would provide salvation to all who believe on Him. God promised eternal life to all believers, this promise too has been kept. God promised to supply all man's needs; again God has faithfully kept His promise. God promised punishment if you disobey, this too has been kept.

Who can find one as faithful as God who has kept every promise made? No one is as faithful as God our creator and sustainer. Therefore, man in obedience to God should be as equally faithful to God and our fellowman. Man's faithfulness shows gratitude to a loving and steadfast God. Believers' rewards for faithfulness are eternal life while unfaithfulness results in eternal separation from God.
Which do you choose!

Aug 24

Draw Near To God: Hebrews 10:19-25

And having a high priest over the house of God; Let us draw near with a true heart in full assurance of faith, having our hearts sprinkled from an evil conscience, and our bodies washed with pure water.

The explanation of these verses tell all believers that Christ is our high priest who is seated at the right hand of the Father making intercession for all believers. Therefore, there is no need for an intermediary because at the cross the priest as the go between was removed. Believers can come boldly to God through Christ with a sincere heart in faith. Believers must believe in the goodness of the Lord and by coming or drawing near to God believers find mercy, grace and God's help (v 1; 4: 16; 7:19). Also, there is salvation, sanctification, and cleansing in drawing near to God (vv 7:25; 14; 22).

It is important to note that drawing near to God through prayer and faith in Jesus Christ is essential to the believer's desire for fellowship with God. What this says about prayer and faith is that the two are inseparable in the believer's Christian walk. It is through prayer that we communicate with God while having faith that He will answer. While having faith it is important to hold fast to our faith without wavering in our beliefs as God sometimes prolongs His answers with not yet, **but stand fast in your faith and remain near to God.**

Anchor in Christ: Hebrews 6:13-20

For when God made promise to Abraham, because He could swear by no greater, He sware by Himself.

What is an anchor? An anchor is an object that is designed to hold something "firmly in place or to secure firmly" Merriam-Webster Dictionary (P. 32). On a spiritual plane the term anchor is referring to Jesus Christ who is all believers anchor. As Christ is the one who holds our salvation firmly in place and this was accomplished through His shed blood on Calvary.

Jesus Christ being God and the immutability of God assures all believers that all promises are kept and salvation is secure and the Faithfull's final destination is guaranteed. This is because we have God the Father who made us, God the Son who saved us, and God the Holy Spirit who keeps us. **What a team working on our behalf!**

It is noteworthy to say that the immutability of God and His promises made to Abraham through the oath of the covenant is the same today as it was in the OT times (vv 18,19). Also, God has proven Himself to be trustworthy and truthful as He cannot lie and what was said through the prophets and written by inspired men many years ago remains true today as these are God's Words. **Our unchanging God!**

It is safe to then say that Jesus Christ is our anchor who has firmly secured all believers place in heaven where all believers will be part of the marriage ceremony. He is the solid rock where all hopes for tomorrow lies and with Jesus all fears are gone.

Jesus Christ our anchor holds!

Aug 26

A Prepared Place For A Prepared People: John 14:1-4

Let not your heart be troubled…in my Father's house are many mansions…I go to prepare a place for you. And if I go and prepare a place for you, I will come again, and receive you unto myself; that where I am, there ye maybe also.

During Jesus' earthly ministry and near the end He was trying to prepare His disciples when He would no longer be present in the flesh with them. Jesus was telling His disciples that He was going back to the Father where in heaven are many mansions prepared for all believers who believe. This is called the household of God—believers' heavenly home. There are rooms enough to accommodate all God's children.

Just as Jesus told His disciples not to be troubled, believers today have the same assurances that Jesus has prepared a place for us. Believers must live with the assurance that one day Jesus will return and receive His faithful to Himself—the church.

What do we know about heaven? We know that it is a place where God lives and joy reigns supreme as it is continuous. Sin is not allowed in heaven, neither is mortality, only immortality and sin free souls who have been washed in the blood of the Lamb—Jesus Christ.

Therefore, Jesus is preparing all who believe for His prepared place—heaven. All believers have been cleansed, sanctified, justified and regenerated so that all will come forth as pure gold.

A prepared people for a prepared place!

Believers Are Living Sacrifices to God: Romans 12:1-2

I beseech you therefore, brethren, by the mercies of God, that ye present your bodies a living sacrifice, holy, acceptable unto God, which is your reasonable service.

Given that Jesus Christ is now seated on the right hand of the Father where He has prepared all believers/Christians heavenly home begs the question what must we do while anticipating His return to take us home? Taken into account all that the Godhead has done and continues to do mankind must do the following; first, all Christians must accept Jesus as Lord and Savior; second, Christians must have a renewed mind to live for Christ. Third, all believers/Christians must present his or her body as a living sacrifice to God as it must be holy, and acceptable to God through our service, dedication and commitment to Him.

An expression of gratitude for God's grace, goodness and mercy is witnessed through our lives of holiness, holy worship and sincere devotion to God. What this means is that believers have separated themselves from the world and no longer conforms to its morals and values. This is because all believers are a consecrated people that have been set apart to a lifetime of worship and services to God.

It is noteworthy to say, believers offer their bodies as living sacrifices to God because all believers have died to sin with Christ and rose with Him and the believer's body are instruments of righteousness and temples where the Holy Spirit resides; for He is God and will not reside in an unholy place.

Believers, live so God can use you in His kingdom building. Make the sacrifice—Christ did.

Aug 28

Be Careful What You Ask For: Matthew 20:20-28

..Jesus answered and said, Ye know not what ye ask. Are ye able to drink of the cup that I shall drink of, and to be baptized with the baptism that I am baptized with? They said unto Him, We are able.

During Jesus' earthly ministry and as His disciples traveled with Him the hunger for position came into play. The Zebedee's mother approached Jesus asking that He give her sons positions where one be seated on His right and the other on the left side of Jesus in His kingdom. Needless to say this mother has no clue of what she was asking of Jesus. If Jesus could have granted her request these men were unworthy because of their sinful nature and lacked the ability to die for humanity's sins. Jesus was the only one found worthy to drink of the bitter cup of salvation as Jesus Christ fulfilled all God's requirements.

The interesting observation here is that when serving God, position should never become and issue or thought because we are all equal in God's eyesight. Just as the disciples suffered many hardships for following Christ so will believers today. Being called to service for God is an honored position within itself. Verses 26-28 gets to the heart of true servant ship and Jesus is the epitome of servant ship without giving thought to position or who He was.

Lastly, asking something of God without regards to the extent of our request can be devastating if granted by God, but thank God for His wisdom and giving what is really needed.

God looked beyond our wants and saw our needs—salvation.

Christian Obligations: Philippians 2:14-18

Do all things without murmuring and disputings:

If the question were raised, What are some Christian obligations? First, according to verse 14 we are to do all things without murmurings and disputing. What this means is to have a pleasant attitude in whatever we as Christians do. Christians are to display joy in the service for the Lord considering what He has and continues to do in the lives of mankind. There is to be no arguments among Christians as we are to love one another as God loves all. Also, Christians are to have the mind of Christ which is to glorify God the Father.

Second, Christians are to be a light in a sin darkened world and this will manifest itself through our daily lives and witnessing Christ to the lost. Third, Christians are to present their bodies as a living sacrifice holy and acceptable to God through our service to Him. Fourth, Christians are to love those who hate us for Christ's sake because the world hated Christ. What benefit is there to love only those who love us? None. Christian growth is seen when we as believers can extend a hand of love to those who despitefully misuse you. What was Christ's stance on the issue? Christ said turn the other cheek and we as Christians are to forgive as God forgave all.

Regarding the issue of love, Christians are commanded by Christ to love because "God so loved the world that He gave His only begotten Son that whosoever believeth on Him shall not perish but have everlasting life" (John 3:16). If God can love that much then why can't you and I love our fellowman that we see daily? Scripture says it is impossible to love God whom we have never seen, but fail to love those we see daily. It is noteworthy to say that love is at the heart of all Christians' obligations.

Christians are obligated to obey God and His commands and one of His commands is that we are to have no other gods before Him and we are to love our neighbors as ourselves. Christians are commissioned by Christ to "go into all the world and teach all nations and baptize them in the name of the Father, Son and Holy Ghost" (Matthew 28:19-20). Christ promised never to leave nor forsake His own, which means in obedience to the commission there is nothing to fear because we have the presence of God through the Holy Spirit.

Lastly, Christians are obligated to persevere in faith until Christ returns for His church. Christians are to remain steadfast in our commitment to Christ and His works. In the words of Paul when he states that the race isn't given to the swift, but to those who endure to the end. What is our end? The Christian end is to see our Savior face to face and be a part of the marriage ceremony---Christ and His church.

Christian obligations are obedience, faith, commitment, dedication and love for all.

Aug 30

Man's Never Ending Supply Source: Philippians 4:19

But my God shall supply all your needs according to His riches in glory by Christ Jesus.

In our scripture text, Paul in his letter to the Philippians believers provides encouragement regarding God meeting all their needs. Like the believers in Paul's day we too sometime need reassuring that God will supply all your needs and from recorded Biblical history as well as personal testimony God has always been faithful to His promise. Throughout the Bible there are many scriptures that talk about God providing for His people and equally as many records with the promised provisions. In God's provisional care He provides for every aspect of human life. He provided for human suffering—a comforter, and our relationship with Him through His Son Jesus Christ and the Holy Spirit. God responds to us in the midst of our afflictions. God ask that we cast all our cares upon because He cares (1 Peter 5:7) and is willing and able to resolve all problems. Exodus 33:14, which states, "And he said, My presence shall go with thee, and I will give thee rest." This scripture supports the fact that God cares and is willing to relieve burdens and resolve problems.

Isaiah 25:4 talks about God being our strength in the time of need, to both the needy and poor. Also, He has been a refuge in a storm, a covering in heat and a warrior in the time of battle.

Whatever you need God's got it and will supply.

A Call To Serve: Ephesians 4:4

There is one body, and one Spirit, even as ye are called in one hope of your calling.

What is a call? According to Zondervan's Pictorial Bible Dictionary (P. 143), the word has over 20 different representations in the Hebrew and Greek text, but it has four different meanings as it relates to our discussion and they are (a) "To speak out in the way of prayer—"Call unto me, and I will answer thee" (Jeremiah 33:3). (b) To name a person or thing—"and God called the light day" (Genesis 1:5). (c) To summon or appoint---"I will call all the families of the kingdom of the earth" (Jeremiah 1:15). (d) To invite men to accept salvation through Christ. Most importantly, a call is by God through the Holy Spirit, and is heavenly (Hebrews 3:1) and holy (II Timothy 1:9). I Corinthians 1:26 and 7:20 use the word in a particular sense, as referring to that condition of life which men (humanity) were when they became Christians.

Given that all Christians/believers have been called by God to serve Him is the basics for being adopted into the family of God and co-heirs with Christ. Additionally, believers are called to service in the kingdom building of God and one day our service record will be read by God. **How will it read?**

Christ is our perfect example of how all believers are to serve which is without reputation seeking only doing the will of the Father.

God And His People

Sept 1

A New Generation Of People: 1 Peter 2:10

Which in time past were not a people, but are now the people of God: which had not obtained mercy, but not have obtained mercy.

Our scripture text is a continuation of verse 9 which speaks to the results of being a chosen people of God. This is because what was lacking in mankind's life prior to accepting Jesus Christ as our personal Savior is now present because of His atoning works at Calvary. All believers then become part of a new generation of people chosen by God to be royal priests, a holy nation that has been called out of darkness and sin into the light of Christ. Believers are to let their "light so shine before men that they may see your good works, and glorify your Father which is in heaven" (Matthew 5:16).

Being members of the new generation of God, all believers are to proclaim the gospel message of Christ the world over and to give praises to His holy name. Believers being members of God's new generation of people are to season the earth/world with their testimonies—righteous living and witness.

What does righteous living mean? Righteous living means that believers as a new generation of people no longer conform to the world and its standards but live by the righteousness of God with the help of the Holy Spirit.

Believers, a new generation of people-chosen by God as His holy nation.

God's Messengers: Mark 1:1-8

As it is written in the prophets, Behold, I send my messenger before thy face, which shall prepare thy way before thee.

The word Messenger is defined as one who brings a word from someone to another. The Bible records that angels were often time messengers of God that delivered messages to His people at different times for different purposes. There were people who served as messengers for God, for example, Judges 3:20 where we find Ehud delivering a message to the king. In 1 John 1:5 we have the word as a message from God that Jesus Christ is God's only begotten Son. Malachi 2:7 records the priest as messengers of God. Malachi 3:1-5 also records God responding to His prophet Malachi of sending the promised Messenger of the Covenant—Jesus Christ.

During the birth of Christ, God used an angel as His messenger to calm the fears and doubts of Mary that she had remained faithful to Joseph as her husband and what Mary was carrying was the works of the Holy Spirit. Angels and the heavenly host made the grand announcement to shepherds abiding in a field of the Savior's birth. At the beginning of Jesus' earthly ministry, God used John the Baptist as His messenger to prepare the way for the coming Christ as Christ's mission were to provide salvation to all who believed.

Is God still using messengers today? Yes, preachers, teachers, evangelists are God's messengers today as each have been called to declare the Word of God.

Are you hearing God's message sent by His messengers? God still speaks through His messengers.

A Way Preparer: Isaiah 40:1-10

The voice of him that crieth in the wilderness, Prepare ye the way of the LORD, make straight in the desert a highway for our God. Every valley shall be exalted, and every mountain and hill shall be made low; and the crooked shall be made straight and the rough places plain.

Verses 3-8 have several implications from a prophetic point of view; what readily comes to mind is John the Baptist the forerunner of Jesus Christ as he preached repentance to his hearers. However, some implications in these verses refer to the restoration of the Jews from exile as they had been in captivity for seventy years due to sin and rebelling against God. The second implication points to the coming Messiah and His salvation to all who believe. The third implication points to the consummation of redemption in the new heaven and the new earth.

Another point of view on our topical discussion is that Isaiah and his prophetic ministry was trying to prepare the exile Jews for the future blessing that was waiting for them upon returning to their homeland and to provide comfort for them while in exile. A broader message was the glory of God was soon to be revealed and all flesh would see it—this was Jesus Christ in the flesh.

Life is limited, frail and weak, but eternal life lasts forever. God's promises shall be fulfilled, and His redemptive truth cannot be annulled. Listen to God the way preparer!

Sept 4

The Messenger's Message: Isaiah 40:6-12

O Zion, that bringest good tidings, get thee up into the high mountains; O Jerusalem, that bringest good tidings, lift up thy voice with strength; lift it up, be not afraid; say unto the cities of Judah, Behold your God...the Lord God will come with strong hand, and his arm shall rule for him; behold, his reward is with him, and his work before him.

After God has answered Isaiah's question as to what to say, Isaiah is told why he was instructed to tell the people that God's Word will last forever. Knowing God's Word lasts forever provides joy, comfort, strength and reasons to shout with victory because the Lord Jesus Christ is coming again with strength and power. He will rule with His supreme power and might, yet with the tenderness of a caring shepherd who tends His lamb—humanity with love and mercy.

In verse eleven, Isaiah paints a vivid picture of Christ's care for His people, and this is the main message Isaiah was to convey to God's people; mainly the Jews during his prophecy. However, this message remains true today.

Therefore, today's messengers are to proclaim God's message of salvation just like Isaiah and other prophets have.

God's salvation invitation remains open and His return is eminent for His faithful people.

Sept 5

God's Promised Messiah: Malachi 3:1-5

..I will send my messenger, and he shall prepare the way before me; and the Lord, whom ye seek, shall suddenly come to his temple, even the messenger of the covenant, whom ye delight in; behold, he shall come, saith the Lord of hosts.

During Malachi's day evil was rampant and some people were asking where is the God of judgment (2:17)? The people had heard of the promised Messiah as well as there would be God's messenger preparing the way for the coming Messiah. God's longsuffering does not mean that He tolerates sin, but it is His desire for sinners to repent and turn to Him and His righteousness. His reassurance is found in our scripture text that answers all skeptics regarding the Lords' return and will judge all unrighteousness.

As promised before the Messiah John the Baptist the forerunner appeared on the scene preaching repentance as he was preparing the way for the Lord—Jesus Christ. Jesus Christ is the promised Messiah who came and brought salvation to all who believed. The second part of this prophecy will be fulfilled at Christ's second coming as He is the messenger of the covenant. At Jesus' second coming He will purify (v.3) and judge (v.5) Israel and He will purge all of the wickedness in the land and only the righteous will remain (Isaiah 1:25; Ezekiel 22:17-22).

If the question were raised, who is Israel in this scenario? Israel is God's chosen people both Jews and Gentile who have accepted Jesus as their personal Savior and remain faithful until the end. In other words, Israel is all believers who is the righteous bride of Christ—the church.

Let's look at each of these messengers in our text first; Malachi is God's messenger speaking to the nation of Israel saying "fear not because God will punish sin in His due time. The second messenger is John the Baptist who was preparing the hearts of man for Christ's earthly ministry. Third, Christ Himself is God's messenger who came to redeem man back to the Father and will ultimately return with all

God's chosen people to rule this earth with power and glory.

It is noteworthy to say from all recorded biblical history and living proof God's promises are with certainty to be fulfilled. If wrath is promised it is sure to come, when blessings are promised, they too are granted. A Savior was promised Jesus came. Salvation was promised His gift is available accept the gift and have eternal live.

Now that we know God's promises are sure, persevere in faith for God will reward the faithful and punish the unfaithful.

Sept 6

John Preaches Repentance: Matthew 3:4-11

I indeed baptize you with water unto repentance; but He that cometh after me is mightier than I, whose shoes I am not worthy to bear; He shall baptize you with the Holy Ghost, and with fire.

Thus far we have discussed God preparing the hearts and minds of His people for the promised Messiah—Jesus Christ. During God's preparatory period He sent many messengers telling the people to repent and remain faithful because His promised Messiah was coming.

From our study text the Messiah—Jesus was to begin His earthly ministry and the people's minds needed cultivating. A farmer who is preparing his fields for planting, the fields must be cultivated, which is turning over the soil and softening it in preparation to receive the seeds. This was John's role in preparing the way for Jesus as he was the cousin of Jesus preaching repentance who was sent by God to prepare the way for Jesus. The seed in this scenario is the Word of God. John's message of repentance was to admit that you are a sinner, confess your sins and then turn to the Lord. John told his hearers that he would baptize them with water, but the one coming after him would baptize them with the Holy Spirit and this baptism would give them the ability and greater powers to live and witness Christ and His message.

God's messengers are still cultivating the hearts and minds of His people, therefore, these questions come to mind. Are you ready to receive the Word of God? Are you ready for true repentance? Hear God's messengers as they preach repentance and be saved.

Salvation is free.

Identifying Christ: Matthew 3:11-17

And lo a voice from heaven, saying, This is my beloved Son, in whom I am well pleased.

Identification devices are for the purpose of identifying someone or the person has someone to speak for them. This is the case in our study text as many saw Jesus as an ordinary son of a carpenter, but He was more than just a man. He was God in the flesh both God and human.

Jesus had been prophesied for many years, yet when He came many failed to recognize Him for who He was. Also, Jesus being baptized by John the Baptist His forerunner fulfilled prophecy in several ways/reasons, which are (a) "to fulfill all righteousness (v.15), as the fullness of time had come that God had sent forth His Son to be Savior of the world (Galatians 4:4-5). (b) Jesus was identifying Himself with sinners who needed a Savior and He was the Messiah sent by God the Father to save mankind. (c) Lastly, Jesus' association with John the Baptist as a fulfillment of prophecy in Isaiah 40:3 and Malachi 3:1.

Verse 17 makes a profound identification as to who Jesus was as all members of the Godhead met together at Jesus' baptism. The sight to behold is Jesus the Son coming up out of the water, God the Holy Spirit descending upon His shoulders in the form of a dove and God the Father speaking from heaven identifying Jesus as His Son.

There can be no greater identification than being identified by God saying "this is my beloved son in whom I am well pleased." **What identification!**

Restoring God's People: Hosea 1:1-11

The shall the children of Judah and the children of be together, and they shall come up out of the land; for great shall be the day of Jezreel

In today's topical discussion God uses the prophet Hosea and his marriage to paint a vivid picture of His relationship with Israel. Throughout scripture God is seen as the husband wooing His bride-His chosen people and in the NT Christ is the head of the church who is His bride. With that being said, God's chosen people are to be of purity and worship only Him. However, in our scripture text we see the nation of Israel turning from God to idol worship and God used the naming of Hosea's three children in getting His message across to Israel as God would soon pronounce judgment on the nation. He allowed them to be scattered and held in captivity for a long period of time.

Verse 6 states that God would have no mercy on His people as well as in verse 6 when God tells the nation that they are no longer His people, but in verse 7 God promises to save the southern Kingdom-Judah because at that time they were remaining faithful to God under the leadership of King Hezekiah. What does this say for all who remain faithful to God? Regardless of your surrounding situations, God will protect you.

Verse 11 brings home the point of God restoring His people because in the final day He will bring all believers together under one kingship—Jesus Christ as every knee shall bow and every tongue shall confess that Jesus is Lord.

What restoration!

Sept 9

Christ Our Incarnated Savior: John 1:10-14

He was in the world, and the world was made by Him, and the world knew Him not.

The word incarnation means in "the flesh", which describes Christ as He took on flesh and became human (Philippians 2-5-9). What this means is that humanity and deity were united together in Christ. Being born as man He dressed Himself in all humanity's limitations and experiences. It is noteworthy to say that Christ's beginning began long before His earthly appearance. He was present during creation as "all things were made by him" (v.2).

If the question were raised, Why was it necessary for Jesus to come as man? There are several reasons for Jesus coming as man; one, previously God had spoken to His people through the prophets, two, now God was speaking through His Son who is the final revelation of God. Three, Jesus met all the necessary requirements to restore the broken fellowship between God and man that resulted from sin. Throughout Christ's earthly days He remained sinless even unto the cross.

Lastly, during His earthly ministry many recognized Him as the promised Messiah and believed while many did not and were lost. In many of His messages He provided authentication that He was the promised Messiah through signs and miracles.

The incarnated Christ came to provide salvation to all who believe all because of God's grace and mercy. He is the Passover Lamb!

Sept 10

God's Power And Wisdom: 1 Corinthian 1:17-31

But unto them which are called, both Jews and Greeks, Christ the power of God, and wisdom of God.

In Paul's letter to the Corinthian church he makes a profound comparison between the power and wisdom of God and that of the world. It is through the foolish preaching of the cross all men are saved who believe. The wisdom of this world is foolishness with God because the world feels that humanity is the highest order of authority and with this kind of wisdom humanity will never come to know God for who He really is and what He has done and continues to do in the lives of all mankind. Preaching the crucified Christ is foolish to the world because it lacks the ability to conceive the magnitude of God's love for mankind that He would give His only Son to take on the sin-debt of man.

Verses 25-29, Paul expounds of the fact that God has chosen the foolish things because His strength and wisdom far exceeds that of man as His moral and standards differ from those of the world. It is noteworthy to say that it is by God's standards the world will be judged.

The question now becomes, will all humanistic philosophies, psychologies and other worldly systems last an eternity? Absolutely not, because God said in His word that His word will stand when all else passes away. If the world looks upon things as wise, then choose the foolishness of God because through Christ Jesus we have wisdom, righteousness, sanctification and redemption unto salvation.

Be wise choose God.

Sept 11

Wisdom A Gift From God: 1 Corinthians 2:6-16

Howbeit we speak wisdom among them that are perfect; yet not the wisdom of this world, nor of the princes of this world, that come to nought.

What is wisdom? According to the Student Bible Dictionary (P. 249) "wisdom is understanding, knowledge gained by experience (2 Chronicles 9:23; 1 Corinthians 1:17), a gift of God (James 1:5). Wisdom is a characteristic of God."

There are several books of the Bible that talk at length about wisdom and the benefits of having wisdom. King Solomon is known throughout biblical history as being the wisest man to ever lived, simply because he asked God for wisdom over material things. With that being said having understanding is more precious than gold because with understanding comes knowledge.

Another school of thought on wisdom is being a characteristic of God because His wisdom surpasses all. Also, believers who gain wisdom come into the knowledge of God and sees things as He sees them. Lastly, wisdom allows all to make wise use of our knowledge.

A truly wise person obeys God and leans not to his or her own understanding and allows God to direct his or her paths Proverbs 3:5-6. Another point of view on being wise is trusting in God with ones total being as this person recognizes who God is as He is the essence of our being from beginning to end.

Given the opportunity to select a gift from God which would you choose wisdom and knowledge or material goods? Given the gift of wisdom, how will you use your gift?

Spiritual Gifts of the Body: 1 Corinthians 12:4-11

But the manifestation of the Spirit is given to every man to profit withal.

Much has been written, talked and discussed regarding spiritual gifts of the body of Christ, as every believer has been gifted with at least one gift from God and given the responsibility to use his or her assigned gift to the edification of the body of Christ.

If we were to apply a theological definition of spiritual gifts we would find that some scripture verses support a definition as being an endowment or abilities or powers that come from God (1 Corinthians 7:7) to each individual. 1 Peter 4:11 states "If any man speak, let him speak as the oracles of God; if any man minister, let him do it as of the ability which God giveth; that God in all things may be glorified through Jesus Christ, to whom be praise and dominion for ever and ever. Amen." This verse supports how our spiritual gifts are to be used; self promotion is not an option. Since spiritual gifts come by the grace of God (Romans 1:11), Why not glorify the one who gave it? These gifts make for good works as we are God's workman (Ephesians 2:10) and through our good works men will know who we are. It is recorded that special gifts have been given to certain persons for special and or specific tasks. Case in point, God called His prophets to speak for Him to the people. Today preachers are to preach the Word of God to His people.

There are many other spiritual gifts that are utilized in and through the church that edifies the body—the church. Some of those gifts are serving others in the way of ushering/being a door keeper, nursing-providing aid when needed, the spiritual gift of singing—all to God's glory. Many have been given the gift of speaking in unlearned tongues, the gift of healing, the gift of prophecy, the gift of discernment (wisdom), and the gift of prayer, but most of all, all believers are gifted with the gift of love as it is the embodiment of God. It is noteworthy to say that all gifts are given by God and distributed by the Holy Spirit according to the will of God (Hebrews 2:4).

If the question were raised, How does one know if manifested gifts are from God knowing that Satan is on the prowl? First, these gifts are distributed by the Holy Spirit and involve both inward motivation and the power to perform the ministry as the Holy Spirit operates in all believers for a common good. Second, testing gifts by doctrinal truths authenticates the gift.

Let's close today's discussion with these questions, What gift has God given you and how often are you using that gift as His workman? In using your gift is God being glorified?

Use your gifts.

Different Members of the Body: 1 Corinthians 12:12-31

For as the body is one, and hath many members, and all the members of that one body, being many, are one body, so also is Christ.

Continuing our discussion on the spiritual gifts of the body by comparing ones body to the many parts that Paul so eloquently outlines in our scripture text.

Verse 13 states that there is only one Spirit who baptizes each believer in the body of Christ at conversion. It is at conversion each believer is given his or her spiritual gift for in his or her edification works.

Let's take a look at our physical bodies and visualize them on a spiritual plane; each body has one head and on the head there are two pair of eyes and ears both having different functions. Let us continue on with the body, there are two arms, two legs and feet and there are many other parts on the outside of the body that make it function. This is to say nothing of the many internal organs that comprises the internal part of the body and each functioning as God designed.

On a spiritual plane Christ is the head of the church, and pastors are His under shepherds of the church. In each church there is the pastor, deacons, trustees, ushers, choir, teacher and many other ministerial gifts that make up the church each functioning as gifted by God.

All believers are members of the body of Christ serving in different capacities.

Redeemed Through The Blood: Colossians 1:14

In whom we have redemption through His blood, even the forgiveness of sins:

In a bit of a reflective mode one can see the power of the blood as well as the significance it plays in all life forms. It was Jesus' blood that was shed on Calvary in the purchasing process of humanity's sins so that all who believe on Him will be ransomed from darkness into light where believers will be united with Christ and His kingdom.

Let us take a further look at the blood as it was a key element in the OT sacrificial system to atone sin. In the NT it was Christ's blood that made a one-time atonement for sin and opened the door to salvation. During the OT sacrifices the blood of a sinless animal was required as this was a representation of the perfect sacrifice to come—Christ.

Christ's blood is the essential concept of redemption in the NT as Christ's blood accomplished the following (a) forgave sin, (b) ransomed all believers, (c) justified all believers, (d) cleanses all believers, (e) sanctified all believers, (f) made a direct path to God through Him so that all who come will find God's grace, (g) guarantees all promises of the new covenant that replaced the old covenant, and (h) it has saving, reconciling and purifying power to all believers who come to God through Him.

There is power in the blood of Jesus-eternal life giving power!

Sept 15

The Beatitudes: Matthew 5:3-12

Blessed are the poor in spirit; for theirs is the kingdom of heaven.

Today we will look at what has been come to be known as the beatitudes and their meanings as they relate to believers.

First, the word blessed is the happiness or well-being of God's people in a world marred by sin. Believers experience this happiness through the indwelling Holy Spirit who over flows our cups with joy and God's love. Second, the phrase "poor in the spirit" is the realization that we as believers lack the ability to be spiritually self-sufficient and need the Holy Spirit's power and sustaining grace if we are to inherit the kingdom.

Third, the phrase "they that mourn" means we as believers grieve because of our own weakness as it relates to God's standards of righteousness. Also, believers are so united with God that we too grieve the things that grieves God. Fourth, the phrase "hunger and thirst after righteousness" means that believers have such desire for the Word of God until there is a constant quest for feeding. This is because His Word gives us His right standards for holy living. Fifth, the phrase "the merciful" means that believers have compassion on the less fortunate. Sixth, the phrase "the pure in heart" means that believers' hearts have been purged of all manner of deceit and replaced with love and honesty. Seventh, the phrase "the peacemakers" means that believers are no longer enemies of God, but are at peace with Him which was made possible by Christ and the cross. Lastly, the phrase "persecuted for righteousness sake" means all believers who refuse to compromise on godly principles and standards will face rejection by the world.

Live godly principles and be blessed.

Sept 16

Christian Conduct: 1 Peter 3:8-15

Not rendering evil for evil, or railing for railing; but contrariwise blessing; knowing that ye are there unto called, that ye should inherit a blessing.

What is conduct? Conduct is how one carries one self. Our scripture verses outline the proper conduct Christians should exhibit and some of the attributes of Christian conduct is for all to be of one mind having compassion for one another in Christ-like compassion. Other attributes of Christian conduct is that believers refrain from doing evil for evil; believers replace evil with good this includes evil speaking, thoughts and deeds.

There are several daily principles in displaying Christian/Christ-like conduct so the world will see Christ manifested in all believers, and they are (a) believers are sons of God, (b) believers are to be light in a sin darkened world, (c) believers are to live holy lives in imitation of Christ, (d) believers are new creatures in Christ who have been redeemed by the blood of Jesus, (e) believers are messengers for Christ, (f) believers have the desire to live as to please God, (g) believers seek peace at every opportunity and avoid evil, and (h) believers have and display Christ-likeness to one another.

With that being said, several questions come to mind, How does the world see you? Are you seen as a Christian or a member of the world? Is Christ-like love and humility being displayed in our daily routine? If Christ came today, what would He say about your conduct?

Believers, "be ye all of one mind, having compassion one of another" most important, have a mind that is stayed on Christ.

Christian conduct is one of good character

Sept 17

Harmonious Living Among God's People
Romans 12:14-21

..If thine enemy hunger, feed him; if he thirst, give him drink; for in so doing thou shalt heap coals of fire on his head.

What does it mean to live in harmony with one another? To live in harmony with one another each person must be at peace within his or herself as the definition of harmony means to be at peace, on accord or agreement.

The question now becomes, How does one obtain inner peace? To have inner peace one must have a right relationship with God, self and then others. Because peace is the absence of conflict and believers are no longer in conflict with God nor an enemy of God. When each individual comes to terms with the fact that God is our creator and sustainer, He then becomes our Savior then humanity is at peace with self and others. Being in harmony/peace with God brings the highest blessing from Him. It is noteworthy to say that God is a God of peace and not confusion.

Another school of thought on harmonious living among God's people is that when each person has peace then this peace reverberates throughout the community thus rendering a community in harmony with one another and God. **What a blessed community!**

Our scripture text outlines the essence of harmonious living which answers the question am I my brother's keeper? Yes in that all believers are to provide need when required and love and compassion always just as Christ did regardless of social status or ethnicity.

Blessings abounds man and community in harmony- live in harmony and be blessed.

Sept 18

An Exhortation To Love: Romans 12:9-12

Let love be without dissimulation, abhor that which is evil, cleave to that which is good. Be kindly affectionate one to another with brotherly love; in honour referring one another.

Why is love so important in the lives of all believers and why are all believers exhorted to love? First, God is love and to be in the family of God, believers are to love as each manifest the godliness of our heavenly father. Second, believers have the God-given ability and desire to love as God's love made this possible through the indwelling Holy Spirit. Third, believers are exhorted to love because all believers have been set aside for a purpose which is to live holy before God. Fourth, believers are exhorted to love because the love command was issued by Christ Himself and in obedience to our Savior we love everyone. Fifth, there is righteousness in love because righteousness is of God and believers are of God. It is God's righteous standards that all believers will be judged-love and be right. Sixth, believers are exhorted to love as believers are new creatures in Christ where love is the core. Lastly, it was love that made salvation possible. **Love and be loved.**

These questions come to mind, given that our salvation is predicated on love, How do you love? Do you love unconditionally?

Unconditional love is fundamental to the Christian walk. Love as God loves!

The Great Separation: Matthew 25:31-46

And He shall set the sheep on the right, and the goats on the left.

Our scripture verses look forward to a time when the Lord will pronounce judgment on all nations and He will separate the unrighteous from the righteous. Notice where the sheep (righteous) and the goat (unrighteous) are placed in respect to God right and left. The righteous are placed on the right hand of the Lord while the goats are on the left to be eternally cast into the lake of fire.

What's so significant about this separation is that the righteous lived by God's holy standards and fed, visited, clothed and gave water to the least of God's children as the righteous looked beyond the fault of the needy and provided what was needed just as Jesus did while here on earth. Also, the righteous recognized that all need God's grace and mercy that He willingly provides because of His love and desire that all be saved and spend eternity with Him. Another point to the righteous is that they displayed the agape love of God to all without respect of person. The righteous' display of their love and compassion is an outward expression of their true faith and salvation while knowing God would reward them in the end. James 2:14-17 talk's about works without faith is dead, but because of our faith we do good works.

With that being said, the question now becomes, What is James 2:14-17 really saying? Those verses are saying that true faith must be active and enduring as it is the ingredient that shapes our existence and with the indwelling power of the Holy Spirit believers have the ability to persevere to the end and be counted righteous before God.

What is the righteous reward for enduring faith? The righteous will be placed on the right hand of God and will spend eternity with Him while the unrighteous will suffer a different fate. The righteous will be with Christ when He returns to earth to begin His earthly reign.

It is safe to say that the great separation will occur after the tribulation and the church have been taken out of the world and preaching, teaching Christ as well as living holy lives for Him will require a steadfast faith in Him.

What does this say for believers today who are determined to show forth their faith through good works? It says that a service record is being kept in heaven and one day will be read and all will have to give an account of his or her stewardship. Also, the date of Christ's return is unknown, therefore, all mankind is to live if Christ's return is today—be ever ready.

The righteousness of God's standards are currently under attack by Satan from many different directions until ones faith is being challenged, but hold fast to the profession of your faith.

Living faithful or unfaithful lives according to God's standards will determine whether man is separated as sheep or goat.

Which do you choose?

Sept 20

Blessed By God: Numbers 6: 22-27

And they shall put my name upon the children of Israel; and I will bless them.

The setting for today's discussion is during Israel's wilderness journey and God instructed Moses to have Aaron speak to the people to what is known as the Aaronic benediction imparting God's blessing.

The blessings outlines in our scriptures are God's response to His people continued purity in the congregations and their heart-felt devotion to Him. Other aspects of these blessings were that blessing denotes protection from evil forces that would befall the nation of Israel as well as believers today. Also, it represents the presence of God as His face would shine upon His people. His grace, love and mercy would be poured out upon them. The greatest blessing of all is salvation for all who believed and remained steadfast in their beliefs. These blessings remain true for all believers today.

Recorded biblical history records God's faithfulness to keep His promises as seen through the lives of the nation of Israel as well as through the lives of heroes of the Bible. When they obeyed God's commands and lived according to His statues they were blessed. When Israel disobeyed punishment followed; this same principle applies to all mankind today.

If the question were raised, Which blessings carry the most value man or God's? It goes without saying that blessings from God are most valuable because His blessing is predicated on God's unconditional love; whereas man's blessing is conditional, temporal and uncertain.

Invest in a sure thing, remain faithful to God and be forever blessed.

Saved To Do God's Will: Matthew 7:21-23

Not every one that saith unto me, Lord, Lord, shall enter into the kingdom of heaven; but he that doeth the will of my Father; which is in heaven.

Man was created in the image and likeness of God to be in fellowship with Him. As a result of sin, and the disobedience of Adam that fellowship was broken and required repair. God in His desire for a harmonious relationship with man provided salvation through His Son Jesus Christ all predicated on His love.

Jesus Christ in total obedience to His Father went to the cross providing salvation for all humanity who believes will live holy lives unto God.

What is the will of God? The Will of God can be defined as "the law of God" and living in total obedience to His moral statues. These laws usually mean God's instruction which includes the entire Word of God for holy living. God has a perfect will and a permissive will; His perfect will is what God desires for all mankind and His permissive will is what He allows to happen.

How do we know and respond to the Will of God? God left His written Word (the Bible) and spoken word so all mankind will know His Will and respond positively. Communicating with God through prayer is critical to our knowing and living in perfect submission to the will of God.

Christ is our perfect example of knowing and doing the will of God. There are many blessings from knowing and doing the will of God.

Believers are saved to live holy lives unto God.

Sept 22

Serving God Against All Odds: Matthew 20: 17-28

Today's lesson setting takes place in Jerusalem during Christ's earthly ministry as Jesus knew His time was nearing the end. During this time Jesus taught His disciples an important lesson regarding serving and being a servant as He shared with His disciples that He would be betrayed and eventually lay down His life for mankind.

It was during this setting the mother of two of Jesus' disciples came to Him requesting positions for her sons, without regard to what she asked as they lacked the ability to go to the cross for man's sins.

It is noteworthy to say that many of Christ's disciples went on to suffer many hardships for preaching Christ. After Christ's crucifixion they hid for their personal safety, but their desire to witness Christ never ceased as they were dedicated to obeying Christ's commission recorded in Matthew 20:19-20. Paul is a great example of serving God in the midst of persecution. He was beaten, bound and thrown in prison, but continued to preach Christ.

These questions come to mind, Are you willing to witness Christ in the face of persecution? Are you willing to give your life for Christ's sake? Are you willing to travel to a foreign land to preach/teach and witness Christ? If our freedom to worship and serve God is removed, What will you do? Will you meet secretly in your homes or hidden caves to worship and serve God?

Obstacles are no excuse for not serving God!

Sept 23

Greatest In The Kingdom: Matthew 18:3-6

Whosoever therefore shall humble himself as this little child, the same is greatest in the kingdom of heaven.

This question was asked of Jesus, Who is the greatest in the kingdom of heaven? Given the humility which Christ displayed from His birth to death makes this question seem strange, but considering the position mind set of man as well as lacking full understanding of heaven and its make-up the question is reasonable.

In verse 3, Jesus provides the answer by stating, "Verily I say unto you, Except ye be converted, and become as little children, ye shall not enter into the kingdom of heaven." What this verse means is that becoming as little children denotes "humility, unpretentious, dependent, weak, teachable and willing to trust God" (JKV commentary). To further expound on this verse and what Jesus meant is that children are totally dependent on their parents to supply all their needs. Little children willingly follow their parents' instructions and are teachable, because little children have willing hearts. It is noteworthy to say that God has no respecter of persons, meaning all are the same in God's eyesight. Therefore, all who enters heaven will have child-like humility and are on one accord-worshipping and praising God.

This child-like attitude begins at conversion as the heart has been convicted by the Holy Spirit and is ready to receive God's gift of salvation. Through the sustaining works of the Holy Spirit all believers are humbly submitted and dedicated to a new life in Christ.

Christ in His greatness served from a position of humility—believers do likewise.

Sept 24

"The Last Shall be First": Matthew 19:30

But many that are first shall be last; and the last shall be first.

What is the true meaning of this verse? In this setting Jesus was addressing the issue raised by Peter when Peter stated that they had forsaken all to follow Jesus and wanted to know what would they have threefold? In Jesus' parabolic teaching used first and last to get His point across to Peter regarding status in the kingdom.

The first in our scripture verse are those persons with positions of wealth, education, status, and talents and are held in high esteem by the world and even the church. The last are the unknown of the world and many unknowns of the world will be exalted in the end. This is because God values sincerity, love and purity of the heart because in the heart is where the truth lies. It is not how much one gives, but the motive in which it is given. Serving and giving is for God's glory, not self-aggrandizement.

How do you give and to what extreme are you willing to give knowing that God promised to supply all your needs.

The story of the widow's mite when she gave her last in the midst of the wealthy giving from their abundance as God viewed the widow's giving more valuable than that of the rich; because she gave sacrificially.

God values the humble and sincere hearts as He and the world values positions and service differently.

Sept 25

The Barren Fig Tree: Matthew 21:18-22

And when He saw a fig tree in the way, He came to it, and found nothing thereof, but leaves only, and said unto it, Let no fruit grow on there henceforward for ever. And presently the fig tree withered away

Today's lesson text is in the proximity of Bethany after Jesus had cleansed the temple of money changers. On His way back to the city Jesus saw a fig tree filled with leaves giving a false sense that there was edible fruit, but upon closer examination there was no fruit. This angered Jesus and He cursed the tree and it immediately withered.

To further this discussion, let's draw an analogy of the fig tree and some religions and believers. The analogy is that many say they are Christians and have all the outward appearances, but upon closer examination there is no fruit as the fruit of the spirit is love, joy, peace, longsuffering, gentleness, goodness, faith, meekness and temperance (Galatians 5:22). True fruit bearing trees are filled with all the fruits of the spirit as a tree is known by the fruit it bears. Where there is love hate cannot reside as this tree is a replica of God's love for humanity. Where there is joy, sorrow is removed. Where there is peace, confusion is dispelled as a tree of peace has the peace of God and it leaves waves with His mercy. Where temperance resides, no restraint is evicted. Where goodness rules decency, honesty, and virtue is the order of the day. A tree that bears the fruit of faith is one whose leaves display confidence, trustworthiness, and a conviction to live for Christ so the world will know this is a tree living on God's grace.

Which tree are you?

Sept 26

I Will Take You For My People: Exodus 6:7

And I will take you to me for a people, and I will take you a God; and ye shall know that I and the Lord your God, which bringeth you from under the burdens of the Egyptians.

What does this verse mean? God is essentially speaking to the young nation of Israel as they had been in bondage to Egypt and their hard task master Pharaoh. The Israelites cried out to God for deliverance and He heard their cry.

God promised to redeem them and would be their God and they would be His people and Israel was to promise to obey the will of God. Also, God was remembering His covenant promise to the patriarchs, Abraham, Isaac and Jacob. God kept His promise whether it was four, forty or 400 years later. This speaks to God's faithfulness both then and now. God promised mankind a Savior and forty-two generations later Jesus came. **What a promise keeper!**

Additionally, by taking Israel as His people through deliverance God was taking ownership as a transfer was being made from the nation itself to God, not to mention He is the creator of all humanity. The redemption of Israel from Egypt's bondage was significant to a far greater redemption from the bondage of sin through the blood of Jesus Christ.

God's ownership of Israel through His redemptive powers parallels that of Jesus Christ for all humanity by accepting Jesus as Lord and Savior all believers become people of God. Therefore, the above statement has a profound meaning for all believers as we have been bought with a price—Christ's blood.

Being people of God means salvation which is deliverance from something to something as it covers all believers from past, present and in the future. Also, being saved and being people of God includes justification which means that all believers have been made right with God and acquitted of his or her sins. Then the believer is sanctified which is being consecrated to God for service to Him. Lastly, the believer is regenerated or born again from a life of sin to one of righteousness.

Another school of thought on God taking Israel as His people speaks to His goodness, grace and mercy as well as His care and concern for the less fortunate. It also, speaks to His love for all mankind. Israel was chosen as God's people so they would be an example to the rest of the world to all God's goodness, grace, love and mercy as He is all sustaining, knowing, and seeing. He is the only true God that exists from eternity to eternity and possesses sovereignty to choose whom He pleases as His people.

It is a blessing to be chosen as God's people.

The People Of God: Jeremiah 30:22

And ye shall be my people, and I will be your God.

Reflecting on Israel's history one can see the merciful hand of God beginning with His deliverance from Egypt to and beyond today's lesson study. Today's lesson deals with the restoration of Israel back to their homeland from being in captivity for 70 years because of their unfaithfulness and disobedience to God. Through it all God never withheld His love from Israel; even in the midst of Israel's suffering God provided protection and He always has His messenger speaking for Him asking the nation to turn from sin and back to Him.

Who are God's people? God's people are the faithful that will and are going to put their trust in God regardless of how rampant sin is. This was true during Israel's early days and is true today as there was a nation of believers within the nation of Israel (Romans 9:6). God's people are those who will not be swayed by every wind of doctrine and have separated themselves from the world as they realize they are in the world but not of the world. God's people are those persons predestined by God as His elect for they have been called, justified, glorified, and are being confirmed to the likeness of Christ. They are adopted sons of God, recipients of an inheritance of the Lord, and have received the indwelling of the Holy Spirit. As God's people we are to give Him praise and glory and do good works.

All for the Master!

The Assurance Of Salvation: 1 John 5:13

These things have I written unto you that believe on the name of the Son of God; that ye may know that ye have eternal life, and that ye may believe on the name of the Son of God.

Much has been written and talked about salvation and how it is achieved, but if the question were raised, What are the assurances of salvation? To answer the question, first let us look at what we know for sure, which is that salvation is provided through Jesus Christ as He is the only way back to God. Second, salvation is a free gift from God to all who accept Jesus as his or her personal Savior. Third, from eye witness and written accounts that Jesus is the Son of God who died on the cross that dreadful Friday afternoon, and from the spectacular events staged by nature solidified Christ's deity.

If doubt still remains, let's examine some facts we hold to be true, which are (a) our salvation is assured if we believe on the name of Jesus. (b) There is eternal life in salvation. (c) We have the assurance of salvation if we love the Lord, God and His Son instead of the world. (d) Our salvation is assured if we yield to the indwelling Holy Spirit. (e) We are assured the benefit of eternal life if we the believer practices with constituency a life of righteousness instead of sin.

God has proven His trustiness time and again; if God said it then that settles it. Take God at His Word, Abraham, Noah, and Enoch trusted God.

Our salvation is sure and all the benefits therein.

Sept 29

Jesus The Man Of Peace: Micah 5:1-5

....Bethlehem Ephratah, though thou be little among the thousands of Judah, yet out of thee shall he come forth unto me that is to be ruler in Israel, whose goings forth have been from of old, from everlasting....And he shall stand and feed in the strength of the Lord, in the majesty of the name of the Lord his God...And this man shall be the peace....

The prophet Micah's hometown was a small place known a Moresheth-gath in the southern region of Judah which was approximately 25 miles southwest of Jerusalem. Micah's prophecy was pointing to God's punishment of Israel long before they were carried into captivity, but Micah looked beyond that time and even their return to their homeland into the future when Jesus would come, rule and restore everlasting peace, He will rule with righteousness and justice will prevail.

When Jesus comes again, He will reign with true peace, which will be restored just as it was before sin entered the world. He will have destroyed all evil, and Israel and all believers will live in safety as Christ will then be established as the true leader of the world.

When Jesus came the first time He forgave sin and provided salvation to all who accept Him in faith and all believers' salvation are assured. Remaining steadfast in ones belief and commitment to Christ will not face God's condemnation.

Jesus is the man of everlasting peace.

Sept 30

The Peace Of God: Jeremiah 33:16

In those days shall Judah be saved, and Jerusalem shall dwell safely; and shall be called, The Lord our righteousness.

What is the true definition of peace? The Hebrew word for peace is shalom; which is far more than the absence of war, conflict, or stress. It is the positive presence of harmony, wholeness, soundness, well being and success in all areas of life (KJV commentary). This peace can be seen when one is at peace within him or herself and God. It can be said to be in acceptance of where you are at that present time. Regardless of physical, mental, or surrounding conditions God is always near. Paul stated that he knew how to be happy whether he had a little or a lot.

Peace or shalom originated when God created the heaven and earth and all that is within was created in perfect harmony and wholeness with God. Remember the harmony that existed between God, nature, animal and man until it was disrupted by sin. When Adam sinned his sense of inner peace was lost forever until Christ returns to restore men shalom.

While waiting for Christ's return and the restoration of God's peace, how can we have peace now? Peace is available to all believers through the Holy Spirit as we remain united with Christ in faith. Also, we are to seek to live in harmony with others as peace is one of the fruit of the spirit, which is an indicator of who and where we are—at peace.

The peace of God rules supreme and is misunderstood by the world.

God's Instructions

Inspired To Know God: Luke 2:41-52

And all that heard Him were astonished at His understanding and answers

If the question were raised, What would inspire one to know God? One motivating factor could be the wonders of creation, and the awesomeness of gravity that holds all the planets, earth included, and all the stars of the universe in place. Another motivating factor is recognizing and acknowledging how wonderfully we are made. Then there is the stimulating factor of wonderment that there must be a God who is bigger and mightier than you and I who loved humanity so much that He breathed His spirit into each and gave mankind the ability and desire to want to know Him so that we may be in fellowship with our creator. **What an awesome God!**

Another thought on being inspired to know God is the fact that God has a perfect will for all mankind and has established a set of rules for holy living so that all mankind can and will live harmoniously with God. How will one get to know the will of God? Our scripture text provides a perfect example of getting to know God and His Will.

At the end of the yearly feast of the Passover, young Jesus stayed behind to study and expound on scripture. The young Jesus began to "increase in wisdom and statue, and in favor with God and man." This was in preparation to doing the will of His Father and to begin His ministry of saving souls. The sweet taste of God's Word is invigorating to our quest for knowledge.

Get to know *Go!*

Oct 2

The Grace Of The Lord: Psalm 147:1-20

Praise ye the Lord for it is good to sing praises unto our God; for it is pleasant and praise is comely

If we were to define grace, it would be that grace is God's unmerited favor, because as stated in our lesson text we see the goodness of the Lord. If it were not enough to sing praises to His holy name for His goodness, some examples of His goodness is spelled out as follows, (a) "The Lord doth build up Jerusalem, He gathereth together the outcasts of Israel. (b) He healeth the broken in heart, and bindeth up their wounds. (c) He telleth the number of the stars; He calleth them all by their names. (d) Great is the Lord, and of great power, his understanding is infinite. (e) The Lord lifteth up the meek; He casteth the wicked down to the ground. (f) Who covereth the heaven with clouds, who maketh grass to grow upon the mountains. (g) He maketh peace in thy borders, and filleth thee with the finest of the wheat."

Throughout scripture God is seen as caring for His people, the meek and during Jesus' ministry, He too ministered to the humble and afflicted. God has displayed His love and support for all who have a humble spirit, because those persons recognize they can do nothing in and of themselves.

Lastly, in our scripture text, the psalmist provides assurances of God's help and victory in all endeavors because of His grace as love is at the core of His grace.

Walk humbly with God in His grace.

The Passover Instituted: Exodus 12; Numbers 9:1-5

And the blood shall be to you for a token upon the houses where you are; and when I see the blood, I will pass over you, and the plague shall not be upon you to destroy you, when I smite the land of Egypt.

The Passover history dates back to 1445 B.C. when the Hebrew /Jewish people celebrated the Passover in the spring of each year. The Jewish people had been in slavery to the Egyptians for 400 years and as a fulfillment of God's promise to Abraham, Isaac and Jacob, He delivered the Jews through the leadership of Moses.

Moses was to deliver God's mandate to Pharaoh "Let my people go" (Exodus 5:1). God knew that Pharaoh's heart would be hardened and it would take a series of plagues before relenting to let the people go. The tenth plague was of the death angel that would pass over the houses where there was blood on the door posts. As God had issued His command to kill all first born both man and beast (Exodus 12:12). This blood was to be from year-old male lamb without defect and kill it at twilight on the fourteenth day of the month. This lamb represented the perfect Lamb of God—Jesus Christ who would die for the sins of the world.

Also, on the night of the Passover, the Israelites were to be dressed and ready to depart on a moment's notice when the Egyptians would ask them to leave. In their Passover meal they were to roast the lamb, prepare bitter herbs and bread made without yeast.

The Passover or Feast of Unleavened Bread is commemorated each year around the 14th of April as this is a memorial to their deliverance from Egypt. From our scripture text we see this memorial being established and kept by the Israelites under Moses' instructions.

There are several important facts regarding the Passover as it relates to Christians in that it contains several prophetic symbolisms that point to Jesus Christ and it teaches that the Jewish feasts are "a shadow of things to come" (Colossians 2;16-17). Also, that redemption is through Jesus Christ. Exodus 12 highlights the following facts regarding the Passover, and they are (a) it is the heart and soul of God's saving grace as He brought the nation of Israel out of bondage, because He loved them and was faithful to His covenant. Also, the salvation that we receive is through Jesus Christ through God's Grace. (b) The purpose of the blood on the door posts was to save the firstborn son from each family from death and this blood represents Christ's blood that would be shed on the cross at Calvary so that all who believed may be saved from death and God's wrath. (c) The Passover Lamb was a "sacrifice" (Exodus 12:27) as this points to the sacrificial death of Christ as He is our Passover Lamb. (d) The male lamb that was "without blemish" (Exodus 12:25) represents Christ, the perfect Son of God (John 8:48; Hebrews 4:15). (d) Eating the lamb represents identification in the Israelite community just as eating of the Lord's Supper represents all believer's partaking in Christ's death which saves us from a spiritual death. The Lord's Supper is a memorial, and is done "in remembrance" of Christ (1 Corinthians 11:24). (e) Sprinkling blood on the doorposts was an act of obedience in faith (Exodus 12:28) this same obedience we must have to receive salvation through Christ (Romans 1:5; 16:26). (f) Lastly, the unleavened bread represents the absence of sin and corruption as yeast usually represents sin and corruption (Exodus 13:7).

The Passover is a memorial that has withstood the test of time so has the Lord's Supper. Observe in commemoration for what God has done in the lives of all mankind.

Passover Observed: Exodus 12:17

And ye shall observe the feat of unleavened bread; for in this self-same day have I brought your armies out of the land of Egypt; therefore shall ye observe this day in your generations by and ordnance for ever.

In our scripture text God is giving specific instructions for the nation of Israel to observe this feast forever and in the preceding verses God is very specific with His instructions on what is to be included in the feast and how it is to be eaten. Case in point, the unleavened bread represents a separation from sin and worldly corruption while the bitter herbs serve as a reminder of the hard times Israel suffered in Egypt. It is prudent to remember the difficult times in ones life and God's deliverance is worthy of constant praises.

It is noteworthy to say that as the Passover observance is significant in the lives of Jewish people so is the Lord's Supper to all Christians worldwide. Both observances denote believers consecrating themselves to God and turning away from sin. The Passover is observed yearly while the Lord's Supper is observed monthly in most churches. However, it can be observed as often as agreed upon by the congregation. Both must be observed with a sincere heart and in obedient faith to God. It must be stated that all believers should be committed to God daily whether Passover or The Lord's Supper is being observed or not.

All believer's lives and households should be leavened/sin free zones.

Observing Traditions: Luke 2:41-45

And when He was twelve years old, they went up to Jerusalem after the custom of the feast.

What is a tradition? According to The Student Bible Dictionary (P. 231) tradition is a belief, teachings, practice, or rule handed down from the past (Matthew 15:2-3; 2 Thessalonians 2:15). There are many traditions that have been handed down from one generation to another. Some of those traditions are the observance of Good Friday and Resurrection Sunday which symbolizes the death and resurrection of our Lord and Savior Jesus Christ. The most significant tradition observed is the birth of Jesus, because without His birth and death there would be no salvation. This begs the question, How should these traditions be observed? The most holy of holy days should be observed with reverence to God for what He did for mankind out of love. He gave the very best that He had to be the propitiator for us as man was unworthy and unable to die for his sins.

It is noteworthy to say that there are some traditions that can and should be omitted as they are not of God; such as setting fires to property around Halloween. However, in our lesson text we see a tradition being observed by Jesus and His parents when He was a young child. The tradition that Jesus was keeping was making the yearly pilgrimage to Jerusalem for the yearly feast of the Passover. It is wise to know the history and meaning of the many traditions in society today and then decide your participation.

Traditions have meanings.

Oct 6

Hear God's Commands: Exodus 20:1-26

Thou shalt have no other gods before me.

Today's focus discussion is on hearing and obeying God's commands for which man is to live by. He was very explicit in what was required for the nation of Israel and these commands apply today. Reflecting on the Ten Commandments, one can see the holy standards by which God expects His people to live by.

Just as Israel was to worship and call upon the name of the Lord because He is the only one who delivered Israel and all humanity from bondage. All worship is to be directly to God for He is the creator and sustainer of all that exist. Worshipping God is to be in honesty, sincerity, and in faith.

If the question were raised, Why were these commands necessary? Exodus 19 explains the reasoning behind God issuing the Ten Commandments, which was because after Israel's deliverance and in the wilderness of Sinai He made a covenant with them to be their God and they would be His treasured possession and reap the benefits of His blessing. They were to be a unique people just as all believers are God's treasured people who are expected to live by His holy standards. Also, believers are to be a nation of priests, and a holy nation. Therefore, obeying the Ten commandment obligations remain in effect today just as they did during biblical times.

Hear and obey God's commands because outward expressions reflect the desires of the heart.

Oct 7

God Teaches His People: Deuteronomy 32:1-3

Give ear, O ye heavens, and I will speak, and hear, O earth, the words of my mouth. My doctrine shall drop as the rain; my speech shall distil as the dew, as the small rain upon the tender herb, and as the showers upon the grass.

This chapter is known as the Song of Moses who sang God's instructions to the people as to what God wanted them to hear. If the question were raised, What was God going to teach His people? God was going to teach His people His ways, His moral, and standards as He expected them to live by.

Verse 2 provides a vivid description of how God was going to shower His teachings upon the people. Reflecting on the purpose of rain as it waters and causes things to grow and in God's watering His people with His doctrines the people would grow in the knowledge of God. Having the knowledge of God increases one's wisdom and results in holy living which is pleasing to God.

Moses, through his song reminds Israel who God is and His faithfulness to His people as well as the consequences for being disobedient. They were asked to remember the generations of their fathers who had powerful testimonies of God's deliverance. With that being said, What is the importance of teachings? Teaching is important because it provides instructions, guidance and gives directions.

Adhere to God's doctrines as they are true and without error.

Adhere to God's Instructions: Proverbs 23:12

Apply thine heart unto instruction, and thine ears to the words of knowledge.

In every aspect of our lives we are guided by instructions; there are instructions or manuals on how to assemble many manufactured products that man has made. These instructions/manuals or procedures are designed to guide the consumer in a step-by-step approach in assembling the particular product. There are procedures on how to make our favorite dishes for eating, many are written and many are passed on from one generation to the next. With that being said, the question now becomes Why are God's instructions so important?

God's instructions are important because they are designed for guidance and directions as His instructions are recipes for holy living. God provides instructions for His people just for that purpose so that they will not go astray or be tempted by Satan and his deceptive schemes. It is noteworthy to say that God's instructions are constantly being revealed to all who read study and meditate on His Word.

It is wise to adhere to God's instructions because He is all knowing and has the ability to guide His people around any and all hurt harm or danger if adhered to. Providing instructions is part of God's provisional care for His people. God's value of teaching children is recorded in Deuteronomy 6:7 where He instructed parents to teach their children in their going out and coming in. In Joshua 4 God instructed Joshua to erect a memorial using stones as a teaching tool to the younger generation of Israelites of where and how they crossed the Jordan.

Adhere to God's Word.

Purpose Of Instructions: 2 Timothy 3:16

All scriptures are given by inspiration of God, and is profitable for doctrine, for reproof, for correction, for instruction in righteous.

Our scripture text provides the answer to the implied question of what is the purpose of instructions. Also, stated in our scripture text is who gave the instructions as there would be no doubt of the legitimacy of the Bible as it is one love story with instructions for man's benefit.

Providing an explanation of doctrines we see that these teachings are to preserve God's holy laws as mankind is to abide by His law that is designed for man's holy and righteous living. Doctrines can be seen as traditions, a policy or conviction as man's convictions are to first believe there is a God who created and sustains all that exist. Also, it is all believers' conviction that God breathed His breath into man and he became a living soul. With that being said, then it is both God and man's (believers) conviction to live in a harmonious relationship with each other.

If the question were raised, What is a conviction? A conviction is a persuasion or belief. The believer's persuasion to obey God's instructions, obey them as they are to correct man when he/she go contrary to God's commands, or provide proof that man is living according to God's laws.

Instructions are guidelines or a plumb line for righteous living as they are good in every way.

Oct 10

The Mind of Christ: I Corinthians 2:16

For who hath known the mind of the Lord, that he may instruct him? But we have the mind of Christ.

In today's discussion we will begin by looking at the word "mind"; first the mind is the mental or intellect aspect of a person. It is referred to as perception, judgment, wisdom, intention, or determination. Second, the mind is where one's thought patterns begin as well as intentions and these are acted out in the physical ream of life. Some may have good intentions and some bad or deviant intentions, but whatever the intentions are there are consequences of ones actions.

If the question is raised, How must one be certain that his or her intentions are of good judgment? One is to practice good judgment and intentions at all times to have the mind of Christ. This is accomplished through knowing Christ and having the mind of Christ as well as being led by the Holy Spirit.

This poses another question, which is, How is one to have the mind of Christ? Having the mind of Christ is to know the Will of Christ, His redemptive plan and purpose (vv 9-12). These verses carry several connotations, which are, seeing things as God sees them, valuing as God values, and love and hating as God does. God hates sin and evil, so must believers as believers have been called out of the world and no longer conform to the world and its ways and beliefs. Additionally, having the mind of Christ means understanding the holiness of God as His thoughts, ways and morals supersedes that of man.

Another thought on having the mind as it relates to His redemptive plan and purpose for mankind is that all should be saved through the shed blood of His Son Jesus Christ. It is noteworthy to say that there are many who will not be saved because they will not believe that Christ is God's Son who came to earth for the sole purpose of being the sacrificial Lamb of God.

Continuing our discussion on how we must know the mind of

Christ is through daily Bible reading and prayer as it is important for all believers to remain in constant communication and fellowship with God. It is important for non-believers to study the scriptures as it has been discussed in earlier readings that instructions are profitable for reproof and corrections. Additionally, reading God's Word provides insight as to who He is and His awesome powers.

Lastly, having the mind of Christ requires a willing and receptive heart as Christ has stated that He will stand at the door and knock and those who are willing He will come in and sup with the person (paraphrased). God through Jesus Christ is still knocking at the door (hearts) of man to establish a loving fellowship with man.

Open the door to your heart and get to know Christ.

All Nature Praise God: Psalm 148:1-6

Praise ye the Lord, Praise ye the Lord from the heavens; praise him the heights. ..Let them praise the name of the Lord; for his name alone is excellent; his glory is above the earth and heaven.

The entire number of this Psalm is singing the praises of God for He is worthy of all praises. Even nature offers its praises to the Lord as nature recognizes the awesomeness of God. Praises to God is seen being song by all the angels, sun, moon and stars even the waters both in and above the earth for they recognize their creator for whom He is.

The writer of this psalm recognized how awesome God is and if all nature can offer praises to God then the question becomes why not all humanity? God is worthy of all the praises that humanity has to offer being that God is man's creator and sustainer as well as having the Spirit of God who lives inside of each believer. **Praise ye the Lord!**

A common saying is that "if I had ten thousand tongues would be inadequate to give God His worthy praise." What this saying means is that all our praises are insufficient because of God's worthiness. **What praise worthiness!**

How do you praise God? Is it with out-stretched hands lifted high in holy reverence to God? Do you praise God with a heart of thanksgiving in both good and bad times?

Praise God as nature praises Him.

Doing God's Work: Luke 2:46-50

....How be it that ye sought me? Wist ye not that I must be about my Father's business?

The scene for today's lesson discussion takes place with the young Jesus and His parents making the annual pilgrimage to Jerusalem as the custom—the Feast of the Passover. Upon their return to their homeland Jesus remained behind to begin His Father's work. Jesus' parents supposing their son was in their company had traveled quite a distance before recognizing that He was missing and turned back to locate Jesus and when doing so questioned Him as all good parents do. Our scripture text provides Jesus' answer to His reasons for remaining behind.

The lesson behind this story is that when it is time to obey God's call then we must obey and be about our Father's business which is doing what we have been called to do. Doing God's work in many times causes us to leave family and friends behind as doing the works of God is far greater than that of man. It is noteworthy to say that all believers have been called to do the work of ministry for God. Some are called to teach, preach, minister to others in different occupational fields, and simply sharing the Word of God. Doing the work of God as His workers we are aiding in kingdom building.

Jesus is our example of doing God's work, He was committed to His task, what about you and I?

"Trust In The Lord": Psalm 37:3

Trust in the Lord, and do good; so shalt thou dwell in the land, and verily thou shalt be fed.

The word trust has been defined as having confidence in someone or something, being trustworthy, being dependable. With that being said, given God's track record He has proven to be trustworthy in all His promises.

If the question were raised, Why trust in the Lord? We are to trust God because He is our creator and sustainer who cannot lie and what God promise's He surely will bring it to pass. Case in point, God encourages all to trust Him and do good (well), because blessings will follow. More specifically, our scripture verse states that all who trust God will dwell in the land and all of our needs will be met. Another point to this discussion on trusting God is that it is right to do good by others as we want others to do for us. This is commonly known as the golden rule.

Also, verse 1 tells us that we are to refrain from worrying about the evils that others may do and to delight ourselves in the Lord (v. 4). Being delighted in the Lord brings blessings galore in that all who delight themselves in Him have a desire to live for and to please God. Delightful living results in all prayers being answered and our hearts desires are granted.

Trust in the Lord because He has proven to be worthy of all trust.

The Joy Of Being In God's Company: Psalm 37:4

Delight thyself also in the Lord; and He shall give thee the desires of thine heart.

What does it mean to delight ones self in the Lord? There is certain jubilation from being in the presence of the Lord as this represents closeness between the believer and God. The Lord desires a close fellowship with His people and welcomes such closeness.

Other joyful results from being in God's company are the jubilation that the world neither gave nor understands. This is because the believer sees things from God's prospective and relish in His presence, nearness and the truth of His Word and righteousness. Also, being in the presence of the Lord, the believer has an extreme desire to do His will because the believer has come to know God's will and purpose, which is to build His kingdom. Knowing the Will of God is achieved through daily Bible reading and meditating on His Word.

Another school of thought on the joy of being in God's company is that the believer has learned patience, trust and humility because through the indwelling Holy Spirit all believers have the ability to persevere with a steadfast hope of vindication for all the wrong this world has inflicted upon believers for Christ's sake. Vindication from this world's injustices is a promise of God which will be kept by Him. The ultimate joy from being in the presence of God is the believer's assured salvation and spending eternity with Him.

O! What a joy to behold for there is no greater joy.

Oct 15

Instructed To Love: Luke 6:27-28; Leviticus 19:17-18

But I say unto you which hear, Love your enemies, do good to them which hate you, Bless them that curse you, and pray for them which despitefully use you.

Verses 27-42 is regarded as the law of love issued by Christ Himself as these commands are given for the purpose of living harmoniously with others in a land where revenge is the norm. These commands are for members (believers) of the new covenant and we as believers are obligated to obey. The meaning of these commands is that we as believers are to love our enemies with a genuine concern for their well-being. Those persons who have hatred in their hearts cannot be of God because He is love. Also, mean spirited people are hostile to God and His people and believers are to pray for those persons that they will have a change of heart to one of faith in Christ. Another thought on loving our enemies is that believers through their prayer lives have decided against sitting idly by while evildoers continue in their wicked ways. Loving and praying for ones enemy is a powerful but effective weapon against Satan and all wickedness.

Our Leviticus scripture text supports the love instructions that were issued to the nation of Israel by God on how Israel was to treat all those who they came in contact with.

Love instructions were issued in both the OT and NT—obey them.

Judge Not: Luke 6:37; Matthew 7:1

Judge not, and ye shall not be judged; condemn not, and ye shall not be condemned; forgive, and ye shall be forgiven.

What is the meaning of this scripture? It means that we are to refrain from criticizing others of their wrong doings while holding self out to be faultless. All are guilty of something, therefore if we judge not then we will not be judged as all wrong doings are worthy of forgiveness. God forgave mankind of his sins when justice was demanded, but mercy prevailed.

With that being said, the question that comes to mind is, Who are we to judge? Man is unworthy of judging our fellowman because there is only one righteous judge—God Himself who in due time will judge the entire world as He pronounced the entire world guilty and this resulted in Jesus Christ coming to redeem mankind.

It is noteworthy to say that in this instruction, Christ is condoning the habit of criticizing others of his or her wrong doing, but Christ did not deny the need for discernment or making value judgments with regards to evil in our fellowman. What are we to do? We are to pray for the person to have a change of heart and turn to God for forgiveness as we are to hate the sin, but love the person.

Concluding our opening question, we are to judge not, forgive and be forgiven--God forgave all. He is the righteous judge.

Oct 17

Give As God Gave: Luke 6:38

Give, and it shall be given unto you; good measure, pressed down, and shaken together, and running over, shall men give into your bosom. For with the same measure that you mete withal it shall be measured to you again.

How did God give? God gave the best that He had in His only begotten Son Jesus Christ to be the Savior of the world. John 3:16 records the magnitude of God giving out of love to redeem man back to Himself. This was made necessary because of sin and man lacked the ability to give his own life as a sacrifice for the sins he committed. Only God would give all that He had to give to restore a broken fellowship and provide salvation for those whom He loved. **Agape love!**

This begs the question, What is agape love? Agape love is God's love that has no beginning, ending or condition except to love Him in return. Who would not give love in return given all the love that has been bestowed upon mankind?

Now that we have discussed how God gave, let us discuss our giving in accordance to how God gave. We are to give out of love for one another and give our best. More importantly, we are to give to those in need as God in His provisional care has made provisions for all mankind; this includes the haves and have not's. We are to remember that God will reward the cheerful giver in accordance to what and how we give to those in need. It is prudent to remember that one day there will be a day of reckoning when our stewardship will be read on how we cared for the less fortunate. Also, we must remember that what we do for the least of God's children it is being done to Him or what we failed to do for the least it too is being done unto God. Also, our scripture text outlines how we are to give, which states that the more one gives the more will be returned two fold. This scripture text incorporated the analogy of having more windows than doors in an effort to receive God's blessings as a result of ones giving. **How do you give?**

Reflecting on the question of how do you give begs other questions and they are, Do you give and then ask for it back? Do you give only to those who love you or you love? Do you give without conditions? Do you give cheerfully? Do you give your last like the widow woman and best or do you give from your abundance or for a show to the world? However you give do it all to the glory of God because He sees the heart and knows your motive for giving and how you gave.

Give as God gave because He gave His love and continues to give His love for all humanity.

True giving is unconditional.

Oct 18

The Golden Rule: Luke 6:31

And as ye would that men should do to you, do ye also to them likewise.

When growing up as a child I was taught the golden rule failing to realize that my mother was teaching me scripture as well as a principle in which to live by that would prove to be a good rule of thumb on treating others.

The question now becomes, What happened to this biblical life principal that was practiced during my early childhood? There are several answers that could be applied, but some are, there is a disregard for human life. Also, many people today fail to ask themselves this question, If this were me how would I want to be treated? This is evidenced by the criminal elements that are committed daily and the perpetrators will go to any lengths in an effort to remain free and avoid paying the consequences of his or her actions. It is safe to say that the Golden Rule is oblivious to many in today's society as they have never heard of this rule.

This reminds me of the time in the OT when sin had become so prevalent that "The Book" God's Word had become lost and was later discovered by the scribes and reported their findings to their righteous king. This occurred as the temple was being restored. The book was read and the king led a spiritual revival and once again God's blessings begin to flow upon the nation of Israel.

Live and let live- treat others as you want to be treated.

Model Prayer: Mathew 6:9-15

After this manner therefore pray ye; Our Father which art in heaven, hallowed be thy name.

The focus of today's discussion is the instructions Christ gave on how to pray as our prayers are our communication with God.

Let's look at our model prayer and our approach to God, first we are to acknowledge who God is and where He is. This is because our heavenly father is one who cares for and provides for all our needs. God does not tolerate sin and all manner of sin will be punished. Second we are to hallow God's name because He is worthy of all adoration and in doing so we are giving God the highest honor and praise for who He is and what He has done and continues to do in the lives of all mankind. Also, we must honor and exalt God in our prayers, daily lifestyles as expressions of reverence for God, and His church and gospel message.

Third, we must pray that His kingdom will come as this too is an expression of our concerns for God's kingdom here on earth and in the future. Fourth, we must pray that God's will be done in our lives and ours be aligned with His as His is far superior to ours. Fifth, we are to pray that our daily needs are met as God promised to do. Sixth, we are to ask for forgiveness as we are to forgive others as God has forgiven all. Lastly, we are to ask God to protect us from evil as this is done through the Holy Spirit.

Follow God's instructions.

Intercessory Prayer: I Timothy 2:1

I exhort therefore that, first of all, supplications, prayers, intercessions and giving of thanks, be made for all men.

What is intercessory prayer? The word intercession is to make a plea for others or the mediation, which is to act as a go between for two or more parties. Also, to be an intercessor is to make a petition to someone for someone else. With that being said, then our intercessory prayers become our petition to God for others as Jesus Christ is our intercessor to God for all mankind.

If the question were raised, Why should we pray for others as many we may not know or what their condition is? First, it is good to pray for others as an expression of our care for all mankind. Second, there will come a time when we will need others to pray for us. Lastly, our scripture text encourages praying for others as this denotes a caring spirit as this spirit exemplifies that of Christ.

This question comes to mind, in our intercessory prayer, what should we pray for others? We should pray for the well being of others as it is the desire of all mankind that all is well in his or her daily lives. Lastly, we are to pray a prayer of thanksgiving as an expression of gratitude for God's many blessings and difficulties as well because problems grow faith.

Intercede for others as Christ intercedes for you and I daily- pray.

Pray Constantly: Luke 18:1

And he spake a parable unto them to this end, that men ought to always to pray, and not to faint.

Jesus taught His disciples many things; in this verse He uses the parable of the widow to teach an important lesson on prayer and the effectiveness of prayers and the continuity of praying.

Jesus taught several important lessons using this parable, which are (a) all believers, must persevere in prayer regarding all life matters until He returns. (b) Believers must realize that our prayers are an effective weapon against Satan our adversary. (c) Believers are to cry out in prayer against sin and evil that is being pressed upon all humanity. (d) Constant prayers by the believer are counted as his or her faith on display. (e) As the end time approaches there will be a diabolical oppression to the prayers of the righteous and our faithfulness to Christ and many will cease to persevere in faith, but true believers are commanded to remain steadfast and pray.

What makes a prayer effective? An effective prayer is one that is constant, sincere and done in faith. This is because an honest prayer begins in the heart with a focus on God and His will. Effective prayer warriors are those persons who have walked and talked with God daily and have established a personal relationship with God. God has gifted many with the gift of praying and they are using this gift to God's glory.

Let's all pray daily.

Oct 22

Prayer And Faith
Psalm 17:6; Genesis 4:26; Psalm 3:4; 25:1; Hebrews 10:22

I have called upon thee, for thou wilt hear me, O God; incline thine ear unto me, and hear my speech.

Yesterday's discussion focus was constant prayers, but today's focus is prayers themselves and the believer's faith that must be exhibited for their prayers to be effective.

First we will discuss the meaning of prayer and its public beginnings. Prayer is ones communication peace with God. Many scriptures refer to prayer from different activity points such as in Psalm 17:6 it is known as "calling on the Lord", and in Genesis 4:26 prayers are referred to as "calling on the name of the Lord." It was with Enoch that public prayer and worship began. In the Psalms 3:4 the prayer activity is "crying with one's voice to the Lord", while in Psalm 25:1 prayer is "lifting up one's soul to the Lord." Isaiah 55:6 refers to prayer as "seeking the Lord", while Hebrews 4:16 refers to prayer as "approaching the throne of grace boldly", and then Hebrews 10:22 refers to prayer as "drawing near to God."

We are commanded by God to pray as this is our link to God for receiving His blessing and power as these are promises made by Him. It is through believers' prayers that one grows and maintains a relationship with God. Jesus prayed and asked that we pray in His name.

Most importantly, our prayers are to be done in faith, which is our belief that God will answer our prayers. Prayer without faith is ineffective; therefore an effective prayer has faith.

Pray with faith.

The Three Components Of prayer: Matthew 7:7

Ask, and it shall be given you, seek, and ye shall find, knock, and it shall be open unto you.

If the question were raised, Why are these three components necessary in one's prayer life? First each represents the sincere desire of the believer in having a harmonious relationship with God. Second Jesus encourages the persistence in the believer's prayer life.

Asking represents perseverance in desiring to receive God's blessing and power that is given through the Holy Spirit. Asking also denotes a desire for a close relationship with God and to remain in His presence. Furthermore asking implies a consciousness of a need whether it is salvation, protection and or guidance while navigating life's journey.

Seeking carries a connotation of honestly petitioning God with an obedient heart to humbly obey His will. Having a humble heart the person has a right view of God, self, and others as well as realizing that one can do nothing in and of his/herself.

Knocking implies perseverance in coming to God while having the patience to wait for God's answer if it is not given immediately.

Prayer components are necessary because believers seek God's kingdom first and being a child of God means salvation has been granted because of His love, goodness and mercy. All petitions are granted according to His will, which is for all men to be saved.

Prayers of the righteous bring God's grace and mercy--they ask, seek and knock.

Gift Of The Holy Spirit: Acts 2:1-4

And when the day of Pentecost was fully come, they were all with one accord in one place. And suddenly there came a sound from heaven as of rushing mighty wind, and it filled all the house where they were sitting. And there appeared unto them cloven tongues like as of fire, and it sat upon each of them.

Today's focus discussion is on who is the Holy Spirit and the importance of Pentecost. Pentecost was the second great feast of the Jewish year. Pentecost was a harvest feast when the first fruits was of the grain harvest was presented to God (Leviticus 23:17). Pentecost also symbolizes the beginning of soul harvesting by God for the church.

Let's clarify who the Holy Spirit is. The Holy Spirit is the third person in the Godhead who was in the beginning with God during creation. He is God and there are plethoras of scriptures that support the fact that the Holy Spirit is God. The Holy Spirit is seen as "the Spirit that moved over the face of the deep" (Genesis 1:2).

Taking a deeper look into our scripture verses, we see there are three observerable manifestations that occurred on the day of Pentecost, and they are (a) the rushing mighty wind is the audible manifestation of the Holy Spirit as He descended upon all 120 disciples that were present. This was a prophetic sign of the Spirit's coming in power. Also, wind is one of the symbols of the Holy Spirit. (b) The visible manifestation was the "cloven tongues like as of fire" that rested on each of the disciples present. Fire is also a symbol of the Holy Spirit, and they were to carry God's message in a fiery, contagious manner. (c) The Holy Spirit's speech manifestation was the disciples "began to speak with other tongues as the Spirit gave them utterance" (v.4). The "other tongues" were the many other native languages that were represented in and understood by the different nations that were present. This threefold manifestation of the Holy Spirit represents the threefold ministry recorded in Acts 1:8, which will be discussed in our next discussion.

If the question were raised, What is the meaning of being filled with the Spirit at Pentecost? It means that God was fulfilling His promise made in Joel 2:28-29 that He would pour out His Spirit on all flesh in the end times. It also meant that His disciples would be "endued with power from on high" (Acts 1:8; Luke 24:49). It is a revelation that the Holy Spirit's nature is for all to be saved and all who received the baptism in the Holy Spirit will have the same longing/desire. The disciples of that day became ministers of the Spirit as they not only preached Christ but were instrumental in leading others to repent and have faith in Jesus Christ and be saved. Lastly, all who are baptized in the Holy Spirit become successors to Christ's earthly ministry as they are followers of Christ.

The gift of the Holy Spirit is a powerful gift for Christ followers as He gives the necessary tools to witness Christ.

Oct 25

The Holy Spirit Amazes Many: Acts 2:5-38

And they were all amazed and marvelled, saying one to another, Behold, are not all these which speak Galileans?

Continuing our discussion on the events that occurred on the day of Pentecost, there were Parthians, Medes and Elamites as well as many other foreigners who had heard about this phenomenon of speaking in other tongues. Those persons were in doubt and stood in amazement of the power of the Holy Spirit and maybe failed to recognize who He was. Those standing in amazement accused Peter and the rest of being drunk with wine early in the daytime hours.

Verses 14-40 is Peter's answer to those persons who lacked the understanding of what occurred at Pentecost as God fulfilled His promise of sending the Holy Spirit. In Peter's Pentecost sermon, he reminded the hearers that God prophesied in Joel 2:28-29 that He would "pour out His Spirit on all flesh." This included sons, daughters, men, women, servants, and handmaidens as all would prophesy. What does prophesy mean? To tell others what God said as well as preach and teach the gospel message of Jesus Christ. This is to take place in the last days. The "last days" includes a time of prophetic witness calling all to repentance and experience the outpouring of the Holy Spirit and these days include the inauguration of God's kingdom when He will come with all power. The OT, "last days" were considered the time when God judges evil and brings salvation to His people. It is noteworthy to say that the "last days" will be complete at the second coming of Christ when He will bring an end to the evil forces that exist.

Therefore, understand the power of the Holy Spirit because when endued with Him believers become drunk with His powers.

Oct 26

Power of the Holy Spirit: Acts 1:8

But ye shall receive power after that the Holy Ghost is come upon you; and ye shall be witnesses unto me both in Jerusalem, and in all Judea, and in Samaria, and unto the uttermost part of the earth.

There are two connotations in this verse and they are (a) receiving power, and (b) becoming witness the world over. If the question were raised, Who will receive this Holy Ghost power? It can be best answered by saying that all believers will receive power to witness Christ just as the disciples did on the day of Pentecost. Their life works verifies the power they ministered in the name of Jesus after that day. They performed many miracles, raised the dead and healed the sick. **Wonderful powers!**

Likewise believers today are powerful in Christ's ministry through the workings of the Holy Spirit.

Therefore, let's look at "power" and what it means in this setting. Power means special powers in operation or action to carry out God's work. This power causes believers to boldly witness Christ, and to live lives with such boldness so that the world can and will see Christ in each believer. Holy Ghost power empowers believers to perform signs, wonders and miracles (2:43; 5:12-16, 8:6-8).

In regards to witnessing Christ as a result of the Holy Ghost; He makes real the person of Jesus Christ. He witnesses to the "righteousness and" "truth" of Christ in both words and deeds. Lastly, being baptized in the Holy Spirit, the believer's witness becomes more effective.

The awesomeness' of the power of the Holy Spirit!

Oct 27

Trust God: Psalm 31:1-5

In thee O Lord, do I put my trust; let me never be ashamed; deliver me in thy righteousness.

Taking a panoramic view of this psalm one can see this it is a personal prayer expressing heart felt grief as it can be the result of mistreatment from ones enemies or desertion by friends, illness, and or persecution from being associated with Christ Jesus. Regardless of what caused the pain, the sufferer realizes that only the Lord will never forsake or leave His children especially in the time of trouble. From OT prophets to Jesus Christ have used this passage of scripture to express the regret they felt. Jesus used these words while hanging on the cross (Luke 23:46).

Another point in this passage of scripture is that it expresses ones deepest feelings of alienation during ones time of afflictions. It also brings to mind that when all else fails try God. It goes without saying that God is the only trustworthy person who has proven His trustfulness time and again. He said in His word "cast all your cares upon Him (1 Peter 5:7). God in His immutability would not have made such a statement if He did not mean it to be so.

Verse 3 denotes the spirit of humility because God is being recognized for who He is and His saving powers, while verse 4 solidifies the need for God's guidance, then verse 14 drives home the point of trusting God---"Thou art my God."

A trustworthy God!

Do Not Hate God's Instructions: Psalm 50:17

Seeing thou hatest instructions, and castest my words behind thee.

The discussions this month have been centered on God's instructions and the benefits from adhering to His wise counsel. One benefit is that He is God the almighty creator and sustainer who knows all and sees all. Second, being that He is sovereign and exists from everlasting to everlasting which makes Him the righteous law giver and all are encouraged to refrain from disobeying or disliking God's instructions.

The third benefit from receiving and adhering to God's instructions are that His instructions are for corrections, reproof; they are doctrinal teachings and guidance. Wise persons readily accept godly instructions and teachings as they are guiding principles in which to live by.

With these thoughts in mind the question now becomes, Why would anyone hate God's instructions? Is it because the lack of wisdom? Is it because the person has failed to accept God for who He is? Believers have learned to obey God's instructions and to lean not to ones own understanding. This is because God's ways are much higher than those of man. But to the unbeliever God's instructions are tossed aside (v.17) as they are looked upon as being foolish.

It is noteworthy to say that the wicked in his or her disobedience to God's instructions is headed for destruction. Case in point, Adam disobeyed and a harmonious relationship was destroyed.

Heed wise counsel for all instructions have a purpose.

Oct 29

Instructed By God: Isaiah 8:11-12

For the Lord spake thus to me with a strong hand, and instructed me that I should not walk in the way of this people, saying Say ye not, A confederacy, to all them to whom this people shall say, A confederacy, neither fear ye their fear, nor be afraid. Sanctify the Lord of hosts himself; and let him be your fear; and let him be your dread.

In our scripture text the prophet Isaiah was giving God's instructions to Judah in his attempt to persuade them to seek God and His ways. Judah had turned its back on God and was facing destruction if it refused to hear the word of God and repent. Isaiah was God's spokes person and for being obedient to God's instruction he was accused of conspiracy and suffered persecution. This is true today of those persons who attempt to call God's church back to Him and away from the many human programs and all unbiblical Christianity. Those persons are often times met with persecution and disrespect and even called old timey, but God's Word is the same today as it was yesterday and will be forever as it is the only thing that will withstand Satan's demonic attacks.

We are to fear only God and be obedient to His call as stated in verse 13, because He our deliverer and in the time of trouble He will deliver His people.

When God gives instructions follow them in spite of nay Sayers.

Oct 30

Instructions For Life: Proverbs 4:13

Take fast hold on instruction; let her not go; keep her; for she is thy life.

When King Solomon wrote the book of Proverbs he had a specific purpose in mind which was to provide instructional guidelines that crossed all boundaries, children and adults so that all could live according to God's holy law.

In proverbs 1:2-7 gives a purpose to provide wisdom and understanding concerning wise behavior, righteousness, and justice. While in verses 2-3 as King Solomon states the purpose is for the simple man to become prudent and verse 4 is for the youth to gain knowledge and discretion, which is to be careful of what one does. In verses 5-6 states that the wise will become wiser; all this says in summary is the life instructions provided by God through King Solomon is the foundation for holy living.

This brings us to our scripture text where instructions are spoken of as "her" giving life as this depicts the wisdom of God for all who gain wisdom will live as God designed. This is to live a long joyful life in God both physically, morally and spiritually and those who die in Christ full of wisdom can be assured of being raised to a new life after this tabernacle has been resolved--died a physical death.

Wisdom can be gained by diligently seeking it as it is given through God's instructions and listening to godly parents.

Get wisdom get understanding and live godly.

Oct 31

Apply Learned Knowledge: Proverbs 23:12

Apply thine heart unto instruction, and thine ears to the words of knowledge.

If the question were raised, What is meant by apply thine heart to instructions? It can be determined that this phrase means when one hears instruction the person is to hide those words in thy heart so that the stated instructions will become meaningful and can be applied to ones daily life. It has been long determined that what's in the heart becomes a part of a person's actions whether good or evil because the heart (mind) is the center of all thought process. A person loves with his or her heart, feels with his or her hearts and reasons with his or her heart.

It is noteworthy to say that people hear words constantly, but until the spoken words are understood they are just words. At the point understanding takes place, then these spoken words become meaningful and then application can take place. What happens next is the person begins to live a godly life and the wisdom of God is manifested just as it was with Christ as He displayed the full wisdom of God the Father.

Speaking from another point of view, God didn't just want man to get wise knowledge, but to apply the learned knowledge so that He may be manifested in all believers. Let's take this instruction from still another point of view, which is so we have just learned to speak correctly, but what good is this new knowledge if one continues to speak the old way. Isn't this the same principle in regards to realizing that one is a sinner and in need of a Savior, but refuses to accept Jesus as ones personal Savior and be saved?

The question now becomes, What good is learned knowledge if not applied? My answer is learned knowledge is of no use. However, persons/believers who have come into the full knowledge of God and His love, this knowledge becomes more meaningful to them, and then God and His love have a positive affect in that the person hungers and thirst for the Word of God and to be in His presence daily. **This is**

applied learned knowledge.

God continues to reveal His wisdom through His written Word and the indwelling Holy Spirit who brings all things into remembrance as He guides, teaches and protects all believers.

It can be concluded then that there are blessings in gaining knowledge then applying the learned knowledge as it is God's desire to have a loving fellowship with mankind. All who have accepted Christ as their personal Savior have applied their new found knowledge of Christ as He provided salvation; God as their creator and the Holy Spirit as their sustainer who lives on the inside.

What awesome knowledge!

Hope In Jesus Christ

God Our Deliverer: Daniel 3:17-30

If it be so, our God whom we serve is able to deliver us from the burning fiery furnace, and he will deliver us out of thine hand, O king.

The setting for today's discussion is where Daniel and his three friends (Shadrach, Meshach, and Abed-nego) were in a strange land where idol worship was prevalent. The three Hebrew boys refused to worship the king's gods and in his fit of anger ordered the three men to be thrown in the fiery furnace.

Our scripture verse provides their answer to the king and for their faith in the true and living God they were delivered. When the king looked expecting them to be destroyed he saw an angel of the Lord in the furnace with the Hebrew boys. **What deliverance!**

It was through their faith in God that the king believed and began to worship their God and declared that there was no other god throughout the land other than their God. The lesson here is that regardless of our situation or surrounding conditions believe on God for His deliverance. Trust and faith plays an integral part in our beliefs as God has proven Himself to be trustworthy and faithful to His people. Just as God delivered the Hebrews boys from the fiery furnace and Daniel from the lion's den He will do the same for you and I today.

These questions come to mind which are, How strong is your faith in God? Do you trust Him in your fiery furnaces and lion's den?
He is still delivering.

Joy In God's Presence: Psalm 16:1-11

Preserve me O God: for in thee do I put my trust.

What is joy? Joy is gladness, or rejoicing in something pleasant. With that being said, the Psalmist is rejoicing in the presence of God and sees no meaningful life apart from God. Paul in Philippians 1:21 and again in Galatians 2:20 expressed the same feeling when it came to being in the presence of the Lord. What does this say for you and I today? Life without God is meaningless because true joy comes from God because the world's joy is empty and short lived.

If the question were raised, What is the significance of joy? First, it is an integral part of our salvation as it brings an inner peace and delight from the Godhead, and blessings flow from being in the presence of God. Second, joy is one of the fruits of the spirit and comes from all believers abiding in a covenant relationship with God. Third, there is an inseparable connection from God and believers as we grow deeper in His Word and obeying His command; the fullness of the joy we feel is indescribable. Fourth, there is the delightful joy in being in the presence of the one who made provisions for all who believe to spend eternity with Him. Lastly, there is pure joy in knowing while in the presence of the Lord we are protected from the world and its turmoil.

There is unspeakable joy in God's presence.

God's Watchful Eye: Psalm 33:18-20

Behold, the eye of the Lord is upon them that fear him, upon them that hope in his mercy.

What are these verses saying? It is saying that for all who have a reverential fear of the Lord that God through His "eye" is protecting them in a special way through His loving and caring provisions. Psalm 34:15 supports this scripture by stating "The eyes of the Lord are upon the righteous, and his ears are open unto their cry." What this means is that the righteous have a special protection upon them from the Lord. This is not to say that God does not see or love and care for all humanity because He does. Because scripture has taught us that God loved us while we were enemy with Him and His love is evidenced by giving His only Son to die for the sins of the world.

It is also noteworthy to say that the Lord's watchful eye is ever present to keep the very souls of all believers as they have placed their hope and trust in God. The unbeliever, God is there as well, but the unsaved must accept God for who He is and His protective powers. From our scripture text (vv 13-14) it plainly tells us that God looks down from heaven and sees and hears all and responds accordingly. Which do you choose righteousness and the extra protective eye of God or rebel and wear a thin layer of protection?

God is watching.

Comfort In The Time Of Trouble: Psalm 39:1-13

Lord, make me to know mine-end, and the measure of my days, what it is; that I may know how frail I am.

In our scripture text we see King David asking the Lord to show him the brevity of his life and all life that is in a short span of time considered the time we will spend in the presence of God or separated from Him. See David was suffering punishment at the hand of God for his sin (Psalm 38) and in our text we see David making an honest confession and commitment that he would take heed to his ways. This should be the attitude of all who sin because God will not allow sin to go unpunished. David wanted to know how much longer he must suffer punishment at the hand of God. It is noteworthy to say that when one is experiencing pain and suffering the time seems forever, but in God's eyesight it is limited and is designed to turn our hearts back to Him.

It is comforting to know that during times of trials and tribulations God is present with out stretched arms waiting for us to repent. If the question were raised, How do we refrain from conforming to this perverse generation? Believers live for God in this world with the aid of the Holy Spirit as He is our comforter, guide and protector. He lives on the inside to teach us God's holy standards and His righteousness.

God the Holy Spirit is our comforter trust Him

A Yearning For God: Psalm 42:2-5

My soul thirsteth for God, for the living God; when shall I come and appear before God?

The writer of this Psalm gives an illustration of life as water is essential to ones physical life so is the presence of God essential to ones spiritual life. Being in the presence of God gives believers a sense of wholeness and satisfaction of life as He is present through the Holy Spirit--as He is God.

Believers must pray that our thirst never cease because there is love, righteousness in His water, and a deep desire to see the fullness of Christ's kingdom. It can also be said that to stop thirsting for God's spiritual water is to die spiritually. Believers have too much at stake for this to happen.

How do we remain spiritually alive? We must commune with God daily through His written word, prayer, and yielding to the Holy Spirit. In John 7:38, Jesus told His audience that if any man thirst let them come and drink of Him because for everyone who believes on Jesus Christ out of "his belly shall flow rivers of living waters." What this means is that when the gift of the Spirit is given then all believers will experience an over flow of His presence. The presence of the indwelling Holy Spirit has such a sweet taste until all believers will yearn for more.

What a blessing to have the bread of life living on the inside to quench our hunger and thirst Glory to God.

Hope In God's Deliverance: Jeremiah 14:7-8

O Lord, though our iniquities testify against us, do thou it for thy name's sake; for our backslidings are many; we have sinned against thee. O the hope of Israel, the Saviour thereof in time of trouble, why shouldest thou be as a stranger in the land, and as a wayfaring man that turneth aside to tarry for a night?

What is the message here? It was during the time when Judah had turned away from God and when that happens punishment is sure to follow. Their punishment was to the point that God had withheld the rain which was important to the land and life. The people cried out to God for rain, but the Lord refused to hear their cry for rain. God was sending a natural disaster to Judah as a form of punishment for their sin and corruption. This is a testimony for modern day society as sin is rampant and man is heading on a collision course for punishment from God and it will come a time when prayers will go unheard to punish the nation's sinfulness.

What are we to do? All who understand the punishment of God must pray for the hearts and minds of the unrighteous to repent because today God is speaking to the wickedness of nations through nature. All who remained faithful to God He spared a remnant and will do so today.

Any hope of deliverance is in God--He is our deliverer.

Nov 7

Jesus Christ Our Living Hope: Acts 24:15

And have hope towards God, which they themselves also allow, that there shall be a resurrection on the dead, both of the just and unjust.

Let's begin this discussion by looking at hope, resurrection and Jesus Christ; first hope from a biblical point of view is "defined as a belief that God will accomplish what He has promised (Psalm 71:5; Ephesians 2:12. The Christian hope is based on the fact that God has always been faithful to do what He said He would do. In the NT, Christian hope is never wishful thinking; it is a divine certainty" (The Student Bible Dictionary P. 115). 1 Corinthians 15:12-34 talks about the resurrection of Jesus Christ and without His resurrection there is no salvation.

Using the same source to define resurrection, we find that resurrection is the raising of the dead to life (Matthew 22:23). Romans 6:9 states, "Knowing that Christ being raised from the dead dieth no more; death hath no more dominion over him. What this says is that God raised Christ from the dead. All who believe died with Christ to sin and rose with Him to a life of righteousness on Sunday morning. So then if the question were raised, why is the believer's hope alive? It is because Jesus Christ is alive and now seated on the right hand of the father making intercessions for all believers. Another thought on believers' hope being alive is that death could not contain Him--Jesus Christ and the grave could not hold Him. ***He is alive!***

Our scripture text tells us that there will be a resurrection of both the saved and unsaved each to a different destination. The righteous to an eternal life with Christ and the unrighteous to a life separated from Him. With that being said, then believers have something to live for in that they will reign with Christ during His reign here on earth. It is noteworthy to say that all believers being raised to a new life in Christ have the power to resist sin and its temptations.

It you don't know Jesus Christ He is the Savior of the world, who died for the sins of the world. He is man's redeemer for all who believe in Him and accept Him as Lord and Savior. He is the believer's intercessor who is seated at the right hand of the Father making intercessions for us. He is our living hope because in Him we live and breathe. It is in Christ Jesus that we hope for tomorrow as He is the one who we can take our burden to and leave them there with the assurances they will be taken care of.

Hallelujah! Hallelujah! Christ is alive--thank God for a living hope.

Jesus Christ No Resurrection No Salvation
1 Corinthians 15:19-22

But if there be no resurrection of the dead, then is Christ not risen; and if Christ be not risen then is our preaching in vain, and your faith is also vain.

In today's discussion it authenticates the importance of believers being raised to a new life in Christ as His resurrection completes salvation. During His earthly ministry, Jesus told His followers that the temple-His body would be destroyed but would rise again in three days. His listeners lacked the full understanding of what Jesus was referring to. Jesus was referring to the fact that He was going to die the horrible death for man's sins and God would raise Him in three days, thus completing man's freedom from the bondage of sin. Verse 17 authenticates this fact when Paul reminded the Corinthian believers of this fact which is the foundation of Christian beliefs.

It is noteworthy to say that if Christ had not died then there would be no resurrection. The question now becomes, What would become of salvation? It is safe to say there would be no salvation, no hope of eternity and man would remain lost marred in sin. The next question is what was the purpose of Christ coming to earth as God-man? If Christ's death and resurrection wasn't a requirement by God the father then Jesus would have remained in heaven, but this was all part of God's plan for salvation.

Resurrection completed man's redemption. Salvation! Salvation!

Nov 9

Charity The Greatest Of All: 1 Corinthians 13:13

And now abideth faith, hope, charity, these three; but the greatest of these is charity.

What is charity and why is it looked upon as the greatest of the three? Scripture (1 Corinthians 13:13 and Colossians 3:14 equate charity to love and this definition is supported in The Student Bible Dictionary (P.59) because God is love and all believers are to have agape like love.

God values charity because it exalts a Christ-like character over possessions or ministry or even faith. This is because God Himself is love and gave the best that He had for humanity's sins and Christ went to the cross to bridge the spiritual divide between man and God.

Therefore, the characteristics of Christ are He is love, honesty, truth, kindness, patience, unselfishness and endurance in righteousness to the end. Although, Christ was man and fully God He remain sinless being tempted by sin and humiliated by man. It is then safe to say that the greatest in God's kingdom are all those who possess the inward godliness and have demonstrated a love for God and others. It matters not how great ones ministry is if love/charity is missing then it mounts to nothing. God provides a perfect example of charity because all He done was in love and because of love.

If the question were raised, What does love have to do with it? Everything because love is the core of our being.
Isn't love great!

The Hope of Righteousness: Galatians 5:5

For we through the Spirit wait for the hope of righteousness by faith.

In an earlier reading we defined hope, but as a reminder hope is our faith in something or someone. The hope of a better life where there is no more sorrow, pain and suffering, hard trials and tribulations and spending eternity with God rests in Jesus Christ as it is His righteousness that we as believers are made right in the sight of God.

The question now becomes, What is righteousness? The Student Bible Dictionary (P.203) defines righteousness as the "rightness of God's standards, justice, and fairness." Isaiah 41:10 and 2 Corinthians 5:21 support the dictionary's definition of righteousness by stating "For he (God) made him (Jesus) to be sin for us, who knew no sin, that we might be made the righteousness of God in him (Jesus Christ)" (5:21).

With that being said, then all humanity will be measured by God's rightness all made possible by Jesus' sacrificial death at Calvary. Through Christ's actions all believers have been justified and God sees us as new creatures in His Son. Believers remain in a right standing with God through our steadfast faith in Jesus Christ and in fellowship with Him.

If the question were to arise, Am I living right or according to God's standards or is my lifestyle pleasing to God? God's Word provides the answer for holy living as our righteousness was made possible by Jesus Christ as He is our hope for tomorrow.

Hope and righteousness =Jesus Christ.

Nov 11

The Full Assurances Of Hope: Hebrews 6:11

And we desire that every one of you do shew the same diligence to the full assurance of hope unto the end.

The writer of Hebrews wanted the readers to remain steadfast in his or her conviction to Jesus Christ as He is the only true source of all believers hope. Our scripture verse provides the writer's heart-felt desire to remain in fellowship with Christ until the end because this would prevent them from becoming spiritually depraved or falling into spiritual apostasy. Our scripture text also expresses Christ-like love and concern for fellow believers as this applies to all believers today.

Let us look at the word assurance and its definition, it states that assurance carries the meaning of "confidence, trust, full conviction, certainty and a firmness of mind" (The Student Bible Dictionary (P.34)). The question now becomes, Who do we put our trust in? The answer is a resounding Jesus Christ. This is because of His atoning work at Calvary. Jesus Christ provided salvation. The next question that comes to mind is what convictions should all believers have? All believers should have such strong conviction that Jesus Christ is God's Son and He died on the cross for our sins so that we are made right with God the Father. If there were any doubt of Christ's deity, His earthly ministry proved that He was the promised Messiah-Christ.

All our assurances rest in Jesus Christ.

Nov 12

Jesus Christ The Hope of Our Salvation: Hebrews 5:9

And being made perfect, He became the author of eternal salvation unto all them that obey him.

What is the meaning of our scripture verse? Jesus Christ is perfect because He is God's Son but suffered human limitations in obedience to His Father. As His mission was to bridge the spiritual divide between God and man which were caused by Adam's disobedience. Another school of thought is that with His atoning work Christ became the author of salvation because He was the only one found worthy to become the human sacrifice for sin. Animal sacrifices were insufficient because it only covered over sin, whereas Christ's blood done away with sin.

For all believers to have this eternal salvation we must obey Christ and His commands. Christ was obedient to His Father unto the end, then why not you and I? Our obedience to Christ shows our love for Him and a desire to live in union with Him. Another point on our obedience to Christ is that believers are being transformed to the likeness of Christ as we will reign with Him one day. This brings into view John 8:31 which speak of continuing in the Word of God--steadfastness.

It can be concluded then that Jesus Christ wrote the manual for our salvation as he was in the beginning with God and understood that in due time He would reconcile man back to God.

He is the author and finisher of our faith--salvation.

Nov 13

Hope In An Unchanging God: Hebrews 6:13-19

For when God made promise to Abraham, because He could swear by no greater, He sware by Himself, Saying, Surely blessing I will bless thee, and multiplying I will multiply thee...That by two immutable things, in which it was impossible for God to lie, which we might have a strong consolation, who have fled for refuge to lay hold upon the hope set before us.

Our scripture verses explain in detail why man has hope in God, it is because He cannot lie and He changes not. God made a promise to Abraham that He would bless him and make him a great nation and God kept that promise. Being faithful believers in God and the seed of Abraham we as believers have assurances of the promised blessings made to Abraham.

Just as Abraham and the other patriarchs had enough faith to believe God for His promise we too as believers must trust God and receive all of His blessings. Biblical history records the many promises kept by God, for example, He promised a Savior, Jesus came. He promised salvation, provided through Jesus' death and resurrection. God promised to supply all your needs, another promise kept. Lastly, God asks you to cast all your cares upon Him (1 Peter 5:7) that He would handle the situation. Take your burden/problems to the Lord-- He is waiting.

It can be concluded that whatever God promised we have the assurances that He will deliver.
Our immutable God!

A New Heaven And A New Earth: Revelation 21:1

And I saw a new heaven and a new earth; for the first heaven and the first earth were passed away; and there were no more sea.

The scene takes place with John on the Isle of Patmos where he was in the Spirit of the Lord and God was showing John what the new heaven and earth would look like. The old would have passed away as the redeemed of Christ will have been transformed into the likeness of Christ.

Believers will have changed from mortality to immortality and the righteousness of God will be ever present as all will dwell in holy perfection with Christ in the New Jerusalem (v.2). The New Jerusalem currently exists in heaven as it is the city being prepared for a prepared people--believers. When He returns this city-Jerusalem will come to earth where God and believers will dwell. All traces of sin will have been erased, the earth as we know it today will have been destroyed; even the stars, galaxies will have been shaken from their foundations and vanished like smoke (Haggai 2:6; Hebrews 12:26-28; Isaiah 51:6).

The new earth will become the dwelling place for all believers and God as there will be peace and harmony, no more tears, sorrow, pain and burdens to bear. This is because all the effects of sin will have been wiped away (v.4). If the question were raised, Why is it necessary for God and His people to live in conditions of perfection? It is because God and His holiness cannot look on or dwell in sin. Therefore, the redeemed will have resurrected bodies like Christ they will be real, tangible and visible, but will lack any form of corruption.

The question now becomes, Who will be in the new heaven and new earth? Verse 7 provides the answer by stating that "all who overcometh shall inherit all things; and I will be his God and he shall be my son." This verse carries a twofold meaning, which are, the over comer are who by the grace of God have received faith in Christ and have become new creatures in Christ. The second meaning is that all who remain faithful to God will share in the blessing of being with Christ when He reigns here on earth. It is noteworthy to say that over comers will eat from the tree of life and will not experience the second death due Christ's atoning work at Calvary (v.11). Of all the many blessings from being an over comer, the most important is forever being children of God and remaining with Him forever and bearing His name. On the other hand for those persons who do not accept Jesus as his or her personal Savior and persevere to the end will be eternally separated from God.

It can be concluded then that being an over comer means living the blessed life in our heavenly home prepared by God Himself.

The new heaven and new earth-a place of heavenly bliss.

A Blessed Hope: 1 Peter 1:3

Blessed be the God and Father of our Lord Jesus Christ, which according to his abundant mercy hath begotten us again unto a lively hope in the resurrection of Jesus Christ from the dead.

The term "blessed" in this scenario means happiness or to be made happy by God (Matthew 5:2-12; Psalm 1:1). This term was used in the OT, it means to praise God (Psalm 18:46). With that being said, then we see believers being blessed by God with His grace, mercy and salvation through Jesus Christ.

Our scripture verse talks about the blessed hope all believer have in being born again in Jesus Christ as we rose with Him to a life of righteousness. The question now becomes, What does it mean to be begotten of Christ? The term begotten carries a connotation of regeneration which is the doctrinal teaching of the Christian faith. This is where the believer begins a new life in Christ as the person has been delivered from a life of sin doomed for eternal separation from God the Father. It is noteworthy to say that the begotten lives a life of devotion to God and His holiness.

Our blessed hope-God the Father begets us, God the Son saves us and God the Holy Spirit keeps us all to spend eternity with Him where there will be continuous praise and worship.

Hope everlasting - Blessings abound! Where is your hope?

Nov 16

Sanctify The Lord: 1 Peter 3:15

But sanctify the Lord God in your hearts; and be ready always to give an answer to every man that asketh you a reason of the hope that is in you with meekness and fear.

What is the meaning of this verse? Peter is saying to all that we should have an inner reverence for and a total commitment to Christ as He is Lord and we must be ready at all times to truthfully expound on the Word of God. In order to know God's Word and effectively tell others one must study His word through daily Bible reading and meditate on His world. This verse also bring into focus II Timothy 2:15 which states, "Study to shew thyself approved unto God, a workman that needed not to be ashamed, rightly dividing the word of truth."

In witnessing Christ to others, John 4:4-26 provides a perfect example of meeting people where they are and then direct the discussion to Christ. Jesus made Himself known to the Samarian woman she then witnessed to the towns people and the whole town was saved.

Another point in this verse is "inner reverence" which is to hide the Word of God in our hearts with deep adoration/respect for God. Inner reverence is setting apart our inner most feelings and desire for God and to live holy lives and witness Christ to others.

Sanctify the Lord for He is worthy.

Looking For That Blessed Hope: Titus 2:13-14

Looking for that blessed hope, and the glorious appearing of the great God and our Saviour Jesus Christ; Who gave himself for us, that he might redeem us from all iniquity, and purify unto himself a peculiar people, zealous of good works.

The phrase "blessed hope" refers to full blessings from God, His favor and the happiness for possessing immortal bodies that are free of decay, suffering and pain caused by all manner of corruption. The hope that all believers are looking for is the time when Christ appears in His glory coming for His bride--the church. The church consists of baptized believers who have been washed in the blood of Jesus Christ as He redeemed all believers from sin. Believers are to prayerfully and in a steadfast faith wait for Jesus as He is the groom coming for His bride; as she is to keep herself in purity as a virgin.

The question now becomes, Why must the church present herself in purity? Jesus Christ gave Himself for the church and He is without sin so must His bride. All believers are a set aside people who are peculiar to the world as they see and do things differently. Also, Christians were sanctified by Christ Himself for the purpose of continuing His kingdom building.

Knowing who we are and whose we are, all believers have a blessed hope to look forward to--the returning Christ.

What a blessing!

Nov 18

Wait And Hope: Lamentations 3:26

It is good that a man should both hope and quietly wait for salvation of the Lord.

At the time of this writing Jesus Christ had not made His earthly appearance and Jeremiah was encouraging the people of his day to continue to quietly wait and hope for Jesus' arrival. We know that many died looking for the Messiah as He was promised and we know also that God is faithful to keep His promises. God made no specific time promise as to when the Savior would come, but just stated that He was sending the Savior--Jesus came. God's time and man's time differs, one day with God is a thousand years with man. Another point of discussion is that Jeremiah was encouraging the nation to remain confident in their faith in God. Why is this? This is because without a steadfast faith, hope is null and void.

The question now becomes, What happened to those persons who died without seeing Jesus? If those persons remained faithful to God they too are believer and will be raised to a life of eternity with Christ.

A noteworthy point on waiting, one must remain patient and persevere with confidence to the end. Paul in one of his writings likened this Christian walk to that of a long-distance runner as the race isn't given to the swift, but the endurance runner.

Be patience- go the distance and never give up hope.

Nov 19

The Lord The Hope Of His People: Joel 3:16-17

The Lord also shall roar out of Zion, and utter his voice from Jerusalem; and the heavens and the earth shall shake; but the Lord will be the hope of his people, and the strength of the children of Israel. So shall ye know that I am the Lord your God dwelling in Zion, my holy mountain; then shall Jerusalem be holy, and there shall no strangers pass through her any more.

Joel's writing had a threefold purpose to the people of Judah which were (a) "to come together before the Lord in a sacred assembly, (b) to exhort the people to repent and return to the Lord, and (c) Joel recorded God's prophetic word to the people of Judah" (KJV Commentary).

In verses 9-16, the people are instructed to prepare for war because he was going to bring His form of destruction on them because of their wicked ways. In verse 13, it talks about "the harvest is ripe" is God's judgment on all nations who refuse His salvation invitation. It is noteworthy to say that the wicked can continue in their ways thinking they have gotten by, but when sin gets to a certain point He says enough is enough then God's punishment is definite. Verse 16 picks up with the prophet Joel outlining the magnitude of God's destruction, while that only God is the hope of believers. This verse gives the assurance to all believers that regardless of our surrounding conditions God is our deliverer and protector.

Hope in the Lord.

Nov 20

Purified In Hope: 1 John 3:3

And every man that hath this hope in him purifieth himself, even as he is pure.

This scripture is speaking of all believers who have placed their trust and hope in Jesus Christ has purified themselves. Believers' being purified in Christ means that we have put on the newness in Christ and His holiness. Being purified in Christ believers become sons of God which carries many blessings (v.2). Being called sons of God, believers have accepted Jesus and his or her personal Savior as this was done out of faith in and trusting God. Some of the blessings from being sons of God and purified in Christ is that believers have the assurances of spending eternity with God. Also, being sons of God and purified in Christ we as believers have been sanctified to a life of righteousness. Believers will reign with Christ when He returns to rule here on earth.

Let's look at having a purified hope is that the love of God is depicted here because while we were enemies of God His love caused Him to give His best to bridge the spiritual divide. The question now becomes, Why was purifying necessary? Purification was necessary because of the immoral purity of sin and blood is one of the purifying agents. Believers have been cleansed by Jesus and our hope rests in Him.

Jesus is all the world to me.

Nov 21

Perseverers In Faith: Romans 4:5

But to him that worketh not, but believeth on him that justifieth the ungodly, his faith is counted for righteousness.

Today's discussion focus is on persevere and faith while examining some notables from the Bible who remained steadfast in their faith until the end. Let's begin by defining persevere/perseverance, it is the act of keeping on, not giving up, endurance, consistency and determination. The person who perseveres is the person who displays attributes of determination and consistency in his or her endeavor. The faith is ones belief and is an aspect of perseverance. This is because the person has a strong faith and steadfast endurance to complete his or her journey.

Our scripture verse counts this type of faith as righteousness. The righteousness spoken of here is the rightness of God by which all will be judged. This is because God has justified the ungodly and this righteousness is a gift from God. Most important, the righteousness of God flows from His love, mercy, grace and His nature. Then all believers can respond to Christ in faith because of God's actions. Another note of faith being counted as righteousness is that it brings forgiveness because of Christ and His atoning work at Calvary and our belief in Him.

If the question were raised, Who are the ungodly? The ungodly are those who have yet to accept Jesus as his or her personal Savior. To answer this question brings into view Romans 3:23, which states "For all have sinned and come short of the glory of God." This means that at one point we were all sinners and the saved are sinners saved by grace. When God looks He sees the hearts of believers who have turned to Him by faith in Jesus Christ and God counts this faith as righteousness. **What a merciful God!**

Lets segway to some of the faithful in the Bible, they are Abraham who was counted as righteous because of his faith. Why? Because he believed the promise God made to him and remained loyal to God throughout his earthly journey. Enoch was so faithful to God and walked closely with God until he was spared death. Noah is another patriarch who took God at His word. When God told Noah it was going to rain, Noah believed God. Noah acted in faith on God's instructions. **What faith!**

This question comes to mind which is, what did these three men have in common? All had faith in God realizing that their salvation came by faith and that the law was not their savior. The purpose of the law was to show the need for salvation---through Jesus Christ.

Paul equated Perseverers in faith to that of an endurance runner who has the determination to endure unto the end. John in Revelation likened Perseverers to over comers because in each scenario the believer have endured persecutions, pain and suffering, temptation, rejection for Christ's sake and all manner of humiliations. Regardless of the terminology all who remain steadfast in Christ is rewarded.

A crown of life is waiting stay the course.

Nov 22

Name In The Book Of Life: Revelation 3:5

He that overcometh, the same shall be clothed in white raiment; and I will not blot out his name out of the book of life, but I will confess to my Father, and before his angels.

Today's scripture text packs a powerful punch in that it is speaking specifically to believers and expresses our reward for remaining steadfast in Christ through faith. All who overcome will be clothed in white raiment as everyone will have been washed in the blood of Jesus our Lord and Savior. Next we have Jesus stating that He will stand before His Father and the angels and witness that these are the believers who have withstood all trials and temptations that the world and Satan have thrown their way. They are worthy to be clothed. **What a blessing it is to have Christ Himself witness on your behalf!**

It is noteworthy to point that this verse also carries an implication that all who fail to remain faithful to the Lord will have their name blotted out of the book of life and will be eternally separated from God. Is this a possibility? One would assume this to be so because all believers have victory in Christ but it is imperative that we as believers walk in the newness of Christ.

We know that chapter 3 was written to the churches as they had become spiritually dead (v.1) as only a few of the members remained faithful. Outwardly these churches appeared alive and were successful by the world's standard, but Jesus saw the true heart of the church. The church is comprised of baptized believers then individually and collectively all must hear what "the Spirit" has to say.

Remain in the book of life by remaining faithful to God.

Christ My Redeemer: Job 19:25

For I know that my Redeemer liveth, and that he shall stand at the latter day upon the earth.

On this life's journey and we as believers become weary with the troubles of this life and it appears as though we can go no further, we are to remember in whose strength we operate---Christ Jesus. It is in Christ we live and breathe as He is the center of all life. With that fact in mind we then can say like Job with assurances that "my Redeemer liveth."

Knowing that Christ is alive and one day will rule supreme on this earth is enough to continue standing for Him; in the end we will be rewarded with a crown of life and will gain our full inheritance for being sons of God. Job's life serves as a perfect example as how one must endure in the midst of suffering and tribulations. Did Job turn his back on God? No, he became weary as this is human nature. As Job remembered who gave him life and who had the power to take his life, then we too must remember we have victory in Jesus Christ because of His victory over sin and death.

A closing note, living in today's society is a whirlwind of sin and spiritual decay, but we as believers have the power through the Holy Spirit who protects us from this spiritual apostasy and the power to remain in Christ.

Christ is alive--our Redeemer.

Redemption In Christ Jesus: Romans 3:24

Being justified freely by the grace through the redemption that is in Christ Jesus

Reading the above scripture text brings to mind this question, Why was man's redemption necessary? Verse 23 provides the answer in that God had pronounced the whole world guilty before Him and there was no man on earth found worthy to pay the penalty of sin. What was required was a human sacrifice without sin. Who was found worthy was His Son Jesus Christ. Because of man being marred in sin he was unworthy and animal sacrifices lacked the ability to remove sin and required a yearly atonement for sin. What did Christ tell His Father, prepare me a body I will go? He suffered human limitations for the purpose of redeeming man back to God.

What qualifies Christ to be man's redeemer is that He is God's Son, second He was and remained sinless until the end and third, Christ being both God and man met all the requirements specified by God, the Father. Christ's death removed sin and requires no yearly sacrifice; just accept Him as our personal Savior for He is our Redeemer.

In the redemption process all who believe have been made right (justified) or found not guilty by our righteous judge--God. Man's justification is part of the salvation process as no man has the ability to justify him or herself.

The conclusion is "No one is justified apart from redemption in Christ" (KJV Commentary).

Nov 25

The Joy Of Thanksgiving: Psalm 26:7; Psalm 100

That I may publish with the voice of thanksgiving, and tell of all thy wondrous works. Make a joyful noise unto the Lord, all ye lands. Serve the Lord with gladness: come before his presence with singing.

This day is set aside for a time of reflecting on the goodness of the Lord and to give thanks for His many blessings bestowed upon us. Traditionally this day was set aside to give thanks for bountiful crops as our fore parents recognized that it was God's blessings that the harvest was sufficient to last until the next planting season.

Our scripture text reminds us how we are to express our thankfulness for God goodness and mercy throughout the year. If each person would take an accounting of his or her blessings they would out number our troubles every time.

God's goodness is witnessed throughout His many wonders as He sends the rain in due season. The sun, moon and stars operate on schedule; the temperature is as He orders and each of us rises each morning to the dawning of a new day as He orders and within His time limits. He supplies all our needs according to His wishes (Philippians 4:19). He hears our cry when we call Him as no problem is too small or large for Him to handle. Every man, woman boy or girl can dial 1 1 1 and never get a busy signal.

God is good, gracious and His mercy is everlasting---be thankful.

The Gift Of Salvation: 2 Corinthians 9:15

Thanks be unto God for His unspeakable gift.

Much has been written and discussed about salvation, but salvation is a topic worthy of continuous discussions because of the blessing it carries. We know that it is a free gift from God through His Son Jesus Christ that was freely given out of love. Salvation was provided for humanity from the foundation of the world as God in His infinite wisdom knew that man was going to sin and would require saving. God also, knew that man was unworthy to redeem himself back to God and regain his right standing with God.

Being that God could not look on sin neither does He tolerate sin implemented the sacrificial systems as a way to atone man's sins knowing that animal sacrifices were insufficient and a permanent human sacrifice would atone for sin once and for all. Christ's one-time death bought man's freedom from the bondage of sin to a life of righteousness. Man has the opportunity to spend eternity with God as opposed to being separated from God our Creator both now and in our after life. ***Salvation-our freedom is the gift.***

To receive and enjoy this gift one must accept Christ as his or her personal Savior because He freed us, redeemed us and then justified us. What a gift to be ever thankful for and offer praises to His holy name.

Have you accepted your gift today? Is joy of thanksgiving for the gift present in your praise and life? Accept the gift.

Christ Our Hope Abideth Forever: John 13:32-34

And if I be lifted up from the earth, will draw all men unto me...The people answered him we have heard out of the law that Christ abideth for ever; and how sayest thou, The Son of must be lift up? Who is this Son of man?

During Jesus' earthly ministry He taught His listeners many thing concerning His deity but still many lacked understanding and failed to recognize Jesus as the promised Messiah. We see in this setting just such a thing taking place where Jesus is speaking of His impending death at Calvary and it was necessary for Him to go by Calvary to provide salvation. Christ's message was that He was going to die on Friday but would rise on Sunday and at His appointed time return to His Father and all who believe in Him He would draw them to Him. **They missed the concept.**

The reality here is that Jesus' listeners had been taught the law and was expecting the Messiah, but because Jesus appeared as an ordinary man they failed to recognize Him neither did they understand Him as being the Son of man. Jesus was both the Son of man and God's Son given His mission here on earth. Jesus was man because it required a man to atone the sins of the world as this person must be sinless--God man.

Therefore, man's hope of salvation, Jesus must live and return to His Father and alive He is.

Nov 28

Love And Hope In Jesus Christ: John 3:16-17

For God so loved the world that he gave his only begotten Son that whosoever believeth in him should not perish, but have everlasting life. For God sent not his Son into the world to condemn the world; but that the world through him might be saved.

Our scripture text provides and answer to an implied question of why would God do what He did? Our answer goes far deeper than just love for all humanity and a restored fellowship with man. Our scripture text depicts the true heart of God for His prized creation--man.

Let's outline what God did out of love; First, He "gave" His only Son knowing that Jesus would die a humiliating death. God willingly gave His Son as no one forced God to take the action He took. Second, man must believe in what God did and who He gave. Third, the assurance that one who believes on Jesus shall not perish. Lastly the promise of "everlasting life" carries the guarantee of spending eternity with God. **What an act of love!**

The second act of love in the Godhead is that Christ God's Son willingly came to earth to be man's propitiator and the third act is that God the Holy Spirit readily takes up residence in the believer to guide, protect, and teach all things that man must know and do to remain faithful to Christ our Savior. **There is no greater love than that of the Godhead working in harmony for mankind.**

With that being said then man has every reason to hope in Jesus Christ and rejoice because of His action we who believe have a brighter tomorrow.

It is noteworthy to say God's actions included all generations, past, present and future---before Christ's birth, after His birth and death and His ascension back to heaven. This is because all who died before Christ's birth was looking forward to the cross and those afterward were looking back on the cross. Needless to say Christ is no longer on the cross but residing in heaven making intercessions for us. The common thread here is faith regardless whether it was during the age of the law or grace. Many of the OT prophets and believers had an unwavering faith in God. It is imperative for new age believers to have the same faith. With that being said then faith is the key to our beliefs as it has been quoted, read and written that it is impossible to please God without faith.

Then our hope through faith in Jesus Christ makes it possible for us to receive the love gift of salvation.

All begins and ends with Christ.

Nov 29

Born Again In Christ: Titus 3:5; John 3:3

...Verily, Verily, I say unto thee, Except a man be born again, he cannot see the kingdom of God. Not by works of righteousness which we have done, but according to his mercy he saved us, by the washing of regeneration, and renewing of the Holy Ghost.

What does it mean to be born again in Christ? Being born again is the doctrinal teaching in the Christian community and faith. It teaches that one must have a rebirth spiritually in Christ. This is the process that takes place in the human heart. What occurs is that the confessing believer confesses his or her sin realizing that he or she needs saving and lacks the ability to do him or herself (repent). Prior to turning to Christ the person was spiritually dead to sin and after repenting they become spiritually alive in Christ. A transformation occurs. Instead of being at odds with God the now believer gains fellowship with God as he or she enters into the family of God. Another note here is that during transformation, instead of rebelling against God the believer turns to a life of righteous living.

How all this occurs is that the believer has been washed in the blood of Jesus Christ. As He died on the cross for sin so did we and we rose with Him. The Holy Spirit's role in this process is that He keeps us in a renewed spirit to remain committed to Christ and His righteousness.

What a blessing to be born again in Christ!

Nov 30

Blessed Hope: Titus 2:11-14

For the grace of God that bringeth salvation hath appeared to all men. Who gave Himself for us, that he might redeem us from all iniquity and purity unto himself as a peculiar people, zealous of good works.

Today's lesson study tells us in plain English why we as believers have a blessed hope. First it says that by the grace of God that salvation came to all men. As some men during Christ's earthly visit recognized Him and some didn't. John 3:16-17 comes into view and expresses why it was by God's grace for sending our Savior.

What is grace? It is God's Righteousness At Christ's Expense--who gave Himself for us. **What a price to pay for someone else's freedom!** However, love is the main artery in the salvation process.

Man was redeemed from a lifetime of iniquity to one of purity to become a special people to God as we as believers are to look and be different from the world. Being redeemed we on the holiness of God are to become dedicated workers for His kingdom building. How are we to do good works for God? This is achieved by righteous living daily and witnessing Christ the world over. It is during our witness that we season the world as this is providing spiritual food to all who will believe. Also, being purified by Christ believers become a peculiar people, a royal priesthood, a holy nation set aside to God by Jesus Christ.

Jesus is our blessed hope.

Salvation Through Jesus Christ

Dec 1

The Meaning Of Salvation: Romans 1:16

For I am not ashamed of the gospel of Christ: for it is the power of God unto salvation to every one that believeth; to the Jew first, and also to the Greek.

During Paul's missionary journeys, he expressed his desire to travel to Rome and preach the gospel of Christ to the Romans and his willingness to preach Christ wherever and to whomever for it is by which all men shall be saved. It goes without saying that all who desire to be saved must first believe that Jesus Christ is God's Son.

If the question were raised, What are we being saved from? All who believe in Jesus Christ are being saved from a life of sin to a life of righteousness, which is in God as this is done in faith. The term "salvation" in itself means being delivered or being brought safely through or from one place to the next. The believer is being delivered from a life of eternal separation from God to spending eternal life with Him.

Jesus Christ is the only way to salvation which is provided through the grace of God that He freely gives. Our beliefs are based on Christ's death (Romans 3:25; 5:8) and His resurrection (Romans 5:10). Salvation is the gift of God that we received through faith in Jesus Christ that God extends to us as a result of His grace.

Salvation our deliverance; accept the gift.

The Promised Savior: Isaiah 9: 6-7

For unto us a child is born, unto us a Son is given: and the government shall be upon His shoulders: and His name shall be called Wonderful, Counseller, The mighty God, The everlasting Father, The Prince of Peace.

The prophet Isaiah was foretelling of a time in the future encouraging the people of his day not to get discouraged because the promised Savior was coming just as promised by God. This scripture coincides with Isaiah 7:14 as the prophet provides details of Jesus' birth and the unique way in which He would be born.

Isaiah's descriptive name of Christ characterizes the functions of the Messiah. The name "Wonderful" symbolizes the miraculous works or supernatural wonders he would perform, such as miracles He would perform. The name "Counseller" represents the incarnation of perfect wisdom as He provided the perfect plan of salvation. The name "Mighty God" embodies the full deity of God as He was God in the flesh. The name 'The Everlasting Father" means that Christ would reveal His heavenly Father and He Himself would have compassion on all mankind as a compassionate father that loves all His children. Lastly, the name "Prince of Peace" means that Christ would bring the peace of God to all humanity through mankind's deliverance from sin. ***Christ is the man of peace.***

A Savior was promised, a promise kept God--Jesus Christ is the promised Messiah.
Accept Him!

Thou Art The Christ: Matthew 16:16

And Simon Peter answered and said, Thou art the Christ, the Son of the living God.

During Jesus' earthly ministry, He began to wonder who people thought He was, some felt that Jesus was "John the Baptist, some took Jesus to be Elias, while others took Jesus to be Jeremiah or even one of the other prophets." The most telling fact to this conversation was between Jesus and His disciples when He asked them "whom do ye say that I am?" It was Peter's faith that gave him the correct answer (v.16). What can be said about Peter's faith is that he believed the promise as well as the many eye witness accounts of the miracles that Jesus had done. Peter's faith was on display when Jesus told them to follow Him and they immediately stopped what they were doing to become soul winners for Christ.

Peter's like faith in Jesus is what He is building His church upon as all believers are to have an unwavering faith in Jesus while knowing that all of Satan's efforts to destroy Christ's church and hinder kingdom building will fail.

With that being said, these questions come to mind, How strong is your faith? Does your faith give you the insight to see spiritual deception? Stand fast in Christ for He is the One.

On Christ the solid rock I stand in Him my anchor holds!

Dec 4

See The Salvation Of The Lord: Luke 2:25-26

...There was a man in Jerusalem, whose name was Simeon; and the same man was just and devout, waiting for the consolation of Israel; and the Holy Ghost was upon him. And it was revealed unto him by the Holy Ghost, that he should not see death, before he had seen the Lord's Christ.

This lesson setting takes place in Jerusalem at the early stage of Christ's birth when He was just an infant. There was a spiritually devout man and woman Simeon and Anna serving in the temple as they had heard of the promised Savior.

The Holy Ghost filled Simeon was devoted to God in the midst of a spiritually luke warm atmosphere. It can be speculated that Simeon prayed and asked God to spare his life until the coming/consolation of the Messiah; God granted his wish.

The birth of Christ ushered in the Messianic era and the surrounding areas of Judea and Galilee saw a spiritual awakening and with the spread of the news of Christ's miraculous birth some knew that the Messiah had arrived. ***Peace on earth and good news to all.***

The lesson from this story is that regardless of our surroundings there will always be persons who will remain steadfast in their faith and devoted to God and His righteousness. A believer's greatest blessing is to one day see Christ face-to-face. Remaining steadfast in Christ is our hope for tomorrow, because one day He is coming for His church.

Christ promised to return and return He will.

Dec 5

Recognize Christ: John 4:25-26

The woman saith unto him, I know that Messias cometh, which is called Christ: when He is come, He will tell us all things. Jesus saith unto her; I that speak unto thee am He.

Let's begin today's discussion with a thought provoking question, given all that had been spoken and presumably written of the promised Messiah would you recognize Him if you met Him? Let's look at the Samarian woman, who had heard that the Messiah was coming, but she like many others of her day was expecting Jesus in another manner. See! Jesus was an ordinary looking man, who could be easily mistaken for just a prophet like John the Baptist. He was humbled in His entire earthly ministry. Being Christ He looked beyond the woman's faults and saw her needs--saving. **He does so today.**

Jesus met the woman at the well getting physical water and offered her everlasting water. **He is still giving everlasting water to all who believe.** Back to our question, many today do not recognize Jesus as He is meeting all unbelievers at his or her well of spiritual apostasy offering living water. Once the unbeliever recognizes Jesus, the person has a testimony like the Samarian woman. Let's reflect on Paul when he met Jesus on the Damascus road, he immediately recognized Jesus as the living Christ; the one who can and will save anyone who confesses that He is Lord. Let's look as others who recognized Christ; Peter recognized Jesus as the Christ and it was this faith that Christ is building His church. Peter preached to thousands and many souls were saved. John the Baptist knew Jesus as the promised Messiah who was preferred before him. Satan recognized Jesus as the Christ, God's Son and tried his level best to tempt Jesus so that God's kingdom building would be derailed.

The question now becomes, can the world recognize Jesus in the believer's lifestyle? Believers are Christ's workman as we are to witness Christ daily both in word and living holy lives before Him.

Believers have recognized Christ as his or her life quenching

thirst and in obedience to the Great Commission recorded in Matthew 28:19-20 is sharing Him with others because He is just too good to keep to ones self. He is like fire shut up in ones bones. Jesus Christ is the perfect conversation piece as there is no argument of His goodness, His grace and mercy and most of all salvation.
    Recognize Jesus--He is very visible.

Dec 6

Harvesting Souls For Christ: John 4:35-38

Jesus saith unto them, My meat is to do the will of him that sent me, and to finish his work....And he that reapeth receiveth wages, and gathereth fruit unto life eternal: that both he that soweth and he that reapeth may rejoice together.

What does it mean to harvest souls for Christ? Harvesting souls for Christ carries several messages one of which that the current believer is obeying the Great Commission (Matthew 28:19-20) commissioned by Christ Himself as His kingdom building must go forth. Who best to share the good news of Christ other than fellow believers who have tasted the sweet herbs of salvation? Believers are to witness Christ the world over as believers are the salt of the earth. As believers we season this world with words and holy living so the world will see Christ manifested in us.

While obeying the Great Commission believers are bringing others to Christ in a saving faith as the consequence of this faith is eternal life. There is great joy when one soul comes to Christ; visualize the scene of rejoicing there is as more souls are harvested for Christ. There will be rejoicing from both the sower and reaper. **What a joyful scene?**

It is God's desire that all be saved and Christ's finished work at Calvary makes God's desire possible. The sower is believers and the hearer is reaping the benefit of coming and knowing Christ.

The harvest fields are ripe with souls to be harvested (v. 36).

Dec 7

Jesus The Branch Of God: Isaiah 4:2

In that day shall the branch of the LORD be beautiful and glorious, and the fruit of the earth shall be excellent and comely for them that are escaped of Israel.

Isaiah's writing looks forward to a time in the future before the coming of Christ and even further into the future when Christ will rule the world with justice, peace, and righteousness. The first part of Isaiah's prophesy was fulfilled some 700 years later when Christ was born as He is of the earthly lineage of Jesse, David's father (11:1). The second part of Isaiah's prophecy will be fulfilled when Christ returns. When Christ returns the world will once again enjoy total peace and harmony as it was when God first created all things.

Jeremiah 33:15 labels Christ as the "Branch of righteousness" because He is the Son of God and His second coming will be different from the first as He will rule with the Grace and love of God for He is God. Revelation 19:1-6 talks about Christ's return to earth to destroy the beast, the false prophets, the ungodly and all ungodliness and will rule with the saints—the church.

Fulfillment of the first part of Isaiah's prophecy was beautiful and gracious because the Savior came and the second part will be more precious and beautiful because peace, harmony, love and righteousness will be ever present.

Jesus the righteous branch—all is complete in Him! Praise Him! Praise Him!

Dec 8

The Prophesied Christ: Isaiah 7:14; Matthew 1:23

....The Lord Himself shall give you a sign; Behold, a Virgin shall conceive, and bear a Son, and shall call his name Immanuel...which being interpreted is, God with us.

All believing saints during the OT era were looking for the Messiah as many believed the promise of God that He would send a Savior who would bring peace to this world. God knew from the foundation of the world what would happen to man and He had prepared a plan of redemption through His Son Jesus Christ. God knew the appointed time of Christ's birth, to whom and His earthly lineage. It is noteworthy to say that there were some during the OT who believed and trusted God; however it was necessary for God to speak to His people through Isaiah.

Isaiah's prophesy was fulfilled with the birth of Christ (Matthew 1:18-23) as His name was given to signify that God was with His people. A virgin birth was necessary because Christ's mission was to pay the penalty of sin and only a holy God was worthy. Christ's worthiness was because of His virgin mother and God as His father as He was conceived by the Holy Spirit—God.

God was with us then and remains so today through the indwelling Holy Spirit.

Dec 9

Christ The Anointed Savior
Matthew 1:1; John 7: 42 Acts 10:38

Jesus Christ, the son of David, the son of Abraham....That Christ cometh out of the seed of David, and out of the town of Bethlehem, where David was?...How God anointed Jesus of Nazareth with the Holy ghost and with power; who went about doing good, and healing all that were oppressed of the devil; for God was with him.

To be anointed is to be consecrated for special service, which usually means to perform a special service for God. Special service anointment was prevalent throughout the OT. This was done for Kings and priests (Exodus 28:4; I Samuel 15:1; 17).

King David was anointed to be King of Israel as Christ would come out of the lineage of David. Oil is used when anointing Kings and priest for services. Jesus Christ was anointed by God Himself to be the Savior of the world as Christ was anointed by the Holy Spirit who gave Him power to overcome Satan and worldly temptation as Christ was both human and divine. God anointing His Son points to Christ's deity and authority to perform the many miracles, healing and other signs and wonders He performed. Christ was anointed Savior because He is God and is worthy of all praise and honor.

Christ was anointed as our Savior so believers have been consecrated for service for Christ—spreading the good news world over.

Jesus The Rejected Stone: Acts 4:11-12

This is the stone which was set at nought of you builders, which is become the head of the corner. Neither is there salvation in any other; for there is none other name under the heaven given among men, whereby we must be saved.

In Peter's bold preaching Christ reminded his audience that Jesus was the builder that earthly builders rejected as Christ was the head corner stone meaning that Christ existed before His earthly ministry began. Christ was the promised Messiah who came to bring salvation to all mankind. Verse 11 is the foundation for Peter's statement as biblical history records that many in Jesus' day rejected Him as the Christ. Many believed that Jesus was Elias, John the Baptist reincarnated or some other prophet, but Peter through the revelation of the Holy Spirit knew Jesus as the Christ.

While Christ walked the earth many rejected Him, the question that comes to mind, Is Christ being rejected today? If so how are we rejecting Christ? One can say that unbelievers reject Christ by failing to accept Him as Lord of his or her life. Believers can reject Christ by failing to obey His commands and live holy lives before Him and yielding to the convicting work of the Holy Spirit, Jesus becoming the head of our lives.

Jesus is the corner stone and one day all will recognize Him as such and confess that He is Lord.

Don't reject the stone!

Jesus The Only Name For Salvation: Acts 4:12

Neither is there salvation in any other; for there is none other name under heaven given among men, whereby we must be saved.

Let's begin today's discussion by looking at why Jesus is the only name that brings salvation. First, salvation was necessary because of man's sin which was ushered into the world by Adam. All humanity born after Adam was born into sin and lacked the ability to save himself. Second, to completely do away with sin required a God-man and Jesus was the only one who fulfilled all of God's requirements. Third, Jesus is God's Son who was in the beginning with God and found worthy to be the Savior of the world. Fourth, due to man's sin and continued wickedness, God pronounced the whole world guilty and to repair the spiritual divide that existed between God and man, a Savior was necessary—Jesus Christ. Jesus restored the broken fellowship with His death and Resurrection; thereby providing salvation to all who believe on His name.

The question that comes to mind, What is salvation? Salvation is the bringing of one safely from harm or danger. Salvation is the freeing one from bondage. In this case man was freed from the bondage of sin and into a life of spiritual freedom one that carries the blessing of spending eternity with God.

In conclusion, the name of Jesus means salvation the one whose blood stain banner removed sin and it's stained; the only name by which men can be saved.

Dec 12

Christ's Work In Salvation: Romans 1:16

For I am not ashamed of the gospel of Christ; for it is the power of God unto salvation to every one that believeth; to the Jew first, and also the Greek.

Yesterday we discussed the name of Jesus and salvation, today's focus discussion is on His work in salvation. Also, we have learned that salvation means deliverance. In Christ saving process He delivered mankind from sin and bondage to that of freedom in Him.

It is noteworthy to say that Christ is the only way to God the Father and salvation is provided to mankind through God's grace that was freely given in His Son Jesus Christ, which is based upon Christ's death, resurrection and continued intercession for mankind to the Father. Even though salvation is a free gift from God it must be received in faith by the believer. Salvation doesn't just include those believers during and after Christ's time but extends to those faithful believers prior to Christ's time. As those OT patriarchs died in faith believing in God's promise. Scripture records many patriarchs who died believing God. With that being said then faith is the key to our salvation.

Let us look at the work done by Christ in the saving process; there is redemption which is to buy back ones freedom. Through Christ's blood mankind's freedom was purchased from the bondage of sin. All who believe are now redeemed by Christ from our previously held bondage to one of spiritual freedom. Jesus Christ paid a heavy price so that man's sin debt can be marked ***PAID IN FULL***. This was done in love by God the Father and God the Son.

Then there is the justification process which is to be declared "not guilty" and "declared righteous" in the sight of God. When God the Father looks at man He sees Christ's righteousness instead of man's sinful nature. Being that God cannot look on sin, therefore, Jesus' blood was required to remove the stain of sin. Another way of looking at justification and what Jesus does for all who believe is that

He acts as our attorney who presents us before God as righteous. This is because scripture states that "all have sinned and come short of the glory of God" (Roman 3:23). It can be said then that our justification comes by God's grace and our faith in Jesus Christ as our Lord and Savior.

Then we have regeneration which is the believer's new birth which is being born in the spirit of Christ. All believers have died to sin and were raised with Christ to a new life of holiness. Being regenerated carries the connotation of being a new creature, not physically, but spiritually as each believer has the indwelling Holy Spirit that aids in the believer living a life of righteousness. It is noteworthy to say that with the aid of the Holy Spirit believers have the ability to live in complete obedience to God.

Being that believers are born again creatures we are then sanctified or set apart from the rest of the world to that of a life of holiness to perform good works for God. Sanctified people are believers who are in the world but no longer of this world. We are a royal priesthood, a holy nation and the salt of the earth to season the world with both our verbal witness and daily living. As our lifestyles are to manifest Christ at all times.

The magnificent work of Christ makes us right with God. What a Savior!

Believers A Sanctified People: Hebrews 13:12

...Jesus also, that He might sanctify the people with His own blood, suffered without the gate.

We have learned that sanctification is being set apart or consecrated for service to God and all believers are those set apart people and being sanctified was accomplished through the shed blood of Jesus. This was so that all believers would be presentable to God. It stands to reason that the "redeemed" are to be made presentable before God because humanity is sin riddled and in that state is unpresentable to God.

Another point of being sanctified is that believers are Sons of God and His goal is to transform us into His likeness—holiness/glory which is sanctification. 1 Peter 2:9 talks about sanctified people as a holy nation which consist of all believers collectively as we represent God's kingdom. God's holiness is to show forth through all believers.

Titus 2:14 explains in detail why Christ did what He did for all who believe and accept Him as his or her Savior. Given the cost of our salvation to Christ and anyone who still struggles with sin should ask this question, given that Christ died for our salvation and conquered sin Would He not make it possible for us to live victoriously over sin and all manner of evil? We have victory in Jesus Christ.

Being that all believers are a sanctified people we are to obey the Great Commission issued by Christ Himself in Matthew 28:19-20 that is carry the gospel to all nations.

Dec 14

The Lord Is My Strength: Psalm 27:1

The Lord is my light and my salvation; whom shall I fear? The lord is the strength of my life; of whom shall I be afraid?

The writer of this Psalm makes several profound statements in asking two questions that should be asked and answered by all believers. First, the writer states implicitly his relationship with God. Second the statement carries the connotation that God is his light with His all seeing eye and salvation means that God is his Savior. Given the knowledge of what a Savior does begs the question that was asked of the writer, which the answer should be no one. Also, given the fact that a Savior means protector and provider there is nothing or no one to fear or be afraid of. God in His provisional care provided for all fears and concerns.

The most profound fact of this scripture is the relationship the writer of this Psalm had with God for recognizing who God is and that the essence of all life begins and ends with the Lord. All believers must possess this kind of understanding of who God is and what He does is the life of all mankind. Paul realized that all of his strength came from the Lord and in God's strength he could do all things--***so can we***.

Fear God in reverence and let Him do the rest for He is our all in all!

Dec 15

Sealed With The Holy Spirit: Ephesians 1:12-14

That we should be to the praise of his glory, who first trusted in Christ. in whom ye also trusted, after that ye heard the word of truth, the gospel of your salvation in whom also after that ye believed, ye were sealed with that holy Spirit of promise, Which is the earnest of our inheritance, until the redemption of the purchase possession, unto the praise of his glory.

What is the meaning of being sealed with the Holy Spirit? The seal of the Holy Spirit is given to all believers who have accepted Christ as his or her personal Savior as God's mark of ownership. Being that we as believers have been bought with a price—Christ's blood. Being sealed with the Holy Spirit gives believers evidence that we are sons of God adopted into His family and the Holy Spirit lives in each of us as He regenerates and renews each believer continually. Also, being sealed with the Holy Spirit provides believers with an ever present consciousness of God as our Father and we have the power to witness for God (Acts 1:8; 2:4).

The Holy Spirit provides wisdom and revelation and helps each believer as we draw near to God. The Holy Spirit builds believers into a holy temple of God and strengthens each believer with power to witness. He motivates unity in the Christian community of faith.

Both God and Satan see our seal, but Satan will attempt to tear us away from God. God—the Holy Spirit is more powerful than Satan.

A New Life In Christ: Ephesians 1:4

According as he hath chosen us in him before the foundation of the world, that we should be holy and without blame before him to love:

Our scripture verse implies that believers are chosen by God to be His sanctified people and the choice was made before the foundation of the world. The scripture also speaks to election and predestination which is to say that God chooses His people who will be loyal and obedient to Him as the chosen ones will be holy and blameless as He is a holy God. This claim is made because God is all knowing and knows who will accept Christ in faith and who will not. This is because God knows the heart of all mankind as He is our creator and sustainer.

Another point of view is that God's objective was to form a people through the redemptive process of Christ's death on the cross that would be called the "church" or the "body of Christ" to be His people. This body of believers would have a new life in Christ and share in the many blessings that being a new creature in Christ has to offer. This decision was made before hand (predestine) as to who would be included in the elect as Christ is the head or first of the elect.

Being part of the elect, believers begin a new life in Christ and it extends to eternity as believers are seen as being on a heaven bound journey.

A new life in Christ is glorious.

Dec 17

Jesus The Bread And Water Of Life: John 6:22-35

....Verily, verily, I say unto, Ye seek Me, but because of the miracles, but because ye did eat of the loaves, and were filled...For the bread of God is he which cometh down from heaven, and giveth life unto the world. I am the bread of life; he that cometh to Me shall never hunger; and he that believeth on me shall never thirst.

During Jesus' earthly ministry, His fame had spread because of the many miracles He performed whether feeding five thousand, healing the sick or giving sight to the blind. Regardless the reason for the people coming to Jesus they knew He was someone special, but they failed to recognized Him as the promised Messiah or God's Son who came into the world to bring light into the world.

Jesus came to provide everlasting life and all who believed on Him his or her hunger and thirst would cease. Jesus met the people's physical needs in order to meet their spiritual need. Jesus made several "I am" statements identifying who He was and His purpose for coming to earth, which was to provide salvation. This is why He is called the bread and water of life. As man requires physical bread and water to sustain natural life so must he have spiritual bread, God's Word and water to sustain ones spiritual life.

God sustained the Israelites in the wilderness with heavenly manna, today we are sustained with his manna ---His Word.

Eat and drink of His Spirit and live.

Dec 18

Believers Given Sonship In God
Romans 8:12-14; Galatians 4:5

For as many as are led by the Spirit of God, they are the sons of God.....To redeem them that were under the law, that we might receive the adoption of sons.

When a child is born he or she is born into that particular family and becomes part of the family and takes on the family name and characteristics. This is true when persons accept Jesus as Lord and Savior; the person becomes a son of God as all believers are reborn into the family of God. In doing so the believer takes on the characteristics of holiness, the righteousness of God and all Christ like character.

If the question were raised, What are the privileges from being sons of God? Some of those privileges are believers are called to a higher calling and have been sanctified by God to be His spokespersons witnessing Christ the world over. Being sons of God assures believers of spending eternity with God where there is continuous praise and worship. There will be no more dying, crying or sickness as all will be done away with. Being sons of God when we get to heaven we will be given a crown of life which will never end. ***What Joy!***

Lastly, being sons of God is a blessing because He has prepared one lavish heavenly feast for His children in His mansion on high (Isaiah 55:1).

Rejoice! Rejoice! Rejoice because being sons of God equals blessings.

Believers Consecrated For Service: John 17:17-19

Sanctify them through thy truth; thy word is truth. As thou hast sent me unto the world, even so have I also sent them into the world. And for their sakes I sanctify myself, that they also might be sanctified through the truth.

The terms sanctify and consecrate are interchangeable as both mean to be set aside, separated or devoted for worship or for a special purpose. In regards to believers we are consecrated/set aside for service to God and His kingdom building. Believers have been called out of darkness into a spiritual light of holiness, a life that manifest Christ in the believer's daily walk. Believers have heard the Word of God and have humbled themselves to do the will of God in obedience to God. In verse 6 of our scripture text which talks about the obedience of the disciples as they were sent out into the world to preach the gospel of Christ. Jesus prayed for their protection, joy, sanctification, love and unity among the people. The disciple needed to present a unified front when witnessing Christ to an unsaved world. This principle applies for believers today as all believers are separated from the world to effectively do the work of God.

What makes believers sanctified is the truth of God and have believed in Jesus Christ as Lord and Savior. Just as Jesus who is God sanctified Himself in obedience to His Father so must we as believers in order to accomplish the works that God has assigned for us. Jesus sanctifying Himself was to be an example as to how all believers must be set apart from the world to fulfill our commission as outlined in Matthew 28:19-20 as it is God's desire that all be saved. How must an unbeliever be saved unless he or she hears the Word of God? It does not matter if we as believers have been called to preach, teach, prophesy, evangelized or simply witness, we must share God's Word with others.

If the question were raised, Why is it necessary for believers to be separated from the world? The answer is found in II Corinthians

6:17-18 which states in part to "come out from among them." "Them" is the world which is controlled by Satan and his demonic systems. Fundamentally believers cannot be friends with the world and God as we will love one and hate the other. Also, it is necessary for believers to be separated because believers must be morally and spiritually free of sin and everything that is contrary to Christ Jesus and the righteousness of God. Being separated provides greater opportunity to draw near to God and His holiness. Being separated from the world and set aside to God allows all believers to persevere in faith, as we are controlled by the unrighteousness of this world that leads to unholy compromises and being separated from the world gives believers the ability to love those in the world but hate the sins of that person.

1 John 2:15-16 sums up why Christians/believers must be separated from the world by stating "Love not the world, neither the things that are in the world. If any man loves the world, the love of the father is not in him. For all that is in the world, the lust of the flesh, and the lust of the eyes, and the pride of life, is not of the father, but is of the world." From these verses we see remaining attached to the world hinders a meaningful relationship with God and further prevents believers from obeying the Great Commission.

Believers are consecrated to serve, obey God's command as we are His elect to do His Will--serve!

Dec 20

The Lord My Redeemer: Psalm 19:14

Let the words of my mouth, and the meditation of my heart, be acceptable in thy sight, O Lord, my strength, and my redeemer.

The above scripture verse gives insight into the proper response that all believers should have for receiving salvation that is provided by God the Father and His Son Jesus Christ. As this is a prayer that all believers should have in their prayer arsenal asking God to keep his or her mouth in holiness with praise of gratitude and thanksgiving. In expressing our heart felt gratitude for salvation which begins in the heart as the heart is the epicenter of all thoughts, actions, words and or deeds. As the believer fully understands the magnitude of salvation and that all our strength, and entire being is clothed in Jesus Christ.

A heart that is focused on Christ and His saving works on the cross at Calvary, then our prayer request is as the Psalmist asking for acceptance of all our thoughts and actions in the sight of God. This is because like the Psalmist, we as believers realize that our strength comes from the Lord and that we can do nothing in and of ourselves.

It is noteworthy to say that Christ is our redeemer and it is His righteousness that makes us worthy to stand before a holy God. Christ made us right (justified) with God.

Thanks You Jesus for Your atoning work of salvation. Christ my Redeemer. Hallelujah!

Dec 21

Redemption Through The Blood
Colossian 1:14; Ephesians 1:7

In whom we have redemption through his blood, even the forgiveness of sin, according to the riches of his grace.

We have learned from prior writings and lessons that redemption is to ransom or to buy back something or someone from another. In this scenario Jesus Christ is our Redeemer as He purchased man from the clutches of sin and restored the broken fellowship between man and God.

Jesus' blood was required because blood is life giving and Jesus was the only one found worthy to make a one-time sacrifice to forgive sin. Earlier animal sacrifices performed by the priests were insufficient because it only covered over sin whereas Jesus' blood did away with sin.

Looking at the last phrase of our scripture text, which talks about the richness of God's (His) grace; for we know that God's grace is rich with His righteousness and holiness. The true meaning of GRACE is God's Righteousness At Christ's Expense, which is to say that God gave His best to redeem man and Christ gave His life which is His shed blood for man's redemption--salvation. Another point of view is that God's grace superseded His justice. ***What love!***

When the song "Nothing but the blood of Jesus" is sang it expresses the truth about Jesus' blood in our salvation.

"I know it as the blood; I know it was the blood, for Jesus died upon the cross."

Dec 22

My Redeemer Liveth: Job 19:25

For I know that my Redeemer liveth, and that he shall stand at the latter day upon the earth.

Our scripture text setting is during the suffering of Job the godly and upright man who God allowed the devil to test because He knew that Job would never turn his back or doubt God for his deliverance. Even three of Job's closest friends tried their best to convince Job that he had sinned and was refusing to admit to the sin.

Even in the midst of Job's suffering he held steadfast to his faith in God for deliverance and he would be vindicated for all his suffering and the false accusations leveled against him. ***Vindicate He did***. Job was blessed with more than before.

What message is there for us today? The message is that we must possess an unwavering faith in God because He is faithful to His promise of deliverance. Regardless of the situation or circumstance we must know that God has the power to redeem if it's His will.

It is noteworthy to say the last phrase of this verse is pointing to a time in the future when Jesus Christ would come and redeem/save His people from the bondage of sin and all who believe in Him would be vindicated for the world to see. We know that after the tribulation Christ will return with His saints and will rule the earth.

What a time that will be, peace and harmony will reign supreme.

Christ's Eternal Sacrifice: Hebrews 9:11-12

... Christ being come a high priest of good things to come, by a greater and more perfect tabernacle, not of this building. Neither by the blood of goats and calves, but by His own blood He entered in once into the holy place having obtained eternal redemption for us.

During the OT era the high priests would enter into the holy of holy and offer sacrifices to God for the people. Their sacrifice offering was the blood of unblemished goats and calves. This ritual was repeated yearly as sin was constantly being committed. When Jesus came on the scene the yearly ritual of sin atonement was no longer required as Jesus became the perfect high priest who made a one-time sin offering with His own blood as He was the perfect sacrificial lamb who came to take away the sins of the world.

Christ's one-time sacrifice accomplished what animal sacrifices could not. His blood forgave sins of all who believe in Him. His blood redeemed all believers from the bondage of Satan and his powers to the power of God and His righteousness. Christ's blood justified all who believes in Him. Christ's blood cleanses all believers' consciences so that they can serve God with a willing and humble heart all in faith. Christ's blood opened the door so that all believers can come directly to God through Him to find grace, help, mercy and salvation. Christ's blood provides saving, purifying and reconciling power that is continuous for believers and all who desire to be saved.

Christ's sacrifice is eternal to the heavens.

Dec 24

The Just Shall Live By Faith: Galatians 3:11-12

But that no man is justified by the law in the sight of God, it is evident; for, The just shall live by faith. And the law is not of faith; but, The man that doeth them shall live in them.

What is faith? Hebrews 11:1 provides the definition of faith, which states "Now faith is the substance of things hoped for, but the evidence of things not seen," but in a short version, faith is the Christian's belief. Those of us who believe that Christ died for the sins of the world and that He is God's Son, we are exercising our faith as well as those who believed on Him during His earthly ministry was exercising their faith as well. So were the OT patriarchs who lived and died in faith.

It is "through faith that we understand that the world was framed by the word of God" (v 3). More importantly, it is our faith that we believe that there is a God who is supreme and the creator and sustainer of all that exist both seen and unseen. ***How great is thy faith?***

The just are all believers who have accepted Jesus Christ as his or her personal Savior and have been justified/made right with God through the redemptive blood of Jesus Christ. So then, what is the purpose of the law? The law acted as a tutor or a guide for God's people until salvation through Jesus Christ. The law also revealed God's will for holy living which was to lead mankind to Christ.

The law is our guide--faith is the catalytic for salvation.

The Savior Is Born: Luke 2:7-14

And she brought forth her firstborn son, and wrapped Him in swaddling clothes, and laid Him in a manger, because there was no room for them in the inn...For unto you is born this day in the city of David a Savior, which is Christ the Lord.

The birth of Christ is the most celebrated day of all time as it commemorates the birth of our Savior who was promised many years before His arrival. He was prophesied by many OT prophets many years before His arrival. Isaiah 7:14 talks about a Virgin conceiving and bringing forth a Son and that His name would be Immanuel which means "God with us." Our scripture verses corroborates Isaiah's prophesy regarding the birth of Jesus and that He would be born to the Virgin Mary, and where He would be born.

Christ's birth was in humility which set an example for all believers in having the right view of God the Father, self and others. Christ's earthly parents were of humble standing and His mother found favor with God to bring forth His Son.

In honor of this day as it is set aside as the birth of our Savior; let's honor the true meaning of our Savior's birth. Therefore, to provide salvation, He was born to die. ***What a Savior!***

Let's sing like the angels "joy to the world a Savior is born".

Dec 26

Anointed For Kingdom Building: Isaiah 61:1; Luke 4:18

The Spirit of the Lord God is upon me; because the Lord hath anointed me to preach good tidings unto the meek; he hath sent me to bind up the broken hearted, to proclaim liberty to the captives, and the opening of prison to them that are bound.

From our scripture texts we see that Isaiah prophesied about the anointing of Christ being the Savior of the world and what He was to do once His earthly ministry began. Then in Luke we have the fulfillment of this prophecy taking place when Jesus repeated the words of Isaiah.

In Isaiah there is the reference to the Trinity, God the Father, God the Holy Spirit and God the Son Jesus working together for the good of all humanity. Jesus' ministry involved preaching the gospel to the poor, healing and binding the spiritually and physically sick and broken hearted, He was to break the evil bonds of sin and Satan domination. Lastly, Jesus was to open the spiritually blinded eyes of the lost (unsaved) thus bringing them into the spiritual light of salvation.

How did Jesus do all that was required in His ministry? Jesus was successful in His earthly ministry because of the anointing of Him by the Holy Spirit who is God in the third person. OT prophets wrote that the coming Messiah would be empowered by the Holy Spirit and this prophecy came true when Jesus began His ministry at His birth, His baptism, while being tempted by Satan, His promise of the Holy Spirit coming to indwell all believers, His Resurrection, His ascension into heaven, the nearness to His people and when He returns for His bride--the church. Therefore, the Holy Spirit has played an active role in the lives of all humanity from their creation and remains active now and when Christ returns. Case in point, the Holy Spirit was instrumental in the birth of Christ, He was present during Jesus' baptism, it was by the power of the Holy Spirit that Christ was raised from the dead, and lastly, He is active in the lives of all believers as He lives within.

If the question were raised, Why did Jesus have to be anointed if He is God's Son? Being God's Son and human, Jesus limited Himself to human limitations, therefore, He relied on the power of the Holy Spirit in all that He did in obedience to the will of His Father. It is noteworthy to say that being God He could do all things, but as human He could not. Christ was present during creation and as recorded in John 1:1-3 which talks about Jesus being the "Word of God and all things were made by Him." This authenticates His deity who possesses all power, but to carry out God's perfect plan of salvation Jesus had to become human and be anointed by the Holy Spirit.

Christ being mankind's anointed Savior because He is God's Son slain from the foundation of the world for the purpose of saving mankind from sin, and who met all the requirements to do so.

Christ the anointed One!

Dec 27

The Almighty Savior: Hosea 13:14

I will ransom them from the power of the grave; I will redeem them from death; O death, I will be thy plagues; O grave, I will be thy destruction; repentance shall be hid from mine eyes.

The prophet Hosea's name means "salvation" who prophesied to the nation of Israel and Judah trying to get the people to repent and turn back to God. In presenting a clear picture of God and His people He allowed Hosea to marry Gomer an adulterous woman as this represented God and His love for His wayward people who had turn to idol worship.

Our scripture verse portrays God's love for His people in spite of their failure to repent and turn back to Him. Our text talks about God redeeming His people from the grave means that a remnant would be saved (11:5), which is to say that some would hear and repent. This principle applies today as many will hear the word of God and turn to Him and many will refuse God's saving grace. In the redeeming process from death means those who die a physical death out of the safety of salvation, then the grave and the stain of death is very cruel whereas dying in Christ death has no victory as Christ won this battle at the cross.

In conclusion, only God is the almighty Savior through His Son Jesus Christ who has overcome the stain of death and washed away our sin only if we believe in Him.
   What a Savior!

Dec 28

Serve The Lord: 1 Samuel 12:20

And Samuel said unto the people, Fear not; ye have done all this wickedness; yet turn not aside from following the Lord, but serve the Lord with all your heart;...Moreover as for me, God forbid that I should sin against the Lord in ceasing to pray for you; but I will teach you the good and the right way.

    Samuel was a praying devout man of God who served the Lord with all his heart and prayed for Israel to do likewise. It was through Samuel's prayers for Israel the nation was delivered from their enemy (7:5-14). Samuel even prayed for Israel when they rejected God (8:6) and he prayed continually for the people of Israel to fear the Lord and serve Him with all their hearts and in truth. Serving God with a truthful heart is the essence of our service to Him as the heart is the epicenter of all motivations, desires and actions.

    We see Samuel's dedication to serving God in that he was fearful to cease from praying for the people as he was God's chosen spokes person who God called to carry His message to the people and to provide for their spiritual well-being. In addition to praying for the people Samuel was committed to teaching the people the right way which is God's way.

    What does this say for today's spiritual leaders? Today's spiritual leaders are to have the same dedicated commitment to God and His people as spiritual leaders are called to stand on God's Word in spite of any and all difficulties society has to offer. ***Serve God despite the cost or situation.***

Serving The One True And Living God
1 Thessalonians 1:9-10

For they themselves shew of us what manner of entering in we had unto you, and how ye turned to God from idols to serve the living and true God. And to wait for his Son from heaven, whom he raised from the dead, even Jesus, which delivered us from the wrath to come.

Idol worship has been a problem throughout biblical history as well as in today's society, and in Paul's writing to the Thessalonian believers he warned them against idol worship and to worship on the true and living God.

In a common sense approach to idol worship, one should ask themselves can a wooden carved image provide salvation or bring comfort in the time of need. Another question that comes to mind is, Can an idol god part the waters of the Red Sea or the Jordan River? The next question to ask is can an idol god serve as a pillar of cloud by day or a ray of sunshine when needed? If the answer is no, then why serve idol gods? Why not serve a God who created all that exist both seen and unseen; a God who gave His Son to be the Savior of the world; a God who through His Spirit raised His only begotten Son from the dead, who through His death burial and resurrection provided salvation only if you believe on Him.

Serving the true and living God we as believers like the Thessalonian believers have a blessed hope in waiting for Christ's return for His saints.

Serve the true God--the Triune God.

Dec 30

Believers Servants Of God: 1 Peter 2:16-18

As free, and not using your liberty for a cloke of maliciousness, but as the servants of God. Honour all men, Love the brotherhood. Fear God, Honour the king. Servants, be subject to your masters with all fear; not only to the good and gentle, but also to the forward.

The definition of servant is one who belongs to another (The Student Bible Dictionary P. 212). Romans 1:1 Paul talks about him being a servant of Jesus Christ. We know that everyone is enslaved to someone or something, but if we chose to be enslaved to Jesus Christ then we are free (Romans 6:6-7; 8:2; John 8:34), because of His atoning work at Calvary.

In our scripture text, Peter is pointing out some helpful suggestions regarding Christian submission and character traits that all believers are to have once set free from the bondage of sin. We must refrain from using our freedom (liberty) in any malicious manner because all true believers have taken on the characteristics of Christ. As Christ is our master and if we are to emulate Him we must love everyone--even the sinner, but hate the sin.

During Christ's earthly ministry, He made it plain that He did not come to be served, but to serve and to do His master's will. When Peter speaks of serving with fear he is referring to reverence to Jesus our Lord as a sign of true servantship.

We are his workmanship (Ephesians 2:10); serve as faithful servants.

Dec 31

Believers Sealed As God's Property: Revelation 7:3-4

Saying, Hurt not the earth, neither the sea, nor the trees, till we have sealed the servants of our God in their foreheads. And I heard the number of them which were sealed; and there were sealed an hundred and four thousand of all the tribes of the children of Israel.

A seal is a mark of ownership and in this scenario God is marking all people so there will be no mistake as to who they belong.

All God's children that have been sealed with His mark is under His watchful eye and protective care (Ephesians 1:13). The sealer is the Holy Spirit. The number of sealed persons which John is referring to are the representatives from the twelve tribes of Israel who have been sealed for identification purposes to preach the gospel during the tribulation. There will be a greater number of believers in heaven as all believers have the seal of God in their foreheads visible to the Godhead. It is noteworthy to say that those sealed believers from the twelve tribes of Israel are not free from suffering persecution and martyrdom from Satan and physical death (v.14), but it does mean that they are protected from God's direct judgment and demonic afflictions (9:4).

What we do know about being sealed by the Holy Spirit is that all believers belong to God and He protects His own. Remember Job and how God protected him, He will do the same for you and I today.

Bio

Dr. WILLIE B. WHITE holds two Masters of Arts degree in Adult education (MA Ed, MA SED and a Doctorate in Ministry).

Ms. White is a certified Dean and instructor in Christian Education, a college professor and special education teacher K-12.

She frequently publishes articles in The Informer magazine of the SSPB. First book, "The Lord is My Shepherd", (2007) PublishAmerica. "An Expose Of The Holy Spirit", released June 2009, "Heavenly Bread", released July 2009, a monthly devotional.

Ms. White publishes a weekly blog discussion Uplifting Insight- http://willie-writing.blogspot.com.

Works in progress, DVD Who is God? An inspirational video, next books, God's Moral laws: The Ten Commandments, and My Faith Journey with Jesus. All material is available through www.amazon.com, www.createSpace.com, www.kindle.com and wherever books are sold.

www.ingramcontent.com/pod-product-compliance
Lightning Source LLC
Chambersburg PA
CBHW062005180426
43198CB00037B/2400